First World War
and Army of Occupation
War Diary
France, Belgium and Germany

39 DIVISION
117 Infantry Brigade
Sherwood Foresters
(Nottinghamshire and Derbyshire Regiment)
17th Battalion
5 March 1916 - 23 February 1918

WO95/2587/2

The Naval & Military Press Ltd
www.nmarchive.com
Published in association with The National Archives

Published by

The Naval & Military Press Ltd

Unit 10 Ridgewood Industrial Park,

Uckfield, East Sussex,

TN22 5QE England

Tel: +44 (0) 1825 749494

www.naval-military-press.com

www.nmarchive.com

This diary has been reprinted in facsimile from the original. Any imperfections are inevitably reproduced and the quality may fall short of modern type and cartographic standards.

© **Crown Copyright**
Images reproduced by permission of The National Archives, London, England, 2015.

Contents

Document type	Place/Title	Date From	Date To
Heading	WO95/2587/2		
Heading	17th Bn Sherwood Foresters Mar 1916-Feb 1918		
Heading	1/17th Battalion Notts & Derby Regiment March 1916		
War Diary	Witley Camp	06/03/1916	06/03/1916
War Diary	Havre	07/03/1916	08/03/1916
War Diary	Steenbecque	09/03/1916	13/03/1916
War Diary	Estaires	14/03/1916	28/03/1916
War Diary	Busnettes	29/03/1916	31/03/1916
Heading	1/17th Battalion Notts & Derby Regiment April 1916		
War Diary	Busnettes	01/04/1916	06/04/1916
War Diary	Bethune	07/04/1916	07/04/1916
War Diary	Annequin	08/04/1916	10/04/1916
War Diary	Hiddn	10/04/1916	10/04/1916
War Diary	Trenches	11/04/1916	14/04/1916
War Diary	Bethune	15/04/1916	16/04/1916
War Diary	Hingette	17/04/1916	23/04/1916
War Diary	Le Touret	24/04/1916	27/04/1916
War Diary	Trenches	28/04/1916	30/04/1916
Miscellaneous	Report On 17th Notts & Derby Regt. Attached to 98th Inf. Bde. 33rd Division.		
Heading	1/17th Battalion Notts & Derby Regiment May 1916		
War Diary	Trenches	01/05/1916	01/05/1916
War Diary	Festubert	02/05/1916	05/05/1916
War Diary	Trenches	06/05/1916	09/05/1916
War Diary	Hingette	10/05/1916	17/05/1916
War Diary	Gorre	18/05/1916	21/05/1916
War Diary	Givenchy Trenches	22/05/1916	22/05/1916
War Diary	Trenches	23/05/1916	23/05/1916
War Diary	Givenchy	26/05/1916	29/05/1916
War Diary	Trenches	30/05/1916	31/05/1916
Heading	1/17th Battalion Notts & Derby Regiment June 1916		
War Diary	Trenches	01/06/1916	03/06/1916
War Diary	Gorre	04/06/1916	06/06/1916
War Diary	Ferme Du Roi	07/06/1916	11/06/1916
War Diary	Trenches	12/06/1916	30/06/1916
Heading	1/17th Battalion Notts & Derby Regiment July 1916		
War Diary	Trenches	01/07/1916	14/07/1916
War Diary	Richebourg St. Vaast	15/07/1916	24/07/1916
War Diary	Les Choquaux	25/07/1916	26/07/1916
War Diary	Givenchy	27/07/1916	31/07/1916
Miscellaneous	17th. Sherwood Foresters.	03/07/1916	03/07/1916
Miscellaneous	17th. Sherwood Foresters.	04/07/1916	04/07/1916
Miscellaneous	A Form. Messages And Signals.	04/07/1916	04/07/1916
Miscellaneous	Battalion Daily Orders by Lt. Col. H.M. Milward. Cmdg. 17th Sherwood Foresters.	04/07/1916	04/07/1916
Miscellaneous	17th. Sherwood Foresters.	03/07/1916	03/07/1916
Miscellaneous	17th. Sherwood Foresters. Operation Order No. 8	17/07/1916	17/07/1916
Miscellaneous	17th. Sherwood Foresters.	18/07/1916	18/07/1916
Miscellaneous	17th. Sherwood Foresters.	20/07/1916	20/07/1916
Heading	1/17th Battalion Notts & Derby Regiment August 1916		

War Diary	Givenchy	01/08/1916	01/08/1916
War Diary	Trenches	02/08/1916	06/08/1916
War Diary	Essars	07/08/1916	10/08/1916
War Diary	Auchel	11/08/1916	11/08/1916
War Diary	Orlencourt	12/08/1916	24/08/1916
War Diary	Doullens	25/08/1916	25/08/1916
War Diary	Vauchelles Les Authie	26/08/1916	28/08/1916
War Diary	Bertrancourt	29/08/1916	31/08/1916
Miscellaneous	17th. Sherwood Foresters. Operation Order No. 11	30/07/1916	30/07/1916
Miscellaneous	117th Infantry Brigade.	01/08/1916	01/08/1916
Miscellaneous	Headquarters. 39th Division	01/08/1916	01/08/1916
Map			
Heading	1/17th Battalion Notts & Derby Regiment September 1916		
War Diary	Bertrancourt	01/09/1916	01/09/1916
War Diary	Trenches	03/09/1916	03/09/1916
War Diary	Bertrancourt	04/09/1916	06/09/1916
War Diary	Mailley Maillet	07/09/1916	07/09/1916
War Diary	Maillet-Mailley	08/09/1916	15/09/1916
War Diary	Trenches	13/09/1916	19/09/1916
War Diary	Beaussart	20/09/1916	20/09/1916
War Diary	Trenches	21/09/1916	30/09/1916
Miscellaneous	17th Sherwood Foresters. Operation Order No. 19	30/08/1916	30/08/1916
Miscellaneous	To Accompany 117th Infantry Brigade Order No. 50, Appendix E	29/08/1916	29/08/1916
Miscellaneous	Time Table To Accompany 117th Bde O.O. 50	28/08/1916	28/08/1916
Miscellaneous	2nd Division	31/08/1916	31/08/1916
Miscellaneous	To All Officers Commanding Units. 117th Infy, Bde		
Miscellaneous	Copy Of telegram received from Headquarters 39th Division	04/09/1916	04/09/1916
Miscellaneous	Report On Operation On Sept. 3 1916	04/09/1916	04/09/1916
Miscellaneous	117th Infantry Brigade	05/09/1916	05/09/1916
Miscellaneous	Copy of letter received from Headquarters 39th Division.	14/09/1916	14/09/1916
Heading	1/17th Battalion Notts & Derby Regiment October 1916		
War Diary	Bertrancourt	01/10/1916	02/10/1916
War Diary	Hedauville	03/10/1916	05/10/1916
War Diary	Trenches	06/10/1916	10/10/1916
War Diary	Martinsart Wood	11/10/1916	16/10/1916
War Diary	Trenches	17/10/1916	20/10/1916
War Diary	Authville	21/10/1916	22/10/1916
War Diary	Thiepval	23/10/1916	23/10/1916
War Diary	Authville	24/10/1916	24/10/1916
War Diary	Trenches	25/10/1916	25/10/1916
War Diary	Authville	26/10/1916	27/10/1916
War Diary	Trenches	28/10/1916	29/10/1916
War Diary	Senlis	30/10/1916	31/10/1916
Miscellaneous	Message From General Officer Commanding Reserve Army.	01/10/1916	01/10/1916
Miscellaneous	17th Sherwood Foresters Operation Order No. 32	18/10/1916	18/10/1916
Miscellaneous	17th Sherwood Foresters	21/10/1916	21/10/1916
Miscellaneous	117th Infantry Brigade	22/10/1916	22/10/1916
Heading	1/17th Battalion Notts & Derby Regiment November 1916		
War Diary	Senlis	01/11/1916	03/11/1916
War Diary	Trenches	04/11/1916	05/11/1916

War Diary	Martinsart Woods		06/11/1916	06/11/1916
War Diary	Trenches		07/11/1916	08/11/1916
War Diary	Pioneer Road		09/11/1916	10/11/1916
War Diary	Senlis		11/11/1916	13/11/1916
War Diary	Spey Side		14/11/1916	14/11/1916
War Diary	Warloy		15/11/1916	15/11/1916
War Diary	Gezincourt		16/11/1916	17/11/1916
War Diary	St. Omer		18/11/1916	18/11/1916
War Diary	Tetinghem		19/11/1916	30/11/1916
Heading	1/17th Battalion Notts & Derby Regiment December 1916			
War Diary	Tetingham		01/12/1916	22/12/1916
War Diary	Boesinghe		23/12/1916	25/12/1916
War Diary	Trenches		26/12/1916	29/12/1916
War Diary	Brielen		30/12/1916	01/01/1917
War Diary	Trenches		02/01/1917	05/01/1917
War Diary	Brielen		06/01/1917	09/01/1917
War Diary	Trenches		10/01/1917	12/01/1917
War Diary	Brielan		13/01/1917	13/01/1917
War Diary	Vox-Vrie		14/01/1917	14/01/1917
War Diary	C Camp		15/01/1917	24/01/1917
War Diary	Kaaie		25/01/1917	25/01/1917
War Diary	Trenches		26/01/1917	30/01/1917
War Diary	Kaaie		31/01/1917	03/02/1917
War Diary	Trenches		04/02/1917	06/02/1917
War Diary	Ypres		07/01/1917	09/01/1917
War Diary	Trenches		10/02/1917	12/02/1917
War Diary	Ypres		13/02/1917	15/02/1917
War Diary	Vox. Vrie		16/02/1917	26/02/1917
War Diary	Trenches		27/02/1917	04/03/1917
War Diary	Ypres		05/03/1916	10/03/1916
War Diary	St Lawrence Camp		11/03/1917	15/03/1917
War Diary	Trenches		16/03/1917	21/03/1917
War Diary	Ypres		22/03/1917	28/03/1917
War Diary	Montreal Camp		29/03/1917	03/04/1917
War Diary	Ypres		04/03/1917	11/03/1917
War Diary	St Lawrence Camp		12/04/1917	13/04/1917
War Diary	Bollezeele		14/04/1917	27/04/1917
War Diary	Y Camp		28/04/1917	28/04/1917
War Diary	A Camp		29/04/1917	01/05/1917
War Diary	C Camp		02/05/1917	15/05/1917
War Diary	Trenches		16/05/1917	23/05/1917
War Diary	Canal Bank		24/05/1917	31/05/1917
War Diary	Trenches		01/06/1917	08/06/1917
War Diary	O Camp		09/06/1917	16/06/1917
War Diary	Trenches		17/06/1917	24/06/1917
War Diary	Canal Bank		25/06/1917	30/06/1917
Miscellaneous	11th Bn. R. Suss. R.		31/05/1917	31/05/1917
War Diary	C Camp		01/07/1917	01/07/1917
War Diary	Moulle		02/07/1917	22/07/1917
War Diary	Bivouac A 30 Central		23/07/1917	29/07/1917
Miscellaneous	17th Bn. Sherwood Foresters		27/07/1917	27/07/1917
Miscellaneous	17th Bn. Sherwood Foresters		25/07/1917	25/07/1917
War Diary	Canal Bank		30/07/1917	30/07/1917
War Diary	Hill Top Sector Trenches		31/07/1917	31/07/1917
Miscellaneous	17th. Bn. Sherwood Foresters. Operation Order No. 43		23/07/1917	23/07/1917

Miscellaneous	Report On Operations On 31st July 1917	07/08/1917	07/08/1917
Miscellaneous	Appendix "A"		
Miscellaneous	Appendix "B" Brigade And Advanced Brigade Dumps		
Miscellaneous	17th Bn. Sherwood Foresters		
Miscellaneous	II Corps	09/08/1917	09/08/1917
Miscellaneous	17th. Bn. Sherwood Foresters		
Miscellaneous	XVIII Corps	01/08/1917	01/08/1917
Miscellaneous	Special Order By Major-General G.J Cuthbert, C.B., C.M.G., Commanding 39th Division.	20/08/1917	20/08/1917
War Diary	Trenches Steenbeek	01/08/1917	04/08/1917
War Diary	Old German Front Line	05/08/1917	05/08/1917
War Diary	Canal Bank	06/08/1917	07/08/1917
War Diary	Le Roukloshille	07/08/1917	13/08/1917
War Diary	Ridge Wood	14/08/1917	14/08/1917
War Diary	Trenches	15/08/1917	19/08/1917
War Diary	Ridge Wood	20/08/1917	23/08/1917
War Diary	Bois Confluent	24/08/1917	26/08/1917
War Diary	Bois Confluent	27/08/1917	27/08/1917
War Diary	Trenches	28/08/1917	29/08/1917
War Diary	Chippewa Camp	30/08/1917	31/08/1917
Miscellaneous	Route Orders by Brigadier General G.A. Armytage, D.S.O. Commanding 117th Infantry Brigade.	12/08/1917	12/08/1917
War Diary	Chippewa Camp	01/09/1917	04/09/1917
War Diary	Steenvoorde	05/09/1917	12/09/1917
War Diary	Trenches	13/09/1917	15/09/1917
War Diary	N 9.b	16/09/1917	16/09/1917
Miscellaneous	O.A. 830/16	01/09/1917	01/09/1917
Miscellaneous	17th Bn. Sherwood Foresters. Operation Order No. 51	18/09/1917	18/09/1917
Miscellaneous	A Form. Messages And Signals.	21/09/1917	21/09/1917
Miscellaneous	A Form. Messages And Signals.	20/09/1917	20/09/1917
Miscellaneous	A Form. Messages And Signals.	21/09/1917	21/09/1917
Miscellaneous	Report On Operations On September 20th/21st. 1917	25/09/1917	25/09/1917
Miscellaneous	17th Bn. Sherwood Foresters		
Miscellaneous			
War Diary	Camp N 9 B	17/09/1917	20/09/1917
War Diary	Trenches Klein Zillebeke	21/09/1917	22/09/1917
War Diary	Brook Camp	23/09/1917	26/09/1917
War Diary	Ridge Wood	26/09/1917	26/09/1917
War Diary	Trenches	27/09/1917	27/09/1917
War Diary	Locrehof Farm	29/09/1917	15/10/1917
War Diary	Vyverbeeke Camp	16/10/1917	19/10/1917
War Diary	Trenches (Tower Hamlets)	20/10/1917	24/10/1917
War Diary	Vierstraat	25/10/1917	28/10/1917
War Diary	No. 2 Camp Vierstraat	29/10/1917	05/11/1917
War Diary	Chippewa Camp	06/11/1917	07/11/1917
War Diary	Trenches	08/11/1917	10/11/1917
War Diary	Canada St Tunnels	11/11/1917	13/11/1917
War Diary	Ridge Wood	14/11/1917	17/11/1917
War Diary	Trenches	18/11/1917	20/11/1917
War Diary	Chippewa Camp	21/11/1917	24/11/1917
War Diary	Watou	25/11/1917	25/11/1917
War Diary	English Farm	26/11/1917	30/11/1917
Miscellaneous	117th Infantry Brigade No BM/308		
Miscellaneous	117th Infantry Brigade.	06/01/1918	06/01/1918
War Diary	English Farm	01/12/1917	09/12/1917
War Diary	Lottinghem	10/12/1917	28/12/1917

Type	Description	From	To
War Diary	Senninghem And Affringues	29/12/1917	29/12/1917
Miscellaneous	17th. Bn. Sherwood Foresters. (Special) Operation Order No. 62	01/12/1917	01/12/1917
War Diary	Alberta Sector	01/01/1918	03/01/1918
War Diary	Corps Line And Steenbeek	04/01/1918	06/01/1918
War Diary	Albert Sector Corps Line And Steenbeek	07/01/1918	07/01/1918
War Diary	Siege Camp	08/01/1918	14/01/1918
War Diary	Irish Fm	15/01/1918	25/01/1918
War Diary	Suzanne	26/01/1918	29/01/1918
War Diary	Moislains	30/01/1918	30/01/1918
War Diary	St Jean	30/01/1918	30/01/1918
War Diary	Alberta Sector	31/01/1918	31/01/1918
War Diary	Gouzeacourt Sector	31/01/1918	03/02/1918
War Diary	Heudecourt	04/02/1918	12/02/1918
War Diary	Haut. Allaines	13/02/1918	16/02/1918
War Diary	Hamel	17/02/1918	20/02/1918
War Diary	Haut-Allaines	21/02/1918	23/02/1918

w30 05/2 587/2

39TH DIVISION
117TH INFY BDE

17TH BN SHERWOOD FORESTERS

MAR 1916 - FEB 1918

117th Brigade.
39th Division.

Battalion disembarked HAVRE 7.3.16.

WELBECK RANGERS

1/17th BATTALION

NOTTS & DERBY REGIMENT

MARCH 1 9 1 6

Army Form C. 2118

WAR DIARY
of
INTELLIGENCE SUMMARY 17th Sherwood Foresters (Welbeck Rangers)
(Erase heading not required.)

Instructions regarding War Diaries and Intelligence Summaries are contained in F.S. Regs., Part II. and the Staff Manual respectively. Title Pages will be prepared in manuscript.

Place	Date 1916	Hour	Summary of Events and Information	Remarks and references to Appendices
WITLEY CAMP	6th March	10 am / 11 am / 12 m	Battalion moved by 3 Trains from Milford Station to Southampton Docks and embarked on 3 Transports "ARCHANGEL" "INVENTOR" and "CONNAUGHT". Sailed 7.30 pm.	J. Capt ? / J. Capt ?
HAVRE	7th	7 am	Disembarked. Encamped at BLEVILLE	J. Capt ?
HAVRE	8th	5.30 pm	Entrained (2 Trains) Travelled to STEENBECQUE Map Sheet 36A. I.5	J. Capt ? / Lt. Capt ?
STEENBECQUE	9th	11 am	Arrived. Battalion to Billets	J. Capt ?
— do —	10th	—	Routine and Parade. Route March 2 pm	J. Capt ?
— do —	11th	—	Routine and Parades. Route March 2.15 pm	J. Capt ? / Lt. Capt ?
— do —	12th	—	Sunday. Divine Service in Open	
— do —	13th	8.30 am	Marched to ESTAIRES, 11th Brigade, Battalion Billets & Map Sheet 36A. L.29.	J. Capt ?
ESTAIRES	14th	8.15 am	Marched to SAILLY by Companies, Battalion Billeted in area of CUL DE SAC FARM. Battalion in Divisional Reserve. Map Sheet 36 G. 1. 1.	J. Capt ?
— do —	15th	—	Routine. Inspections. Parades. Short Route March.	J. Capt ?

E.A. Hall —............Lt. Colonel,
Comdg. 17th (S) Bn. SHERWOOD FORESTERS

WAR DIARY
INTELLIGENCE SUMMARY

(Erase heading not required.)

17th Sherwood Foresters (Welbeck Rangers)

Army Form C. 2118

Place	Date 1916	Hour	Summary of Events and Information	Remarks and references to Appendices
ESTAIRES	March 16th	5:15 pm	Routine Inspections, Parades. Battalion Inspected by Gen. Sir C. Monro, Commanding 1st Army.	1/C.2118/1
–do–	17th	–	Routine Inspection, Parades, Company Route March. 1st Men Wounded. No 27/335 Pte. Tree 8/184	1/Cp.18/1
–do–	18th	–	Lecture Inspection, Parades, Platoon Route march. Company Officers inspecting "A" Company.	1/Cp.17/1
–do–	19th	10 am	Marched to new Billeting Area. Map Sheet 36A L.23.2.4. "A" and "B" Companies into TRENCHES for instruction. Attached to the 2nd MIDDLESEX REGT. "C" & "D" Companies remain in Billets.	1/Cp.17/1
–do–	20th	–	Routine Inspection, Route march.	1/Cp.17/1
–do–	21st	–	Routine Inspection, Route March	1/Cp.17/1
–do–	22nd	16:30	Routine Inspection, Route march. C and D Companies now into TRENCHES for instruction, attached to 2nd DEVON. Regt. A and B Companies from TRENCHES to Billets.	1/Cp.17/1
–do–	23rd	–	Routine Inspection, Route March, 300 Men Bathing.	1/Cp.17/1

W. Kelly .... Lt. Colonel,
Comdg. 17th (S) Bn. SHERWOOD FORESTERS.

Army Form C. 2118

WAR DIARY
or
INTELLIGENCE SUMMARY

(Erase heading not required.)

17th Sherwood Foresters (Welbeck Rangers)

Instructions regarding War Diaries and Intelligence Summaries are contained in F.S. Regs., Part II. and the Staff Manual respectively. Title Pages will be prepared in manuscript.

Place	Date	Hour	Summary of Events and Information	Remarks and references to Appendices
ESTAIRES	March 24th	—	Routine Inspection. 300 men Bathing. "C" + D Companies from Trenches in Billets about 11 pm. (Casualties during intervention of Companies. Killed 2 wounded)	1 Appx 1
—do—	25th	—	Routine Inspection. 400 men Bathing.	1 Appx 1 / Appx 1
—do—	26th	—	Divine Service. Routine Inspection.	/ Appx 1
—do—	27th	—	Routine Inspection. 17th KRR attached to the Battalion for the day. Larry to Belles.	1 Appx 1
—do—	28th	8.30 am	Marched to new Billeting Area. Map Sheet 36. V. 15 and 16. Distance about 10 miles. (one man fell out)	1 Appx 1
BUSNETTES	29th	—	Routine Inspections.	1 Appx 1
—do—	30th	—	Routine Inspections.	/ Appx 1
—do—	31st	—	Routine Inspections.	/ Appx 1

.... Lt. Colonel,
17th (S) Bn. SHERWOOD FORESTERS.

117th Brigade.
39th Divisen.

1/17th BATTALION

NOTTS & DERBY REGIMENT

V   APRIL 1 9 1 6

Army Form C. 2118

WAR DIARY
or
INTELLIGENCE SUMMARY
(Erase heading not required.)

17th SHERWOOD FORESTERS (Welbeck Rangers)

Vol 2

XXXIX

Place	Date 1916	Hour	Summary of Events and Information	Remarks and references to Appendices
BUSNETTES	April 1st	—	Routine, Inspections, half Battalion Bathing	W/Capt 241
—do—	2nd	—	Routine, Inspections, Divine Service, half Battalion Bathing	W/Capt 241 V/Capt 241
—do—	3rd	—	Routine, Inspections.	V/Capt 241
—do—	4th	10am	Battalion Inspected by Lieut General Sir R.C.B. HAKING. K.C.B. Commanding XI Army Corps. Battalion performed in its turn out. General saying "I am glad to have you"	V/Capt 241 V/Capt 241
—do—	5th	—	Routine, Inspections, Battalion Bathing and charge of linen.	V/Capt 241 V/Capt 241
—do—	6th	9.00am	Marched to new Area. BETHUNE E.11.d. & O. Battalion Billeted.	V/Capt 241
BETHUNE	7th	5.30pm	Marched to new Area ANNEQUIN. F.30.a. & 8. Headquarters & A and B Companies at Billets. A and B Companies to Trenches for instruction with 20th Royal Fusiliers but holding their own trench, viz AUCHY LINE about A.2.c.d. running N.W. S.E. Battalion right flank, 7th Royal SUSSEX Regt. on left flank, 2nd ROYAL WELSH FUSILIERS.	2.C L. Alby [A. Hall] V/Capt 241

[A. Hall] .... Lt. Col.

COMDG. 17th (S) Bn. SHERWOOD FORESTERS.

Army Form C. 2118

WAR DIARY
INTELLIGENCE SUMMARY

(Erase heading not required.)

of 17th Sherwood Foresters (Mellons Rangers)

Instructions regarding War Diaries and Intelligence Summaries are contained in F.S. Regs., Part II. and the Staff Manual respectively. Title Pages will be prepared in manuscript.

Place	Date 1916	Hour	Summary of Events and Information	Remarks and references to Appendices
ANNEQUIN	8th April	—	Routine Inspection. C and D Companies relieved A and B Companies in same line as stated on 7th April 1916. Remainder of Battalion in Billets.	
—do—	9th	—	A and B Companies out at full strength working parties in Annequin. Patrols by C and D Companies from Trenches to Billets Annexe. Complete by 11.30pm. Total Casualties during 2 days: 3 Other ranks wounded.	
—do—	10th	—	Routine. Various working parties. Battalion moves into Trenches at AUCHY RIGHT SUB-SECTION (BETHUNE MAP, Contoured Sheet)	
Auchy	11th	6pm	from A.27.d.8.6.6 to G.H.a.8.8J.) "A" on Right "C" in Centre "B" on left. "D" in Reserve. Battalion on Right 2/K Royal Sussex on Left 2/A & S. HIGHLANDERS. Trench, Patrols, Wire, Work. "SITUATION NORMAL"	
TRENCHES	11th	—	Trench, Patrols, Wire Work. "SITUATION NORMAL" "D" Company move into front line relieving "B" Company. "B" Company moves into Reserve	
—do—	12th	—	from Trenches.	

B. Hall, Lt. Colonel
17th (S) Bn. SHERWOOD FORESTERS

Army Form C. 2118

WAR DIARY
or
INTELLIGENCE SUMMARY
(Erase heading not required.)

17th SHERWOOD FORESTERS (Welbeck Rangers)

Place	Date 1916	Hour	Summary of Events and Information	Remarks and references to Appendices
TRENCHES	Aug 13th	—	Trench Routine normal. Situation normal. 2 Mines were sprung on our immediate right (HOHENZOLLERN REDOUBT) which was followed by a heavy Bombardment on Both sides at 6.30 pm. During the day about 40 Rifle Grenades dropped between our Fire and Support Trenches.	J. Carey
—do—	14th	7.0 bh	Trench Routine work. Situation normal.	J. May 241
		7.0 b h	Battalion relieved (in Trenches) by 1st MIDDLESEX REGT. Marched to BETHUNE and Billetted at ECOLE DES JEUNES FILLES. Map reference (BETHUNE Caitured Sheet E 11. a. 12. 9.)	
		10.6 pm	Total Casualties during this period in Trenches 3 other ranks Killed 10 other ranks Wounded 39 which remain at duty.	
BETHUNE	15th	—	Routine Inspection. Battalion Bathing and Change of underwear. BRIG. GEN. R.F. OLDHAM D.S.O. passing (temp) Command of Brigade Inspected Battalion.	H. Smith 241
BETHUNE	16th	10.30 am	Marched to New Area. HINGETTE. Map reference (BETHUNE Captured Sheet W.17. a. 3. 8.) Settled at in Billets. Inspection Routine. Battalion in DIVISIONAL RESERVE.	M Murray 241
HINGETTE	17th	—	Routine. Inspections.	
—do—	18th	—	Routine Inspections.	R. Taylor

Lt. Col.
Commdg. 17th (S) Bn. SHERWOOD FORESTERS

Army Form C. 2118

WAR DIARY
INTELLIGENCE SUMMARY
(Erase heading not required.)

17th Sherwood Foresters (Welsh Borderers)

Place	Date 1916	Hour	Summary of Events and Information	Remarks and references to Appendices
HINGETTE April 19th	—	—	Routine and Inspection. Inspection of "A" Company by Comdg. Officer. 3 Other ranks killed 3 other ranks wounded while carrying R.E. Tunnelling.	Y/Cap/24/1
—do—	20th	—	Routine and Inspection. 1 other rank killed. 1 other rank wounded while attached to 181st Tunnelling Coy R.E.	Y/Cap/24/1
—do—	21st	—	Good Friday. Divine Service. Inspection of A and D Coys by Comdg Officer. 640 Bathed and Change of underlinen.	Y/Cap/24/1
—do—	22nd	—	Routine. Inspection.	Y/Cap/24/1
—do—	23rd	9.30am	Marched to new area. LE TOURET. (BETHUNE Ordnance SHEET. X.16 a + 9) Battalion Billets. Brigade in front line. Battalion Brigade Reserve.	Y/Cap/24/1
LE TOURET 24th	—	—	EASTER MONDAY. Routine. 300 all ranks working up in front line. FESTUBERT SECTION. Report on Battalion by G.O.C. 98th Brigade Report attached and marked "A". 2nd to Second Tour in Trenches.	Report attached and marked "A" Y/Cap/24/1

W. Hall — Lt Colonel,
COMDG. 17th (S) Bn. SHERWOOD FORESTERS.

WAR DIARY / INTELLIGENCE SUMMARY

Army Form C. 2118

M. Kennard Master (Sherwood Foresters)

Place	Date	Hour	Summary of Events and Information	Remarks and references to Appendices
LE TOURET	April 25th 1916	—	Strength 375 all ranks. Working up to Army for FESTUBERT SECTION.	24 April
—do—	26th	—	Routine. 300 all ranks working up to in front for FESTUBERT SECTION	25 April
—do—	27th	—	Routine. B Company Bathed and Change of underwear. Battalion moves from Brigade Reserve into TRENCHES, FESTUBERT SECTION SUB-SECTION "C.I." (BETHUNE Contoured SHEET) from A.8.b. H.3 to S.26.a.3.7) OLD BRITISH LINE. A Company on Left. B.C.D Company in Regtl Companies held Salients in front as follows:- D Company Princes Salient and no platoon in George Street C Company nos 1, 3, 5, 9. B Company 10. 10a. 11. A Company 12, 13, 13a. Battalion on Right 12th Royal Sussex Regt. Battalion on Left 17th R.P.O. Relief complete at 10.20 p.m.	1 May 1916
TRENCHES	28th		Trench Routine Work. 8.30 pm Priority Message received for GAS. Battalion Stood to Arms. Nothing from Salient reported. No gas in our immediate front. Enemy attack on our Right	

W. Hoskell .... Lt. Colonel,
COMDG. 17th (S) Bn. SHERWOOD FORESTERS.

WAR DIARY
or
INTELLIGENCE SUMMARY

(Erase heading not required.) 17th Sherwood Foresters (Welbeck Rangers)

Army Form C. 2118

Instructions regarding War Diaries and Intelligence Summaries are contained in F.S. Regs., Part II. and the Staff Manual respectively. Title Pages will be prepared in manuscript.

Place	Date 1916	Hour	Summary of Events and Information	Remarks and references to Appendices
	April		Heavy Bombardment on our Right. Our artillery - edge of up trench for an hour. Stood down. Situation normal.	Appx 1
TRENCHES	29th	3 am	TEST. STAND TO. by order of BRIG. GEN. R.D. OLDMAN. D.S.O. Comdg. 117 Infantry Bde. Two tunnels Posted and French Wires. Situation normal.	Appx 1 Appx 1
TRENCHES	30th		Trench Routine. Situation normal.	Appx 1

G.H. Fulle Lt. Colonel,
Comdg. 17th (S) Bn. SHERWOOD FORESTERS.

C O N F I D E N T I A L.

Report on 17th Notts & Derby Regt.,
attached to 98th Inf. Bde. 33rd Division.

OFFICERS. The Officers are keen, and with more experience should do well. Some do not seem to be able to get all the work possible out of their men, due to inability to exercise their powers of command fully at present.

N. C. O's. The N.C.O's. are good material and willing to learn. They are of good stamp and suitable age. They need to acquire more definite control over the men.

MEN. The men are good material and should make good soldiers. They work hard and cheerfully. They are not quick to act on orders but this is probably due to the fact that they are slow thinkers.

DISCIPLINE AND ORGANISATION. Discipline is on the whole good. Officers and N.C.Os. need to learn a rigid enforcement of discipline. The men were alert and careful of their smartness and appearance in the trenches. A stricter attention to trench standing orders is necessary.

Organisation is good down to the smallest unit.
Communication by orderlies requires to be placed on a more satisfactory footing. Attention should be paid to sanitation.

SHEET 2.

MORAL. There is a good tone in the Battalion - and the right offensive spirit exists. Keenness was shown in Rifle Grenade Work.

The general impression which the Battalion made was a very favourable one. The average age of the men seems to be a suitable one. A certain number of the men are quite young, but they are of a good type and should improve rapidly. The chief point which requires improvement is the power and method of exercising commands by Officers and N.C.Os.

117th Brigade.
39th Division.

1/17th BATTALION

NOTTS & DERBY REGIMENT

MAY 1916

WAR DIARY or INTELLIGENCE SUMMARY

Army Form C. 2118

XXXIX Vol 3

(16) 17th SHERWOOD FORESTERS (Welbeck Rangers)

Place	Date 1916	Hour	Summary of Events and Information	Remarks and references to Appendices
TRENCHES / FESTUBERT	May 1st		Trench Routine. Situation normal. Battalion relieved in trenches by 16th Bn. Rifle Brigade. Relief complete by 10.40pm. Total casualties during past 4 days 2 other ranks wounded. Battalion billets in VILLAGE LINE, Rue L'EPINETTE from (Map reference) S.19.t.1.6 to LE PLANTIN. Battalion BRIGADE SUPPORT. (Appx I)	1/5/1916 J. Murray
FESTUBERT	2nd		Routine. 350 all ranks working in front line at night.	J. Murray
—do—	3rd		Routine. 350 all ranks working in front line at night. Gas alarm at 9.30 pm. Stand to. No Gas. Situation normal.	J. Murray
—do—	4th		Routine. 350 all ranks working in front line at night.	J. Murray
—do—	5th	8.30pm	Battalion moves from Brigade Support into Trenches FESTUBERT Section, Sub-Section C.I. high reference as handed over here on April 27th 1916. Companies leading same details and routes & relieving the 16th Rifle Brigade. Relief complete by 10.23pm.	S.C. J. Murray

COMDG. 17th (S) Bn. SHERWOOD FORESTERS. .... Lt. Colonel

Army Form C. 2118

WAR DIARY
INTELLIGENCE SUMMARY

(Erase heading not required.)

17th SHERWOOD FORESTERS (Welbeck Rangers)

Instructions regarding War Diaries and Intelligence Summaries are contained in F.S. Regs., Part II. and the Staff Manual respectively. Title Pages will be prepared in manuscript.

Place	Date 1916	Hour	Summary of Events and Information	Remarks and references to Appendices
TRENCHES	May 6th	—	Trench Routine. Work strong in front of Soliers at night all Companies. Situation normal.	1/Cup.24.1
—do—	7th	—	Trench Routine. Work strong in front of Soliers at night all Companies. Situation normal.	1/Cup.24.1
—do—	8th	—	Trench Routine. Work strong in front of Soliers at night all Companies. Situation normal.	1/Cup.24.1
—do—	9th	—	Trench Routine. Work. Battalion relieved in trenches by 14th HAMPSHIRE REGT. Relief complete by 10 to 3 pm. The Casualties during final 4 days 3 Other Ranks Killed, 1 Other Rank Wounded. Battalion to Billets at HINGETTE (See Diary 16 April 1916) Battalion in Divisional Reserve.	1/Cup.24.1
HINGETTE	10th	—	Routine, Inspections, Companies at Training. 200 men Bathed.	1/Cup.24.1
—do—	11th	—	Routine, Inspections, Companies at Training Battalion Bathed.	1/Cup.24.1
—do—	12th	—	Routine, Companies at Baptures, Company Commander to Tanangaffre form	1/Cup.24.1

.... Lt. Colonel,
COMDG. 17th (S) Bn. SHERWOOD FORESTERS.

Army Form C. 2118

WAR DIARY
or
INTELLIGENCE SUMMARY

(Erase heading not required.)

17th SHERWOOD FORESTERS (Notts & Derbys)

Instructions regarding War Diaries and Intelligence Summaries are contained in F. S. Regs., Part II. and the Staff Manual respectively. Title Pages will be prepared in manuscript.

Place	Date 1916	Hour	Summary of Events and Information	Remarks and references to Appendices
HINGETTE	MAY 13th	—	Routine Conference at Drapeau. Company Commanders for Training before use of programme issued.	[illegible]
—do—	14th	—	Routine Conference at Drapeau. Company Commanders for Training before [illegible] programme issued.	[illegible]
—do—	15th	—	Routine Conference at Drapeau. Company Commanders for Training before [illegible] programme issued.	[illegible]
—do—	16th	—	Routine Conference at Drapeau. Company Commanders for Training before [illegible] programme issued.	[illegible]
—do—	17th 11.30pm	—	Routine. Battalion moved to BRIGADE RESERVE, GORRE (Map reference F.3 & F.5.5.) to billets. Casualties during last 8 days: Killed T (Others), 1 other rank.	[illegible]
GORRE	18th	—	Routine. 250 all ranks working in front line. 1 Coy "A" Training. 240 men Bathed and Change of underclothing.	[illegible]
—do—	19th	—	Routine. 300 all ranks working in front line. 1 Coy "B" Training.	[illegible]
—do—	20th	—	Routine. 280 all ranks working in front line. 1 Coy "C" Training. Remainder of Battalion bathed and change of underclothing.	[illegible]

J. Bottomley Lt. Colonel,
COMDG. 17th (S) Bn. SHERWOOD FORESTERS.

WAR DIARY

INTELLIGENCE SUMMARY
(Erase heading not required.) 17th SHERWOOD FORESTERS (Welbeck Rangers)

Place	Date 1916	Hour	Summary of Events and Information	Remarks and references to Appendices
GORRÉ	May 21st	—	250 All ranks working in front line until Regt. Divine Service. Casualties during 4 days 5 O.Ranks wounded. Battalion known from BRIGADE RESERVE into Trenches with GIVENCHY SECTION, SUB-SECTION "B" I. Map Reference LA BASSÉE CANAL A.16.c.0.6. Right, to A.9.d.5½.2. Left. relieving 16th RIFLE BRIGADE. "A" Coy Complete, 11.10am. 3 Companies FRONT LINE B & "C" Coys Right, 6th ("D" Coy in SUPPORT. Battalion Right. 1st 8th/10th SEAFORTHS. Battalion on left. 1st/11th 16th K.R. RIFLE CORPS.	
		12 M.N.	Enemy Blew up a mine in front of D Company accompanied by heavy bombardment of Trench Mortars and Rifle Grenades. No Casualties from mine explosion from enemy's fire 3 O.Ranks killed 6 O.Ranks wounded	
GIVENCHY TRENCHES	22nd	3 am	Situation Normal.	
		7 pm	Trench Mortar heavy Bombardment about Sides of Battalion frontage on our left.	
		8 pm	Situation Normal. 7 O.Ranks wounded.	
TRENCHES	23rd	—	Trench Routine. Situation Normal. 3 O.Ranks killed. 11 O.Ranks wounded	

B.W. Hacket Pain Lt. Colonel,
COMDG. 17th (S) Bn. SHERWOOD FORESTERS.

Army Form C. 2118

WAR DIARY
INTELLIGENCE SUMMARY

(Erase heading not required.) 17th SHERWOOD FORESTERS (Welbeck Rangers)

Instructions regarding War Diaries and Intelligence Summaries are contained in F. S. Regs., Part II. and the Staff Manual respectively. Title Pages (19) will be prepared in manuscript.

Place	Date 1916	Hour	Summary of Events and Information	Remarks and references to Appendices
TRENCHES	May 24th	—	Trench Routine. Situation normal.	
–do–	25th		Trench Routine. Situation normal. 1 S/O Casualties during past 4 days. 7 other ranks killed & 9 other ranks wounded. Battalion relieved by 16th S/F Brigade. Relief complete 11.45 pm. Battalion moved BRIGADE SUPPORT in VILLAGE LINE area LE PLANTIN – CUINCHY – ROAD from LA BASSEE CANAL, right to WINDY CORNER left, with 2 Platoons in GIVENCHY KEEP and Lay Patrol in HERTS REDOUBT (Map Reference) A, B, C, and A. 14. a, b, and c.	1/May 24th
GIVENCHY	26th		Routine. Inspections. Working Parties. Situation normal.	1/May 26th
–do–	27th		Routine. Inspections. Working Parties. Situation normal.	1/May 26th
–do–	28th		Routine. Inspections. Working Parties. Situation normal.	1/May 28th
–do–	29th		Routine. Working Parties. Casualties during past 4 days 1 Other rank killed	

[signed] .... Lt. Colonel,
COMDG. 17th (S) Bn. SHERWOOD FORESTERS.

Army Form C. 2118

WAR DIARY
INTELLIGENCE SUMMARY

(Erase heading not required.) 17th SHERWOOD FORESTERS (Welbeck Rangers)

Instructions regarding War Diaries and Intelligence Summaries are contained in F. S. Regs., Part II. and the Staff Manual respectively. Title Pages (20) will be prepared in manuscript.

Place	Date 1916	Hour	Summary of Events and Information	Remarks and references to Appendices
GIVENCHY	May 29th (Continued)		3 other Ranks wounded. Battalion move into Trenches GIVENCHY SECTION "B.1" See Map reference 21. 5. '16 FRONT LINE "A" Company Ref. U.B. Company in Centre "C" Company Ref. U., D Company in Reserve.	M/Murray 1/Murray
TRENCHES B.O.1	30th		Trench Routine. Situation normal.	J Slack Givenchy 31.5.16
—do—	31st		Trench Routine. Situation normal.	

W.B. Wallett .... Lt. Colonel,
COMDG. 17th (S) Bn. SHERWOOD FORESTERS.

117th Brigade.
39th Division.

1/17th BATTALION

NOTTS & DERBY REGIMENT

JUNE 1916:

WAR DIARY
INTELLIGENCE SUMMARY

Army Form C. 2118

VOL 4

17th SHERWOOD FORESTERS (Welbeck Rangers)

Place	Date 1916	Hour	Summary of Events and Information	Remarks and references to Appendices
TRENCHES	JUNE 1st		Trench Routine. Situation normal.	1/Coy 24h
—do—	2nd		Trench Routine. Situation normal.	1/Coy 24h
—do—	3rd		Trench Routine. Situation normal. Casualties during past 5 days. Other ranks 4 killed, other ranks 11 wounded. Battalion relieved by 16th Rifle Brigade. Relief complete 10.30 p.m. Battalion moved to GORRE (Map reference) see map for 17th May 1916. Battalion became Brigade Reserve — with "D" Company in VILLAGE LINE see close support. Map reference see map for 25th May 1916.	1/Coy 24h
GORRE	4th		Routine Inspection. Itf. Off. to "A" Company Bathed and Change of under-Clothing. Bathing Parties. "B" Company here up to full Company in Close Reserve, dup. reference. (A 1st & Central) Retaliation formed to Billets 2 a.m. 5/6/16	1/Coy 24h 4/Coy 24h Tally
—do—	5th		Routine Inspection. Working Parties "B" & "C" Companies.	4/Coy 24h

Commdg. 17th (S) Bn. SHERWOOD FORESTERS.

Army Form C. 2118

WAR DIARY
or
INTELLIGENCE SUMMARY
(Erase heading not required.) 17¼ SHERWOOD FORESTERS (Welbeck Rangers)

Place	Date 1916	Hour	Summary of Events and Information	Remarks and references to Appendices
GORRE	Aug 6th		Routine Inspections. Working parties. Blighty Ball Charge (underclothing). Battalion relieved by 1/Herts Regt relief Complete at 10.15 pm. Battalion to Billets at FERME DU ROI. Settled at 12.15 am 7/6/16. Map Reference E.6.c.4.6. Battalion in Divisional Reserve.	Mayzas Hayzas
FERME DU ROI.	7th		Routine. General clean up. Inspections.	Mayzas
—do—	8th		Routine. Training under Company Commanders and Specialists. 1 pm Holiday programme issued.	Mayzas
—do—	9th		Routine. Training under Company Commanders and Specialists. 1 pm Holiday programme issued.	Mayzas
—do—	10th		Routine. Training under Company Commanders and Specialists. 1 pm Holiday programme issued. 120 new Baths and Change of underclothing.	Mayzas

Ainsworth .... Lt. Colonel,
Comdg. 17th (S) Bn. SHERWOOD FORESTERS.

Army Form C. 2118

WAR DIARY
INTELLIGENCE SUMMARY
(Erase heading not required.)

17th SHERWOOD FORESTERS (Welbeck Rangers)

Instructions regarding War Diaries and Intelligence Summaries are contained in F.S. Regs., Part II. and the Staff Manual respectively. Title Pages will be prepared in manuscript.

Place	Date 1916	Hour	Summary of Events and Information	Remarks and references to Appendices
FERME DU ROI.	June 11th		Divn Serves Paraded. Battalion Bathed and change of underclothing. Battalion moves into trenches FESTUBERT Right Sub Section. See April 27th 1916. Companies occupy sub Section. Relieving 17th Bn ROYAL SCOTS. Relief Complete 11.30 pm. Situation normal.	J/Clark
TRENCHES	12th		Trench Routine. Situation normal.	J/Vaughan
—do—	13th		Trench Routine. Situation normal.	J/Vaughan
—do—	14th		Trench Routine. Situation normal. Major H.M. MILWARD 16 R Bn. SHERWOOD FORESTERS assumed Command of the Battalion vice Lieut. Col. E.B. HALES to ENGLAND.	J/Curzon
—do—	15th		Trench Routine. Situation normal.	J/Carthew

H. Milward............Lt. Colonel,
COMDG. 17th (S) Bn. SHERWOOD FORESTERS.

Army Form C. 2118

WAR DIARY
INTELLIGENCE SUMMARY
(Erase heading not required.)

17th SHERWOOD FORESTER'S (Welbeck Rangers)

Place	Date 1916	Hour	Summary of Events and Information	Remarks and references to Appendices
TRENCHES	JUNE 16th		Trench Routine. Situation normal. Adjustment of the BRIGADE frontage. 'A' Company move to LE PLANTIN. 'C' Company in Reserve. (Map Reference A.2.c.) 'B' Company in O.B.L. See trench diete April 27th 1916. 'C' Company relieving Strands 1 - 10 inclusive. 'D' Company PRINCES ISLAND and one Platoon in GEORGE STREET.	See Map 241
do	17th		Trench Routine. Situation normal. One half of 'A' Company Bathed and Change of underclothing.	See Map 241
do	18th		Trench Routine. Situation normal. No half of 'A' Company Bathed and Change of underclothing. 'A' Company relieve 'C' Company in front line (prior to 16th June 1916) 'C' Company to Reserve in front line (prior to 16th June 1916) 'B' and 'D' Companies change places in front line. (See April 27th 1916)	See Map 241

W. Winshurst Lt. Colonel,
COMDG. 17th (S) Bn. SHERWOOD FORESTERS.

Army Form C. 2118

WAR DIARY
~~INTELLIGENCE SUMMARY~~
(Erase heading not required.)

(13) 17th SHERWOOD FORESTERS (Welbeck Rangers)

Instructions regarding War Diaries and Intelligence Summaries are contained in F.S. Regs., Part II. and the Staff Manual respectively. Title Pages will be prepared in manuscript.

Place	Date 1916	Hour	Summary of Events and Information	Remarks and references to Appendices
TRENCHES	June 19th		Trench Routine. Situation normal, one half of C Company Bathed and Change of underclothing.	Weather
—do—	20th		Trench Routine, Situation normal, one half of C Company Bathed and Change of underclothing. C and D Companies relieve each other. D Company to Reserve LE PLANTIN. C Company to front line.	Weather
—do—	21st		Trench Routine. Situation normal, one half of D Company Bathed and Change of underclothing.	Weather (papers)
—do—	22nd		Trench Routine, Situation normal, one half of D Company Bathed and Change of underclothing. D Company Move into front line. The Battalion relieves its normal Position as for 27th April 1916. Order of Companies from left to right D. C. A. and B. Compared.	Weather

H. Newland Lt. Colonel,
COMDG. 17th (S) Bn. SHERWOOD FORESTERS.

WAR DIARY
or
INTELLIGENCE SUMMARY

Army Form C. 2118

(Erase heading not required.) 17th SHERWOOD FORESTERS (Welbeck Rangers)

Place	Date 1916	Hour	Summary of Events and Information	Remarks and references to Appendices
TRENCHES	June 23rd		Trench Routine. Situation normal. 2½ Platoon of 'B' Company bathed and chay! underclothing.	1/Jun 23rd
— do —	24th		Trench Routine. Situation normal.	1/Jun 24th
— do —	25th		Trench Routine. Situation normal.	
— do —	26th		Trench Routine. Artillery Bombardment of Enemy line opposite our front. "Popes Nose" (A.3, 4, 2, 4 and 5) much damage to German left sector Trenches were caught by snipers. Enemy retaliated on O.B.L. Situation in Sherry normal.	1/Jun 26th
— do —	27th		Trench Routine. Enemy Bombarded our line in O.B.L during day. Situation in evening normal.	1/Jun 27th
— do —	28th		Trench Routine. Situation normal.	1/Jun 28th
— do —	29th		Trench Routine. Situation normal.	1/Jun 29th

.... Lt. Colonel,
COMDG. 17th (S) Bn. SHERWOOD FORESTERS.

Army Form C. 2118

WAR DIARY

INTELLIGENCE SUMMARY

(Erase heading not required.) 17th SHERWOOD FORESTERS (Notts & Derby Regt)

Place	Date 1916	Hour	Summary of Events and Information	Remarks and references to Appendices
TRENCHES	June 30th		Trench Raids. Situation normal. The casualties since 11th June 1916. 1 Officer wounded. 2nd Lieut G. REECE. 9 Other ranks killed. 1 Other Rank died of wounds. 33 Other ranks wounded.	J.H. Warde Capt & Adjt.

J.H. Warde Lt. Colonel,
COMDG. 17th (S) Bn. SHERWOOD FORESTERS.

117th Brigade.
39th Division.

1/17th BATTALION

NOTTS & DERBY REGIMENT

JULY 1916

Attached:-

Reports on Raids.

WAR DIARY

INTELLIGENCE SUMMARY

No 18 No 3 B C July
No 13 17th SHERWOOD FORESTERS (welled Regt)
Army Form C. 2118

Vol 5

Place	Date 1915	Hour	Summary of Events and Information	Remarks and references to Appendices
TRENCHES	July 1st		Trench Routine. Situation Normal.	W/[Ay1245]
do	2nd		Trench Routine. Situation Normal. LIEUT. C.M. WOOD. Wounded 3 other ranks Killed 12 Other Ranks Wounded. 120 men Bathed and change of underclothing.	W/[Ay1245]
do	3rd		Trench Routine. MAJOR H.M. MILWARD. Proceeded LIEUT. COLONEL to Command 1/8 Battalion. Battalion took part in raid on German Trenches. Strength 2 Officers (2/Lieuts W.N.N. DIXON and A.T. BULLIVANT.) and 1/8 7/C O and men. Raid most Successful. Casualties 2nd Lieut AT BULLIVANT wounded 1 Other Rank Killed, 1 Other Rank Missing 11 Other Ranks wounded. In addition during day Casualties went to Other ranks Killed 6 Other Ranks wounded. Total 1 Officer wounded, 5 Other Ranks Killed, 10 Other Rank Missing, 17 Other Ranks wounded. Operation Orders Resume of	W/[Ay1245] W/M/1 4/[Ay1245] 5.C

WAR DIARY
INTELLIGENCE SUMMARY

(Erase heading not required.) 17th SHERWOOD FORESTERS (Welbeck Rangers)

Army Form C. 2118

Instructions regarding War Diaries and Intelligence Summaries are contained in F.S. Regs., Part II. and the Staff Manual respectively. Title Pages will be prepared in manuscript.

Place	Date 1916	Hour	Summary of Events and Information	Remarks and references to Appendices
TRENCHES	July 3rd (Continued)		RAID and Congratulatory MESSAGES and other relating to raid attached as APPENDICES. Number B.1. to B.5.] OPERATION ORDER ACCOUNT OF OPERATION. XI CORPS WIRE 3rd Division WIRE Battalion Order by Lieut Col H. M. MILWARD. In conjunction with 16th Bn RIFLE BRIGADE.	B.1. B.2. B.3. B.4. B.5. 4/Cyp74) 4/Cyp74)
			The raid was carried out in conjunction with 16th Bn RIFLE BRIGADE. Trench Routine. Situation normal.	
TRENCHES 41	5th		Trench Routine. G.O.C. 117 INFANTRY BRIGADE (BRIG GEN R.F. OLDMAN. D.S.O) spoke to Raiding Party on the 4th July 1916 and stated how pleased he was with the fighting Spirit Shown, and that they had brought Great Credit to the

17th (S) Bn SHERWOOD FORESTERS

WAR DIARY
INTELLIGENCE SUMMARY

(Erase heading not required.) 17th SHERWOOD FORESTERS (Welsh Ridge)

Army Form C. 2118

Instructions regarding War Diaries and Intelligence Summaries are contained in F. S. Regs., Part II. and the Staff Manual respectively. Title Pages will be prepared in manuscript.

Place	Date 1916	Hour	Summary of Events and Information	Remarks and references to Appendices
TRENCHES (Cuinchy)	JULY 5th		Battalion try their gallant Conduct, it moved up then in line with Coming and billed in fight when forming part of 16 Brig. Bulut Yenture in infantry plane. Situation normal. Lieut J. LAWSON wounded.	N/Capt 74) C.I
		1030 P.M.	Report in mean that who performed good work night 3/1st July 1916. Heavy Artillery bombardment on enemy line on our right. (GIVENCHY) ROYAL WELSH FUSILIERS raid enemy front line enemy reply by placing Barrage on our lines and later Continued to 2.30pm 6/7/1916. Very slight damage during the day. 120 men were bathed and change of underclothing	H/Capt 74) N/Capt 74)
TRENCHES	6th		Trench Routine, Situation normal	N/Capt 74)
-do-	7th		Trench Routine, Situation normal	N/Capt 74)
-do-	8th		Trench Routine, Situation normal 120 men were bathed and change of underclothing during the day.	N/Capt 74)

H. Michael Lt. Colonel
COMDG. 17th (S) Bn. SHERWOOD FORESTERS.

WAR DIARY

INTELLIGENCE SUMMARY

(Erase heading not required.) 17R SHERWOOD FORESTERS (Welbeck Rangers)

Army Form C. 2118

Place	Date	Hour	Summary of Events and Information	Remarks and references to Appendices
TRENCHES	July 9th		Trench Routine. Situation normal. 100 men Bathed and change of underclothing during the day.	A.1.9/7/16
—do—	10th		Trench Routine. Situation normal. 100 men Bathed and change of underclothing during the day.	A.1.10/7/16 J.1. Cypher
—do—	11th		Trench Routine. Situation normal.	
—do—	12th	1.30 am	Trench Routine. 120 men bathed and change of underclothing during the day. Lieut. F. RENSHAW. Killed. In conjunction with raids by 16th Bn. SHERWOOD FORESTERS and 16th Bn. K.R.R. CORPS. on our right, we Put up a SMOKE BARRAGE against the GERMAN front line with the wind blowing from the WEST. from the enemy, which when he was placed them in a panic as he at once lit-flares and opened Rapid and Machine Gun fire and his Querry-opening Rapid and Machine Gun fire. It is doubted that the enemy thought we were about to discharge a gas attack.	

..................................Lt. Colonel
COMDG. 17th (S) Bn. SHERWOOD FORESTERS.

Army Form C. 2118

WAR DIARY
INTELLIGENCE SUMMARY

(Erase heading not required.) 17th SHERWOOD FORESTERS (Welbeck Rangers)

Instructions regarding War Diaries and Intelligence Summaries are contained in F.S. Regs., Part II. and the Staff Manual respectively. Title Pages will be prepared in manuscript.

Place	Date	Hour	Summary of Events and Information	Remarks and references to Appendices
TRENCHES (continued)	July 1916 12th		at once replied with an intense bombardment. Our O.C.-D. BRITISH LINE and all communication trenches got a very bad hurt with batteries to avenge. The Barrage was expected and called forth. Smoke barrage. Our up to divert the artillery from the raiders worked. On the whole we were fortunate. 3.15 am Situation normal.	1 (Appx 24)
TRENCHES	13th		Trench Routine. The Raiding Party of the 3rd July 1916 was inspected by the 1st Army Corps Commander GENERAL SIR CHARLES MONRO, G.C.M.G. K.C.B. He congratulated them on their work, and informed them it was the same work as their comrades were doing in the South at the Battle of the SOMME. He expressed himself as being very pleased with their turn out and smart appearance, stated that they were very much satisfied from what he saw. Item that Situation normal.	1 (Appx 25)

J. W. Hanson Lt. Colonel,
COMDG. 17th (S) Bn. SHERWOOD FORESTERS.

WAR DIARY
INTELLIGENCE SUMMARY

Army Form C. 2118

(63) 17th SHERWOOD FORESTERS (Welbeck Rangers)

Place	Date 1916	Hour	Summary of Events and Information	Remarks and references to Appendices
TRENCHES	July 14th		French Rohn, Strailing Normal Battalion relieved by the 1/ Cambridgeshire Regt. Battalion relief complete 11.50pm. The Casualties since 3rd July 1916. 1 Officer Killed, 1 Officer wounded, 5 other ranks Killed, 29 other ranks wounded. Battalion's tour in the trenches 34 days. The Casualties during this period. 1 Officer Killed, 1 Officer wounded, 30 other ranks Killed, 95 other ranks wounded. Battalion move into BRIGADE SUPPORT at RICHEBOURG ST. VAAST. (Map Reference S.2. a. 2. 7.) Battalion Hd Qr at the place with A and B Companies. C and D Companies in an area of Lufking within Regiment.	
RICHEBOURG ST. VAAST.	15th		Battalion relieved 1/Lufking within Regiment. General Route, Rest, and Clean up.	

.... Lt. Colonel
COMDG. 17th (S) Bn. SHERWOOD FORESTERS.

Army Form C. 2118

WAR DIARY
INTELLIGENCE SUMMARY

(Erase heading not required.) 17th SHERWOOD FORESTERS (Welbeck Rangers)

Instructions regarding War Diaries and Intelligence Summaries are contained in F.S. Regs., Part II. and the Staff Manual respectively. Title Pages will be prepared in manuscript.

Place	Date 1916	Hour	Summary of Events and Information	Remarks and references to Appendices
RICHEBOURG ST. VAAST	16th July		Routine. Working Parties. Bathing.	M. [signed] 1/Aug/4
—do—	17th		Routine. Working Parties. Bathing.	J. [signed] 1/Aug/4
—do—	18th		Routine. Working Parties. Bathing.	J. [signed] 1/Aug/4
—do—	19th		Routine. Working Parties. Bathing. Battalion took part in small raid on enemy's trenches without success. Order etc attached in appendices to D.1. & 3	J. [signed] 1/Aug/4
			OPERATION ORDER	D.1.
			AMENDMENT TO SAME	D.2.
			ACCOUNT OF OPERATION	D.3
			2nd Lieut W.R. BEAMER Wounded.	
			1 Other rank missing	
			4 Other Ranks wounded.	
—do—	20th		Routine. Working Parties. Bathing.	J. [signed] 1/Aug/4 / 1/Aug/4
—do—	21st		Routine. Working Parties. Bathing. 7641167 A.T. BULLIVANT DIED of his wounds at BETHUNE.	J. [signed] 1/Aug/4

COMDG. 17th (S) Bn. SHERWOOD FORESTERS
.... Lt. Colonel.

Army Form C. 2118

WAR DIARY
or
INTELLIGENCE SUMMARY
(Erase heading not required.) 17th SHERWOOD FORESTERS (Welbeck Rangers)

Instructions regarding War Diaries and Intelligence Summaries are contained in F. S. Regs., Part II. and the Staff Manual respectively. Title Pages will be prepared in manuscript.

(35)

Place	Date 1916	Hour	Summary of Events and Information	Remarks and references to Appendices
RICHEBOURG	July 22nd		Routine. Working Parties. Bathing.	Appx 1 / Appx 2
—do—	23rd		Routine. Working Parties. Bathing.	
—do—	24th	5.25 pm	Royal Battalion relieved by 10th Battalion E. YORKSHIRE Regt. Relief Complete 5.25 pm. 1/5th Canadians during stay in Brigade Support. 1 Officer wounded. 1 Other Rank wounded and Prisoner. Other rank killed. 4 other ranks wounded. Battalion marched to LES CHOQUAUX. Companies being scattered in Billets Battalion Hd. Qrs. (W.D.H.6.1.8.)	Appx 3
LES CHOQUAUX	25th		Routine. Company Training from 7 am to 1 pm	Appx 4

[signature] Lt. Colonel,
COMDG. 17th (S) Bn. SHERWOOD FORESTERS,

WAR DIARY
INTELLIGENCE SUMMARY

Army Form C. 2118

17th SHERWOOD FORESTERS (Nottes Rangers)

Place	Date 1916	Hour	Summary of Events and Information	Remarks and references to Appendices
LES CHOQUAUX	July 26th		Routine. Battalion moves into GIVENCHY SECTION, Sub-Section B I and II. See map reference 21st May 1916. Battalion occupies VILLAGE LINE and becomes BRIGADE SUPPORT, relieving 1/6 CHESHIRE REGT. Disposition "A" Company GIVENCHY KEEP. 2 Platoons HERTS REDOUBT. 1 Platoon HILDER'S REDOUBT. ½ Platoon MOAT FARM. ½ Platoon. "B" Company PONT FIXE S. "C" Company PONT FIXE N. 3 Platoons. 1 Platoon "D" Company WINDY-CORNER. 3 Platoons ORCHARD KEEP. 1 Platoon LE PLANTIN. S. 1 Platoon relief complete 8.30 p.m. Battalion Hd Qrs. (Map Reference A.14.a.9.2.6.)	W Murphy / W Carter / W Carter / W Carter
GIVENCHY	27th		Routine. Working parties.	
—do—	28th		Routine. Working parties.	
—do—	29th		Routine. Working parties.	

Army Form C. 2118

WAR DIARY
INTELLIGENCE SUMMARY
(Erase heading not required.) 17d SHERWOOD FORESTERS (Welbeck Rangers)

Place	Date 1916	Hour	Summary of Events and Information	Remarks and references to Appendices
GIVENCHY	July 30th		Routine. Working Parties.	
-do-	31st		Routine. Working Parties. "B" Company Raided Enemy Trenches. Full details to follow with 1st August 1916.	

J Kirkman
Lt. Colonel,
COMDG. 17th (S) Bn. SHERWOOD FORESTERS.

SECRET.   17th. SHERWOOD FORESTERS.   B1

Small Operation Order to be carried
out on the night 3/4 July-16.

1. OBJECTIVE.   To make a demonstration on the German
Front Line trench at (A.3.a.5½.4.) on
a front of about 60 yards, do as much
damage as possible and remain in about
15 min, thereafter remaining in NO MANS
LAND - to guard the right flank of the
raid on A.3.b.3½.5½.

2. COMPOSITION OF PARTY.
A. Party. Cpl. Wintle and 8 men.
B.   "   L/Cpl. Cawthorne. and 8 men.
Liason " 2/Lt. Birkin, 1 N.C.O. & 11 men.
Support" 2/Lt. Bullivant, 1N.C.O.& 8 men.
1 L.GUN. L/Cpl. Freeman and team.

3. PLAN.   A and B. Parties will leave No.3. Island
and advance as quietly as possible, rush
through the gaps in the German wire and
bomb outwards, down the German front line
trench.

LIASON PARTY.

Will follow A and B Parties at a distance
of about 15 yards - as soon as the
leading parties are clear they will at
once enter the German trench and remain
at the point of entry and keep
communication with both flank parties.

SUPPORT PARTY.

Will follow 10 yards in rear of the
Liason Party and lie down just on the
near side of the German wire-
They will remain to the last and cover
the withdrawal of the first 3 parties

SHEET 2.

In addition they are responsible for collecting and evacuating the wounded. Four Stretchers will accompany this party.

LEWIS GUN. Will take up a position in NO MANS LAND at pre-arranged spot.

WITHDRAWAL. On the order being given to withdraw, the party will withdraw and take up a position in NO MANS LAND with the L.G. and cover the right flank.

4. STORES TO BE CARRIED.
Bombers and Carriers, 10 Bombs each.
Support Party, 20 Bombs each.
Bayonet Men, 3 Bombs each.
A and B Parties will carry 5 Wire-cutters each.

5. DRESS. Skeleton Marching Order, no Entrenching tools.

6. PASSWORD. - WELBECK -

7. ARTILLERY. Will fire on agreed on points.

8. TIMINGS. Zero will be notified later.
O.O. to 10 hrs. Intense Artillery Bombardment.
O.O. Assembly of Inf. parties in NO MANS LAND.
O.6. Assault of German Trenches.
O.10. Demonstration at point 34 by 17th. Sherwood Foresters.
O.12. Switch off Artillery to form barrage.
O.12. Light Trench Mortars open fire.
O.12. Rifle and L.G. fire on German Trenches from Islands 22-24.

SHEET 3.

0.55.	Withdrawal begins on "Inf.Clear" Artillery drop to German front line.
9.	The word RETIRE will not be used throughout the operations, everyone must understand that if heard it will not come from anyone in authority.
10. ASSEMBLY.	The party will be in position at No.3. Island 20 mins. before time.
11.	A complete roll of Officers N.C.O's. and men will be taken at the Junction of FIFE Rd and O.B.L. by the Regtl. Sgt. Major at a time to be notified later. He will also take charge of all personal effects of the party. On completion of the operation a roll will be checked at the same place.
12.	Regtl. Aid Post at Junction of BARNTON Rd. and O.B.L.
13.	Garrisons of all Islands, BARNTON T. Trench, GEORGE St. will stand to during the operation. Artillery patrols from Islands 1 - 13a will withdraw until the operations are finished. All Companies in the O.B.L. will stand to.
14.	Watches will be synchronized at 8 p.m. and 10 p.m.
15.	Position of O.C. at Bn.Hd.Qrs.
16.	The party will have black corked faces.
3.5.16.	(sd) H.M. Milward. Lt.Col. Cmdg. 17th.Sherwood Foresters.

17th. SHERWOOD FORESTERS.   B.2

117th Infantry Brigade.

I beg to report for the information of the G.O.C. a brief account of the small operation carried out by the 17th Sherwood Foresters on the night 3/4th July 1916.

The party of 5 N.C.O's. and 43 men under 2/Lts. W.N. Birkin and A.J. Bullivant, left No.3. Island at 12.30 a.m. to make a raid on the German Trench at (A.3.d.5½.4½.)

On arriving 20 yards from the German wire they encountered a party of the enemy lying out on our side of their wire who they drove in, with bombs. They then went forward to the wire which was 20 yards deep and only cut half way.

While cutting their way through the remaining distance, the Germans opened fire with four Machine Guns, and rapid rifle fire.

This part of the Trench was held very strongly. In spite of the heavy fire, and under cover of our bombs twelve men actually got into the German

SHEET 2.

Trenches, and bombed the Germans with great success; Pte. Taylor accounting for a number of the enemy himself.

At 1.10 a.m. the party withdrew under cover of the Support party to a selected position in NO MANS LAND where they covered the right flank, with one Lewis Gun which had been left there for this purpose when the party advanced.

At 1.50 a.m. the whole party withdrew on to No.3. Island.

The Total Casualties were:-

1 Officer Wounded.
1 Man killed.
1 Man Missing.
5 N.C.O's. Wounded.
6 Men.   Wounded.

I have one or two names which I desire to bring to the notice of the G.O.C. These will be forwarded tomorrow.

4.7.16.
          H.M.Milward. Lt.Col.
         Comdg. 17th.Sherwood Foresters.

"A" Form.
MESSAGES AND SIGNALS.
Army Form C. 212

TO	O.C. 17th. Notts & Derby. R.	

Sender's Number.	Day of Month.	In reply to Number.	
*117/B.M./A368	4th		A A A

This message is on a/c of:

B 3 Service.

Eleventh Corps wire begins AAA
Corps Commander congratulates 18th Rifle Brigade
and 17th Sherwood Foresters on the successful raids
last night.

From H.Q. 117 Inf. Bde.
Place —
Time 12.25 p.m.

E. Krolik Lt.

"A" Form.
MESSAGES AND SIGNALS.

Army Form C.2121.

TO: O.C. 17 Notts & Derby R.

Sender's Number.	Day of Month.	In reply to Number.	
B.M./A367	Fourth		A A A

Copy of wire received from 39th Division AAA
The Divisional Commander heartily congratulates
the 16th Rifle Brigade and 17th Sherwood Foresters
on their successful raids last night AAA He
considers that the fighting spirit shewn was
excellent AAA ends.

From H.Q. 117 Inf. Bde.
Place
Time 12.5 p.m.

(Z) E.Krolik. Lt.

COPY.

B5

No. 92.   Battalion Daily Orders by
           Lt.Col. H.M. Milward,
           Cmdg. 17th. Sherwood Foresters.

       X   X   X.

5, OPERATIONS.

      The Officer Commanding wishes it conveyed to all ranks who took part in the small raid into the German Trenches last night his great appreciation in the way in which it was carried out, against the strong opposition which it met.

       X   X   X

4.7.16.   (sd) T. Thornton. Capt & Adjt.
                17th. Sherwood Foresters.

17th. SHERWOOD FORESTERS.

C I

Headquarters,
117th. Infantry Brigade.

Herewith the names of the Officers, N.C.O's. and men who I wish to bring to the notice of the G.O.C. for good service rendered during the operations on the night 3/4 July 1916.

2/Lt. W. N. BIRKIN.

This Officer was in charge of the party - he showed exceptional cool and good leadership.

After the withdrawal of the party he repeatedly went out and assisted in bringing in wounded men under fire.

This Officer on several previous occasions has done very valuable work on reconnoitring patrols.

No. 27846. L/Cpl. E. CAWTHORNE.

Although wounded himself remained in the German Sap after the withdrawal had been ordered with a badly wounded man until he died; he then brought back under heavy fire another man who was also wounded.

No. 30499. Pte. J. T. BELFIELD.

Remained in the German Sap after the withdrawal had been ordered with L/Cpl. E. Cawthorne looking after a badly wounded man until he died.

He then carried another wounded man back from the German wire.

No. 27598. Pte. F. TAYLOR.

Accounted for a great many of the enemy - he bayoneted one of the enemy in the German trench and being suddenly attacked had not time to withdraw his bayonet and fought his way out with bombs inflicting considerable loss.

This man has done very well on several previous occasions.

2/Lt. A. J. BULLIVANT.

Did very valuable work during this raid until wounded.

SHEET 2.

This Officer has done very good work on several previous occasions, especially in reconnoitring the enemy's front line and wire.

In the Field.
3.7.16.

H. Millward
Lt. Col.
Cmdg. 17th. Sherwood Foresters.

COPY.

SECRET. 17th. SHERWOOD FORESTERS.
OPERATION ORDER No. 8.
To be carried out night of 18/19 July 1916.

D.I.

1. OBJECTIVE. To raid the German Front Line trench at S.16.a.8.0. at all costs, capture a prisoner, and on completion of object, withdraw.

2. COMPOSITION OF PARTY. A. Party 2 N.C.O's. 8 men.
Liason " 2/Lt. Benner and 8 men.
Four Stretcher bearers.

3. PLAN. A. Party will leave R.B. Front Line trench at S.16.c.3.9. advance in file as quietly as possible, rush through the gap in the German wire, and bomb outwards down a distance of about 50 yards.

Liason Party, will follow the first party in file at a distance of about 10 yards and remain in the German front line trench at the point of entry. They will then bomb all dug-outs and endeavour to capture a live prisoner.

4. STORES TO BE CARRIED. A. Party. 10 Bombs each.
4 prs. Wire Cutters.
Liason " 5 Bombs each.

5. DRESS. Shirt Sleeves, no equipment. Rifle and Bayonets, caps.

6. PASSWORD. HELEN.

7. ASSEMBLY. The party will assemble in the R.B. front line trench at S.16.c.3.9. at 9.45 p.m.

8. The word Retire will not be used and if heard will only come from a HUN.

9. A complete roll of N.C.O's. and men will be taken at R.B. Hd. Qrs. at 9.30 p.m. (S.9.a.8.5.)
On completion of operations the party will be marched back and the roll called at the R.B. Hd.Qrs. S.9.a.8.5. by the Regtl. Sgt. Major.

10. The R.B. Aid Post at S.9.d.2.7½. will be used. Stretchers from the front line will go by way of COCKSPUR ST.

11. Position of O.C. will be at R.B. Hd.Qrs. S.9.a.8.5.

17.7.16.
(sd) H.Milward. Lt.Col.
Comdg. 17th. Sherwood Foresters.

SECRET. 17th. SHERWOOD FORESTERS.
Amendment to Operation Order No. 8.
Alternative plans for small operation
to be carried out night of 19/20 July 1916.

1. Form up in NO MANS LAND as per sketch opposite gap in German wire.
    Centre party at P. try and entice German patrol to come out and rush them. "If he does so" the two flank parties A1 & A2 allow him to get right up to P. they will then rush in and capture German patrol.
    If a prisoner is captured they will at once return to our line covered by Liason Party.

2. If he does not rise to the occasion as per Plan 1. the O.C. party at P. pulls strings running back to LIASON PARTY and the operation is carried out as previously arranged in operation orders.

3. If the German spot the party taking up their position as per Plan 1. they will at once rush through the wire and attack the German trench as arranged in original Operation Order.

18.7.16.   (sd) H.Milward, Lt.Col.
                        Cmdg. 17th. Sherwood Foresters.

COPY.

SECRET.

No. L.

17t. SHERWOOD FORESTERS.
Raid on night of 19/20 July 16.

At 10.45 p.m. the party of 1 Officer & 18 other ranks left out front line trench at S.16.c.3.9. They advanced as arranged and took up their allotted position after laying there for some time. A German patrol started to come out but being suspicious went back before it had entered his wire - they evidently spotted something, because a few minutes afterwards they at once threw bombs and opened rapid fire from their parapet wounding the Officer in charge of the party and the two N.C.O's. at once.
A considerable amount of wire had been put out just in rear of the gap.
The parapet was strongly manned.
All the leaders being wounded the Officer i/c ordered them to withdraw, they got back to our Front Line, at 12.30 a.m.

The following casualties occured:-
    1 Officer wounded.
    1 N.C.O. Missing, believed killed.
    1 " Wounded.
    2 Ptes. "
    1 Pte. Wounded at duty.

20.7.16.   (sd) H.Milward.Lt.Col.

117th Brigade.
39th Division.

1/17th BATTALION

NOTTS & DERBY REGIMENT

AUGUST 1 9 1 6

Attached:-

Report on Raids.

Army Form C. 2118

WAR DIARY
INTELLIGENCE SUMMARY
(Erase heading not required.)

17th SHERWOOD FORESTERS (Welbeck Rangers)

Place	Date	Hour	Summary of Events and Information	Remarks and references to Appendices
GIVENCHY	August 1916		Ranks. Battalion relieve 16th Rifle Brigade in GIVENCHY Right Sub Section. (map reference See Sh1 new 1/916). A Company & Right 'C' Company in the centre. B Company on left. B Company in Support. Pork and Beef Red. A Coy. 1 Platoon Spoilbank 1 Platn GUNNERS SIDING. "C" Company 1 Platoon Orchard Redt. 2 Platoons 1 Platn MARIE REDOUBT. Relief complete 10.55 pm Account of Raid carried out on the night of 31st August B Company. Raiders Trench Ferrule (?) (MAP REFERENCE A,10, c, 4, 3.) Selected. O.Rs & attached in afternoon dies. Casualties Killed 2nd Lieut. H.A. LANGFORD. 2nd Lieut F.G. DENNIS. 2nd Lieut. G.C. BOLTON. Wounded Captain F.B. LUDLOW. 2nd Lieut. M.A. KENT. 2nd Lieut L.E. FLINT. Other ranks Killed 8. Missing 12. Wounded. 43. Total casualties Died 68.9	6.C. Operation Order E.1. Account of Operation E.2. Officers, NCOs recommended for gallantry E.3. Brigade Report of Raid E...

K.M. Ward
Lt. Colonel.
COMDG. 17th (S) Bn. SHERWOOD FORESTERS.

Army Form C. 2118

WAR DIARY
INTELLIGENCE SUMMARY
(Erase heading not required.) 17th SHERWOOD FORESTERS (Welbeck Rangers)

Place	Date 1916	Hour	Summary of Events and Information	Remarks and references to Appendices
TRENCHES	August 2nd		Routine. Situation normal.	[appx]
—do—	3rd.		Routine. Enemy shelled front line & left Company Cmdrs. Dug out. Our heavy artillery replied (about 6 effec.) Situation normal about 6.30 p.m.	[appx]
—do—	4th.		Routine. Situation normal.	[appx]
—do—	5th.		Routine. Situation normal.	[appx]
—do—	6th.		Routine. Situation normal. Battalion relieved by the 11th Bn. ROYAL SUSSEX Regt. Relief complete 11.15 p.m. Battalion then into Billets at ESSARS (map reference X 25.a Central.) Brigade now in DIVISIONAL RESERVE. This Casualties during period in trenches. Other ranks 6 Killed, 14 wounded.	[appx]
ESSARS.	7th.		Routine. General Clean up. ENEMY bombed BETHUNE with heavy Gun Causing great damage.	[appx]

H. Mellish ..... Lt. Colonel,
COMDG. 17th (S) Bn. SHERWOOD FORESTERS.

Army Form C. 2118

WAR DIARY
INTELLIGENCE SUMMARY

(Erase heading not required.) 17th SHERWOOD FORESTERS (Welbeck Rangers)

Instructions regarding War Diaries and Intelligence Summaries are contained in F.S. Regs., Part II. and the Staff Manual respectively. Title Pages will be prepared in manuscript.

Place	Date 1916	Hour	Summary of Events and Information	Remarks and references to Appendices
ESSARS	August 8th		Routine Training. Confirmed as per Programme. After 4 pm GAS TEST to GAS CHAMBER at LE TOURET after 2:30 pm by Commander of the whole Battalion.	J. Milward
–do–	9th	4 pm	Routine Training by Companies during forenoon. Inspection of the Battalion by Major Gen. G.T. CUTHBERT, C.B, C.M.G. Commanding 39th Division. The General himself as being exceedingly pleased with the turn out of the Battalion. Remarking that it was the best turn out he had seen since taking over the Division. He also congratulated the Battalion and BCoy on what [he] said "it is on the 31st August remarking that it was the first queen he said turned out by any Battalion since the Brigade". Staying in front the G.O.C. remarked very highly of the Battery and was appreciated by all ranks after the Men (Brewery) by the Forward 3 ranks. The Battalion appeared & left the parade in a very high state of efficiency. J. Milward	J. Milward

COMDG. 17th (S) Bn. SHERWOOD FORESTERS.................. Lt. Colonel,

Army Form C. 2118

WAR DIARY or INTELLIGENCE SUMMARY
(Erase heading not required.) 17th SHERWOOD FORESTERS (Welbeck Rangers)

Instructions regarding War Diaries and Intelligence Summaries are contained in F.S. Regs., Part II. and the Staff Manual respectively. Title Pages will be prepared in manuscript.

Place	Date 1916	Hour	Summary of Events and Information	Remarks and references to Appendices
ESSARS	Aug. 10th	4 pm	Route Training by Companies in the forenoon.	
AUCHEL	11th	4 pm	Battalion Moved by Route March to AUCHEL (Map Reference SHEET 36B. C 21 & Central.) arriving in Billets at 9.0 pm. 2 men fell out.	M/Ay 24
ORLENCOURT	12th	4 pm	Battalion moved by Route March with Brigade to L.A. THIEULOYE. Battalion acts as advance Guard to Brigade, arriving in Billets at 10 pm. Battalion Billeted at ORLENCOURT. (Map Reference SHEET 36 B. T. 6 a 8 6.) 1 man fell out.	M/Ay 25
			No. 27846 Lee Cpl. E. CAWTHORNE granted the MILITARY MEDAL for operations on the 31st July 1916. No. 27103 & No. Nn. ROACH. and 87497. Corporal A. PEET. granted the MILITARY MEDAL for Operations on the 31st August 1916.	M/Ay 24
—do—	13th		Battalion commenced Training in Training Area	

J. W. Wingate Lt. Colonel,
COMDG. 17th (S) Bn. SHERWOOD FORESTERS.

WAR DIARY
INTELLIGENCE SUMMARY

(Erase heading not required.) 17th SHERWOOD FORESTERS (Welbeck Rangers)

Army Form C. 2118

Place	Date 1916	Hour	Summary of Events and Information	Remarks and references to Appendices
ORICOURT	Aug 13th Continued		as follows. NORTH MONCHY-BRETON – ROCOURT – MAGNICOURT. EAST and WESTERN Boundaries running South to a Point at CHEERS. Work under Company commenced from 9 am to 3 pm. The following orders from 17th Infantry Brigade Orders. "Under authority delegated by H.M. THE KING, the General Commander-in-Chief has awarded the MILITARY CROSS to the undermentioned officers for gallantry and devotion to duty in Action 8/1. August 1916. CAPTAIN F.O. LUDLOW. 2nd LIEUT. M.A. GENT.	
-do-	14th		Company Training under Company Officers from 9 am to 3 pm.	
-do-	15th		Continued Training under Company Officers from 9 am to 3 pm.	

W. Vincent .... Lt. Colonel,
COMDG. 17th (S) Bn. SHERWOOD FORESTERS.

Army Form C. 2118

WAR DIARY
INTELLIGENCE SUMMARY
(Erase heading not required.)

17th SHERWOOD FORESTERS (Welbeck Rangers)

Place	Date	Hour	Summary of Events and Information	Remarks and references to Appendices
Rhien Cd Camp	August 18th		Company Training under Company Officers from 9am to 3pm	Murray
-do-	19th		Company Training under Company Officers from 9am to 3pm	Murray
-do-	18th		Battalion Training under C.O. from 9 to 3pm	Murray
-do-	19th		Battalion Training from 9 to 3pm	Murray
-do-	20th		Battalion Training from 9 to 3pm	Murray
-do-	21st		Battalion Training from 9 to 3pm	Murray
-do-	22nd		Battalion Training from 9 to 3pm	Murray

H. Murray, Lt. Colonel,
COMDG. 17th (S) Bn. SHERWOOD FORESTERS.

WAR DIARY
INTELLIGENCE SUMMARY

Army Form C. 2118

(Erase heading not required.) 17th SHERWOOD FORESTERS (Welbeck Rangers)

Instructions regarding War Diaries and Intelligence Summaries are contained in F.S. Regs., Part II. and the Staff Manual respectively. Title Pages will be prepared in manuscript.

Place	Date	Hour	Summary of Events and Information	Remarks and references to Appendices
ORENCOURT	August 23rd		Battalion Training from 9 to 1 pm. Transport move to BOURVE MAISON in 2 days. Rallying for the night at NUNCQ.	V/Capt App
ORENCOURT	24th	8.30 am	Battalion marched to LIGNY-ST-FLOCHEL and entrained.	V/Capt App
		1.15 pm	DETRAINED at BOURVE MAISON and marched to DOULLENS. Billets for the night.	V/Capt App
DOULLENS	25th	9.0 am	Battalion marched to VAUCHELLES-LES-AUTHIE and encamped in huts.	V/Capt App
VAUCHELLES LES AUTHIE	26th		Bathing, Arms Drill, and clean up.	V/Capt App
—do—	27th		Divisional Training under Company Commanders.	V/Capt App
—do—	28th 2.15 pm		Battalion moved by March Route to BERTRANCOURT and encamped in huts etc.	V/Capt App

J. .... Lt. Colonel,
COMDG. 17th (S) Bn. SHERWOOD FORESTERS.

Army Form C. 2118

WAR DIARY
INTELLIGENCE SUMMARY

(Erase heading not required.) 17th SHERWOOD FORESTERS (Welbeck Rangers)

Instructions regarding War Diaries and Intelligence Summaries are contained in F.S. Regs., Part II. and the Staff Manual respectively. Title Pages will be prepared in manuscript.

(45)

Place	Date 1916	Hour	Summary of Events and Information	Remarks and references to Appendices
BERTRAN-COURT	August 29th		Routine. Officers mess went Treveles.	1/Appx 64
—do—	30th		Routine Officers mess went Treveles. 3.0 Res Battn Marched whilst availing Treveles.	1/Appx 65
—do—	31st		Routine. Battalion moves by Route march to VITERMONT and encamps.	1/Appx 66

J. W. Williams .... Lt. Colonel,
COMDG. 17th (S) Bn. SHERWOOD FORESTERS,

1875 Wt. W593/826 1,000,000 4/15 J.B.C. & A. A.D.S.S./Forms/C. 2118.

COPY.
SECRET.   17th. SHERWOOD FORESTERS.   OPERATION ORDER No.11.

                To be carried out on the night 31st/1st. Augt.16,
                Ref. Trench Map 1 10,000.

1. OBJECTIVE.
   (a) To raid German Trench immediately in rear of DUCK'S BILL
       CRATERS.
   (b) Capture as many prisoners as possible.
   (c) Kill Germans.
   (d) Destroy two mine shafts.

2. COMPOSITION OF PARTY.
   A. Party.   2/Lt. Flint, and 25 rifles.
   B. Party.   2/Lt. Dennis   "   "
   C. Party.   2/Lt. Langford   "   "
   D. Party.   2/Lt. Bolton   "   "
   LIAISON "   Captain.Ludlow   12   "
                                 8 Runners.
                                 8 Stretcher Bearers.
                                 4 Telephonists.
   Z.   "   R.E. Demolition Party.

3. PLAN.
   (a) A. and B. Parties will leave Front Line Trench at A.9.a.8½.1¼ and
       will form up in NO MANS LAND until time for assault. Will advance,
       each party in file as quietly as possible right up under the
       Artillery barrage, rush through the gap in the German wire and
       enter the front line trenches at A.10.C.2.3. they will then work
       up enemy's trenches as per attached sketch, remaining there for
       approximately two hours.
   (b) C. and D. Parties will closely follow A. and B. parties in the
       same formation and work down enemy's trenches as per plan.
   (c) LIAISON PARTY will follow R.E. Party, C. and D. Party and take up
       a position at point of entry.

4. ASSEMBLY.
   The party will assemble at A.9.d.7.1. at an hour to be notified later.

5. ARTILLERY.
   (a) Heavy Trench Mortars will bombard area of objective and then
       switch to Northern Craters.
   (b) Group Artillery; Heavy and Medium Trench Mortars will bombard
       Northern Craters - Group Artillery will then switch to DUCKS
       BILL CRATERS.
   (c) Light Trench Mortars will remain on fixed targets on flanks on
       objective area and fire on NORTHERN CRATERS with remainder of
       guns as ordered.

6. TIMINGS.
   Zero to be notified later.
   00. to 0.25.   Medium Trench Mortars bombard area of objective.
   0.25.   Heavy and Medium Trench Mortars bombard NORTHERN CRATERS
                  slowly, and continue.
   0.25 to 0.35. Group Artillery bombards NORTHERN CRATERS.
   0.28 to 0.38. Infantry Raiding Party assembles in NO MANS LAND.
   0.36 to 0.38. Group Artillery bombards area of objective under which
                  Infantry advances.
   0.40.   Box barrage established in rear of area of objective.
   2.40.   Signal for withdrawal.

7. STORES TO BE CARRIED.
   A. Party.)   5 picks.
   B. Party.)   5 shovels.
   C. Party.)   10 bombs per man.
   D. Party.)   4 large wire cutters.
                  10 small   "   "
                  50 P. bombs.
   LIAISON PARTY. 20 bombs per man as a reserve
                  at point of entry.

SHEET 2.

8. **DRESS.**
Skeleton Marching Order, no Entrenching Tools or Gas Helmets.

9. **PASSWORD.**
WOODBINE.

10. The word retire will not be used, and if heard will only come from a German.

11. **WITHDRAWAL.**
The Signal for the withdrawal will be bouquets of 4 RED ROCKETS sent up from Front Line and CAMBRIDGE TERRACE in the direction of the German Trenches.

12. A complete Alphabetical Roll of Officers, N.C.Os. and men taking part in the raid will be handed in to Orderly Room before leaving. The Regimental Sergeant Major will check all returning at "B" Company Headquarters.

13. The Battalion Aid Post at WINDY CORNER will be used. Casualties via WOLF ROAD.

14. **TRAFFIC.**

      UP. ORCHARD ROAD.
             ORCHARD TERRACE.

      DOWN. WOLF ROAD.

15. Watches will be synchronized at 8 p.m. Bn. Hd.Qrs. 17th. Sherwood Foresters.

16. The position of O.C. will be in CAMBRIDGE TERRACE at the Left Company Headquarters.

30.7.16.   (sd) H. Milward. Lt.Col.
                          Cmdg. 17th. Sherwood Foresters.

Issued to:-
117th Infantry Brigade   1
16th R.B.   1
O.C. "B" Company   1
O.C. R.E. Party.   1

SECRET.

117th Infantry Brigade.

Report on raid of 17th. Sherwood Foresters on rear of DUCKS BILL CRATERS on night 31 July/ 1st. Aug. 1916.

At 11.43 p.m. the party assembled in NO MANS LAND and advanced towards the point of entry under cover of our Artillery Barrage, three men were hit during the advance by our own shells.

During the advance the party got rather too much to the left and close up under the action, they then right inclined and made for the correct point of entry.

When up by the German wire they came under very heavy machine Gun and Rifle Grenade fire from the rear of the RED DRAGON CRATER. A. and B. parties got through the gap and into the German trenches, A. party bombed several dug-outs and actually had four German prisoners but where bombed out of it. About this time from some unknown source the order to withdraw was given and some men started to go back, when the mistake was found out some of these men rallied and brought back and re-entered the German trenches at a different point of entry.

During the time the parties were in the German trenches they were under Machine Gun and Rifle Grenade fire from the Craters.

Sgt. Brooks reported a mine shaft, but I cant get any information as to whether the R.E. party was informed of this. D. Party and part of C. also got in.

Getting off the right line of advance in the first instance seems to have caused a great deal of confusion, to which the Machine Guns and Rifle Grenade fire from the Craters added considerably.

The total amount of casualties were;-

Officers	Killed	2
"	Wounded	4
Other ranks	Killed	3
" "	Wounded	47
" "	Missing	12
		68

1.8.16.   H. Milward. Lt.Col.   Comdg. 17th. Sherwood Foresters.

COPY.

117th. Infantry Brigade.

Ref. the operations on the night 31st July/1st. August 16.

I wish to bring to the notice of the G.O.C. the following names for his consideration;-

2nd. Lt. M. A. KENT.

This Officer was not actually part of the raiding party but was up in the front line at the point of exit.-
After the raiding party had gone over Capt. Ludlow the O.C. party was hit, this Officer at once on his own initiative went over, joined the party and took Capt. Ludlow's place with the Liaison party.
In the first instance this party had got slightly too much to the left.
2nd. Lt. Kent got together the two leading parties and guided them through the gap in the German wire remaining with the Liaison party himself until severely wounded.

2nd. Lt. L. E. FLINT.

This Officer was in charge of ½ "A" party, he succeeded in getting a considerable way up the German trenches and successfully bombed dug-outs and killed several Germans, at one time he actually had four German prisoners but he was bombed out by a superior party losing nearly all his men.
When this Officer got back he went out again and brought in several wounded men, in spite of being slightly wounded himself.

L/Sgt. W. LOACH.)
Cpl. A. PEET.)

These two N.C.Os. were conspicuous for their gallantry during the whole raid, when all the Officers had been killed or wounded they reformed their parties who had got very mixed up, and re-entered the German trenches.
After the withdrawal they continued bringing in wounded men.

1.8.16.   H. Milward. Lt. Col.
                    Comdg. 17th. Sherwood Foresters.

COPY.
SECRET.

To/
  Headquarters,
    39th Division.

Report on a minor enterprise carried out by the 17th. Notts & Derby Regt.
on the night of the 31st July and 1st August.

Objective. 1. To enter the German trenches at A.10.c.2.3. (a) bring back prisoners and identifications (b) kill Germans (c) destroy 2 mine shafts.

Action. 2. For 4 nights prior to the raid the enemy trenches behind the Northern Craters had been bombarded at stated times to find out what his probable course of action would be on our bombardment covering the entry of the raiding party. It was found that these preliminary bombardments provoked, on the 1st night, heavy artillery retaliation with rifle and M.G. fire; on the 2nd night, less retaliation by artillery but still machine gun and rifle fire, decreasing nightly as regards artillery retaliation.

Plan. 3. The Plan actually adopted was ; First bombardment with heavy and medium trench mortars of the Northern Craters, accompanied by 10 minutes intense bombardment by Group Artillery. A pause, and then the bombardment actually covering infantry entry. This was carried out according to the programme. The infantry assembled without any difficulty in NO MANS LAND and advanced under 2 minutes bombardment up to the German trenches without trouble from M.G. or rifle fire. Their advance was, however, slightly more left-handed than the line reconnoitred, which caused a slight pause before the actual entry. The 2 leading parties moved however, to their right and entered the German trenches. The trenches were found to be so wrecked by the heavy trench mortars' fire that their shape according to the rehearsed plan was very considerably altered. This led to a certain amount of confusion. The 2 leading parties however, forced their way into the German trenches, having several times to take to

Sheet No. 2.

the top to avoid the heavy trench mortar craters.

They bombed right-handed for a considerable distance and encountered 4 German dug-outs which were bombed. At this point 4 German prisoners were captured. A counter-attack by the enemy was made on this party, with the result that the officer leader and 2 men became casualties; 1 man was killed, the prisoners being re-captured.

The left party bombed up what appeared to be their allotted trench, but so unrecognisable had the ground become that there was no certainty that this was so.

About this time a runner came to the liaison party, which included the R.E. demolition party, to inform them that a mine-shaft had been discovered. These went forward and the Officer investigated the mine-shaft, which, he states, had been completely wrecked by a heavy shell. To this R.E. party an order was given at this moment to withdraw, but it is of course not known from whom it emanated. They did so, but an N.C.O. in charge of the infantry rallied about three-quarters of the infantry party and returned into the German trenches. The left party appear to have bombed into the crater area since an officer of the Tunnelling Company on his return went through the crater area and actually looked over the Northern edge, where he saw our men, who were bombing in a Northerly direction. They did not, however, get very far. The 3rd party went over the top from the point of entry a short distance, got into the German trench and no further. The enemy retaliation on the raiding party was very heavy and consisted of machine gun fire from machine guns apparently on the Northern enemy side of the RED DRAGON CRATER, evidently machine guns posted in a sap. This caused a considerable number of casualties. Rifle grenade fire was brought to bear from a rearward support line and also caused casualties.
/all
It should be stated that the officer leaders became casualties and in fact, the Officer Commanding the Company was knocked

Sheet No.3.

out very early in the proceedings. Another officer who was a party of the Liaison party in our own trenches went forward to take his place and most gallantly took the party, which had momentarily halted, towards the German trenches. He subsequently became a casualty. The artillery retaliation over the whole of the GIVENCHY Section was very severe, all calibres up to 5.9" being freely used. Artillery observers intimate that there were a certain number of 8" shells, which fell about GIVENCHY KEEP, which appeared to be the case from my observation post.

The number of Germans actually met with was not great, but M.G. and rifle grenade fire was heavy, and there is no doubt that great confusion in the raiding party was caused by the numerous craters formed by the heavy trench mortars. All ranks who have been questioned agree that this area had been completely knocked out of shape. The switch of the heavy trench mortars' fire was taken gradually some way along the support trench to the Northern Crater area, and it is hoped that a corresponding amount of damage was done along these lines.

4. The heavy trench mortars fired 60 rounds during the action; the medium trench mortars fired 156 rounds; the Light Trench mortars (Stokes) fired 790 rounds, The Group Artillery kept up a barrage during the whole operations which lasted from first to last 1 hour and 23 minutes, by which time all the infantry were back in our lines.

General. 5. It cannot be claimed that the objects of the raid were entirely achieved. No prisoners were taken and identifications seemed to the troops to be out of the question. It has already been said that not many Germans were encountered by the Infantry, which may be due either to their having run away owing to the heavy trench mortar bombardment or to their having been buried. The N.C.Os. questioned are very emphatic about the wrecked appearance of the German trenches. It is also not possible to give an estimate of the number of casualties caused to the enemy for the same reasons. A considerable measure of success may, however, be claimed in

Sheet No. 4.

that we entered the German trenches and there remained for upwards of 1 hour and 10 minutes. The loss of the Officer leaders makes it difficult to give an exact account, which may be regarded as inevitable in any raid which is carried out at the present moment. Heavy fighting is the only method whereby an entry can be obtained into the enemy trenches. Our casualties were severe, amounting to 6 Officers and upwards of 70 other ranks wounded and missing.

The artillery and trench mortar bombardment was magnificent and must have accounted for many Germans.

1st August 1916.

W.G.Maxwell. Capt, Bde. Major,
for Brig.Gen.
Commanding 117th BRIGADE.

117th Brigade.
39th Division.

1/17th BATTALION

NOTTS & DERBY REGIMENT

SEPTEMBER 1 9 1 6

Attached:-

Report on Operations 3rd September.

Army Form C. 2118

117/39 VOL 2

WAR DIARY
INTELLIGENCE SUMMARY

(Erase heading not required.) 17th SHERWOOD FORESTER (Welbeck Rangers)

Place	Date 1916	Hour	Summary of Events and Information	Remarks and references to Appendices
BERTRAN-COURT	Sept 1st		Routine. Company Training before noon. The move to VITERMONT mentioned in DIARY on the 31st August 1916 was cancelled.	1/a/1731
-do-	2nd		Battalion was Ready to take part in the 2nd Offensive on the SOMME. OPERATION ORDER No. 9 attached and marked as appendix F.1. Battalion move into Trenches with aforementioned Operation order which are situated 1500 yds due South of the village of BEAUMONT-HAMEL, about 1000 yds due north of HAMEL and about 3,000 yards "north-West of THIEPVAL". The assembly was Complete about 10.10 pm. Before going into action message from the following General were read to the Battalion before are attacked as appendices marked and V Army Corps. LIEUT GENERAL E.A. FANSHAWE. CB Cmdg. V Army Corps. BRIG GENERAL R.F. OLDMAN Cmdg. 117th Infantry Brigade. Battalion Strength going into action 19 Officers, Other ranks 650 Other ranks.	F.1. F.2. F.3. 7.C Labrum. 1 Captain

W.W. Wood Lt Colonel
17th (S) Bn. SHERWOOD FORESTERS.

WAR DIARY
INTELLIGENCE SUMMARY

(4) 17th SHERWOOD FORESTER (Welbeck Rangers)

Army Form C. 2118

Place	Date	Hour	Summary of Events and Information	Remarks and references to Appendices
BERTRAN-COURT.	Sept 2nd 1916		All details were left at BERTRANCOURT with Transport. The Division were situated as follows in the attack:— 117th Infantry Brigade on the Right; 118th Infantry Brigade on the Left; 116th Infantry Brigade in Reserve. The Brigade were situated as follows in the attack:— 17th SHERWOOD FORESTERS on the left; 10th R.R.C. on the right; 17th 16th R.R.C. in Support; 16th SHERWOOD FORESTERS & 10th Rifle BRIGADE in Reserve. For further particulars See Afterwards F.I.	
			Draft of 1 officer and 16 men arrive from 10th SHERWOOD FORESTERS (Note 24)	
TRENCHES	3rd	5.10am	Battalion turn to attack under Artillery Barrage at 6 am. Kenyon received from MAJOR G STODDARD orders to occupy the line recaptured FIRST LINE & GERMAN TRENCHES. At 6.10am Kenyon receives from CAPTAIN H V Walker that	

H.W. Walker .... Lt. Colonel
OO MDG. 17th (S) Bn. SHERWOOD FORESTERS.

WAR DIARY
INTELLIGENCE SUMMARY

Army Form C. 2118

17th SHERWOOD FORESTERS (Welbeck Rangers)

Place	Date 1916	Hour	Summary of Events and Information	Remarks and references to Appendices
TRENCHES Continued	Sept 3rd		The enemy's 2nd LINE is strongly held with machine guns and that our casualties are very heavy and reinforcements are urgently needed.	
		At 1.15 2 Companies 16 R.R. Corps are up to reinforce. The action is at present stationary, the enemy being very strong in Artillery and Machine Guns and at 2 o'p.m. them there are despatches for all two withdraws to our trenches. At 7.30 pm the Battalion remaining withdraws to an hill-side at MAILLY-MAILLET WOOD left of the by L. Our casualties are very heavy.	(Captures)
BERTRAN-COURT		At 5 pm the Battalion have late Bivouacs at BERTRANCOURT. Casualties in yesterday's action as follows:—	
			KILLED. MAJOR G. STODDARD, CAPTAINS R.G. HOPEWELL, S.F. BROOKFIELD, F.C. SINGLETON, G.P. LITTLE WOOD. WOUNDED. CAPTAINS F. TURNER, R.B. WIGHT, LIEUT. B.T. ROSS, 2nd LIEUTS. W.N. BIRKIN, E.P. ACRILL-JONES, T.C. NUGENT.	

17th (8) Bn. SHERWOOD FORESTERS.

WAR DIARY

INTELLIGENCE SUMMARY

17th SHERWOOD FORESTERS (welsh Rangers)

Army Form C. 2118

Place	Date 1916	Hour	Summary of Events and Information	Remarks and references to Appendices
BERTRAN-COURT. (Contd)	Sept 4th		WOUNDED Contnued 2nd Lieut. T.W. SALSBURY. MISSING. Lieut. A.F. BUCK. WOUNDED and MISSING. CAPTAIN. H.V WALTERS, 2nd LIEUT. M.A. ELLISSEN. TOTAL 15. OTHER RANKS. KILLED. 59 WOUNDED. 155 MISSING. 22 WOUNDED at DUTY 3 Total 4 — 239 LIEUT. L.D WOODHOUSE, attached to LT. M. BATTERY. KILLED. Other Ranks 1. Wounded attached 117th MACHINE GUN Coy. 1 Other Rank Wounded. 3 //Gun That Casualties so far an known Officers 16. Other Ranks 4 + 8.	

.... Lt. Colonel,
COMDG. 17th (S) Bn. SHERWOOD FORESTERS.

Army Form C. 2118

WAR DIARY
INTELLIGENCE SUMMARY

(Erase heading not required.) 17th SHERWOOD FORESTERS (Welbeck Rangers)

Instructions regarding War Diaries and Intelligence Summaries are contained in F. S. Regs., Part II. and the Staff Manual respectively. Title Pages will be prepared in manuscript.

Place	Date 1916	Hour	Summary of Events and Information	Remarks and references to Appendices
BERTRAN-COURT. (continued)	Sept 4th		A good for by him & other ranks reported missing with forgoing and thorn to be WOUNDED but no details are to hand. Draft of 70 men arrive from 11th Bn. SHERWOOD FORESTER'S. Organization of Battalion.	/Names/
-do-	5th	11.0am	Bry Gen R to F. Oldman inspects remainder of Battalion and sympathises with them in the loss of their Comrades and Brothers, then addresses the men — they devoting the Drh to Duty: he remarks that their sacrifice was not in vain. Message Reeves from Army Commander. Reserve Army. H.P. GOUGH GEN. SIR K.C.B. attaches as appendices and sheppen. A Copy of Officer Commandy Report on action 3rd Sept 1916 is attached as an Appendix and handed	F Lt /10/9/44/ F.S.

J [signature] Lt Colonel,
COMDG. 17th (S) Bn. SHERWOOD FORESTERS

Army Form C. 2118

WAR DIARY
INTELLIGENCE SUMMARY
(Erase heading not required.) 17th SHERWOOD FORESTERS (Welbeck Rangers)

Place	Date 1916	Hour	Summary of Events and Information	Remarks and references to Appendices
BERTRAN-COURT.	Sept. 6th		Parades under Coy. officers before noon. Reorganization of Battalion. 1st Drafts forwarded to 17th Infantry Brigade. On completion the 3rd September 1916 marched and attached as any apportenure Battalion moved to MAILLEY MAILLET WOOD (Map Reference Sheet 57d. P.18.h.) Battalion Reserve BRIGADE SUPPORT.	F.6
MAILLEY MAILLET.	7th		Training By Companies. Indent Contact Shell fine day and ny.tr. (110 men Working Parties. The following names are submitted for gallantry and devotion to duty during the action of the 3rd September 1916. Recommended for Military Cross 2nd Lieuts. W.N. BIRGIN and M.A. ELLISSEN. DISTINGUISHED CONDUCT MEDAL No.27/75 Sergt. W. BROWN, No. 31267 Corporal J.W. PORTER, No.31928 Corporal J.T.S. HARVEY, No 32471 Private A. CLARKE. MILITARY MEDAL No.32566 Private F. WHALE, No.28515 Private C. NIND, No.29331 Private T. SCOTNEY, No.28189 Private L. PINKETT, No. 28218 Private E. COPLEY.	(illegible) M/Cross

M. Marshall Lt. Colonel,
COMDG. 17th (S) Bn. SHERWOOD FORESTERS.

Army Form C. 2118

WAR DIARY
INTELLIGENCE SUMMARY
(Erase heading not required.) 17th SHERWOOD FORESTERS (Welbeck Rangers)

Place	Date 1916	Hour	Summary of Events and Information	Remarks and references to Appendices
MAILLET-MAILLEY	Sept. 8th		Draft of 70 N.C.O. Men arrive. Rations, Training Program. Draft of 22 Men arrive.	11th/Sept/1916
—do—	9th		Rations, Training Program. 5 Officers arrive.	11th/Sept/1916
—do—	10th		Rations, Training Program. 7 Officers arrive. 20 O.R.s & 250 men attached to Bn. H.Q.	11th/Sept/1916
—do—	11th		Rations, Training Program. Draft of 67 men arrive.	11th/Sept/1916
—do—	12th		Battalion less 1 Coy. Transferred in relief of 16th Bn SHERWOOD FORESTER'S occupying A & B Company Fronts. Map reference 57 D 110,000. Relief starting at Q. 10 a & 5.2. Right Resting on Q.17. a 4.3. A Company Right front Company. B Company left front Company. D Company in support of A Company, C Company in Reserve. Relief of B Company by D Company complete by 12 noon.	11th/Sept/1916

W.M. Wintrup Lt. Colonel,
COMDG. 17th (S) Bn. SHERWOOD FORESTERS.

Army Form C. 2118

WAR DIARY
INTELLIGENCE SUMMARY

(Erase heading not required.) 17th SHERWOOD FORESTERS (Welbeck Rangers)

Instructions regarding War Diaries and Intelligence Summaries are contained in F.S. Regs., Part II. and the Staff Manual respectively. Title Pages will be prepared in manuscript.

Place	Date 1916	Hour	Summary of Events and Information	Remarks and references to Appendices
TRENCHES	Sept 13th		Trench Routine. Situation normal.	Appx 241
—do—	14th		Trench Routine. Situation normal. Copy of letter received from G.O.C. 39th Division attached as appendix.	Appx 241 G.1.
—do—	15th		Put through the 6th Part in Demonstration and raided outside trench Part 6 and left fire in enemy trench with two guns and rifle fire in an enemy trench with rifle and Verey lights. who made an attempt on my left. Also was observed intermittent rifle & trench mortar German Salient at G.10.d. which he is enfiladed in his front supports and reserve trenches. The officer and 20 other ranks attempted a raid on the German trenches with the object of securing a Prisoner but failed to find a gap in the left enemy wire. Situation normal.	11 pages

A. H. Williams Lt. Colonel, COMDG. 17th (S) Bn. SHERWOOD FORESTERS

WAR DIARY
INTELLIGENCE SUMMARY

(Erase heading not required.) 17th SHERWOOD FORESTERS (Welbeck Rangers)

Army Form C. 2118

Place	Date	Hour	Summary of Events and Information	Remarks and references to Appendices
Trenches	Sept 16th		Trench Routine. Situation normal.	1 App 24/1
-do-	17th		Trench Routine. Situation normal	1 App 24/1
-do-	18th		Trench Routine. Situation normal. 2nd Lieut. BLACK killed	1 App 24/1
-do-	19th		Trench Routine. Situation normal. Battalion relieved by 1st Black Watch Regt. Battalion moved to Billets at BEAUSSART. Casualties during this tour. 1 officer killed 1 other rank killed 6 other ranks wounded.	1 App 24/1
BEAUSSART	20th		Battalion moved into Trenches SERRE SECTOR — RIGHT SUB-SECTION holding front line (map reference (57.D.) K.29.5. to K.29. & S.S. "B" and "C" Companies in front line. "A" Company in support. "D" Company in Reserve.	1 App 24/1

K. Wilman Lt. Colonel,
O.C.mdg. 17th (S) Bn. SHERWOOD FORESTERS.

WAR DIARY
INTELLIGENCE SUMMARY

Army Form C. 2118

(Erase heading not required.)

17th SHERWOOD FORESTERS (Notts & Derby)

Place	Date	Hour	Summary of Events and Information	Remarks and references to Appendices
TRENCHES	Sept 21st 1916		Trench Routine. Situation normal.	
-do-	22nd		Trench Routine, Situation normal. 10 Officers joined for duty.	
-do-	23rd		Trench Routine, Situation normal.	
-do-	24th		Trench Routine, Situation normal.	
-do-	25th		Trench, Routine, Situation normal.	
-do-	26th		Trench Routine. Intense Artillery bombardment very heavy to reply. Slight damage. 2 Officers joined.	

O.C. 17th (S) Bn Sherwood Foresters

WAR DIARY

INTELLIGENCE SUMMARY

(Erase heading not required.) 1/7л SHERWOOD FORESTERS (Robin Hood Rangers)

Army Form C. 2118

Place	Date	Hour	Summary of Events and Information	Remarks and references to Appendices
TRENCHES	Sept 1916 27		Trench Routine, Situation normal.	1/Nov/1916
–do–	28h		Trench Routine. Situation normal. The following were granted the MILITARY MEDAL for gallantry and devotion to duty. 31928 Corporal T.J.S. HARVEY. 32471 Private A. CLARKE. 27675 Sergeant W. BROWN. 31289. Corporal J.W. PORTER. 27399 Private. T. CLARKE (attached 117 TRENCH MORTAR BATTERY	1/Nov/1916
–do–	29pt		Trench Routine. Situation normal.	1/Nov/1916
–do–	30h		Trench Routine. Situation normal. Battalion relieved by 1st Bryce Derbyshire Regt. The Casualties during last 10 days Other Ranks killed. 2 Other ranks wounded 7. Battalion moved to Hutments BERTRANCOURT. Relief Complete. 6.45pm	
				1/Nov/1916

Kirkwood Lt Colonel
COMDG. 1/7th (8) Bn. SHERWOOD FORESTERS.

SECRET.   17th. SHERWOOD FORESTERS.   OPERATION ORDER No.19.

REFERENCE.   1.5,000 BEAUCOURT Trench Map 57.d.S.E. 1 and 2.
             1.20,000 Sheets 57.d.S.E.

Note.   In these Orders the day of Attack is referred to as
             "A Day" throughout.

1. INTENTION.   The Battalion will attack and hold the enemy's system of
                 trenches from Q.17.b.4½.1¾. inclusive to Q.17.b.1.3.
                 inclusive.

2. OBJECTIVES.   (a) First Objective. "A" Company. Will attack the German
                     Front Line from Point 41 exclusive to Point 13
                     inclusive.
                     Second Objective. "B" Company. Will attack the German
                     Second Line from Point 43 exclusive to Point 36
                     inclusive.
                     Third Objective. "C" Company. Will attack the German
                     Third Line from Point 66 exclusive to Point 68.
                     inclusive.
                     Protective Flank. "D" Company. Will take up the Line
                     Points 05. - 36. - 68. as follows;-
                     One Platoon with "A" Company Point 05.
                     One Platoon with "B" Company about Point 36.
                     One Platoon with "C" Company about Point 68.
                     One Platoon about Point 45 in Support.
                 (b) Machine Gun Company. 2 Guns will assemble with "A"
                     Company and follow over in line with the Carrying
                     Party and will take up a position about Point 05.
                     2 Guns will assemble with "B" Company and follow
                     over in line with the Carrying Party and will take
                     up a position about Point 36. In both cases to cover
                     the Left Protective Flank.
                 (c) Light Trench Mortars. Will follow "C" Company and
                     will assemble at the Junction of ROBERTS TRENCH -
                     WORCESTER TRENCH as close to the Company as possible
                     following them over. The actual position of the
                     Mortars being left to O.C., T.M.B.
                 (d) Lewis Guns.
                     (i) Company Lewis Guns will accompany Companies.
                     (ii) Battalion Lewis Guns. One with "B" Company and
                     one with "C" Company. 2 in Battalion Reserve.

3. PLAN.   (a) The leading Company will deploy parallel to Objective
                     as close as possible to barrage in "NO MANS LAND", each
                     Company making good its objective. Companies in rear
                     passing those in front 50 paces distance between
                     each wave. On the Left Flank, Trenches will be blocked
                     for at least 50 yards beyond the line taken up by the
                     Left Protective Flank Company as each successive wave
                     reaches its objective.
                 (b) Captured trenches will be immediately consolidated
                     special attention being paid to the consolidation of
                     the Second Line. Troops consolidating the Second Line
                     will be reinforced, if necessary, for this purpose
                     on information being received that its capture is
                     complete.
                 (c) Strong points will be constructed in the neighbourhood
                     of the following points;-
                     First Line,   13. - 05.
                     Second Line,   45. - 36.
                     Third Line,   68.
                     A deep dug-out should be included in each strong point
                     if possible. Regard must be paid to their existence
                     when planning the strong point.
                     VICKERS GUN CREWS have prior claim to dug-out
                     accommodation.

SHEET 2.

  (d) Definite Clearing parties are being told off in each wave and not less than 2 Sentries placed on the door of each dug-out. "P" bombs should not be thrown into the dug-outs unless the enemy cannot be disposed of by other means.
  (e) Care must be taken that no communication trenches are left unblocked.
  (f) Companies will attack in the following formations:-
    Front Line, 2 Platoons.
    Second Line, 1 Platoon Support.
    Third Line. 1 Platoon Carrying.

4. ASSEMBLY.

The Battalion will assemble in the following order:-
A. C. D. Companies, GORDON TRENCH from RECTOR STREET inclusive to WORCESTER STREET inclusive.
"B" Company, ROBERTS TRENCH Junction RECTOR STREET inclusive to Junction LONG SAP inclusive.
The Battalion will move to the position of assembly by the following Route.
PICADILLY - JAMES STREET - LONG ACRE and WORCESTER TRENCH.

5. ARTILLERY.

  (a) Artillery Barrages are shown on the attached Time Table, every Officer and N.C.O. should be in possession of a copy of this Time Table, which must be strictly adhered to.
  (b) The first barrage starts 50 yards short of the German First Line.
  (c) Only Percussion Shrapnel will be fired for the last minute prior to each lift.
  (d) A Liaison Officer will accompany the Battalion.
  (e) The S.O.S. Signal is THREE GREEN ROCKETS.

6. TRAFFIC.

A series of Traffic Control Posts will be established throughout Brigade Area under Asst. Staff Captain. (See Traffic Map and Appendix D) They will wear a Green Brassard. Up to half an hour before Zero upward movement will be allowed by all Trenches; after that no movement contrary to the arrows will be allowed from half an hour before Zero except Runners with the proper Armlet on, or a bona fide message. All other Stragglers will be turned into GORDON AND ROBERTS TRENCHES, where they will be collected by Officers of the 17th. K.R.R. Corps and forwarded to the German Trenches. Traffic Control Posts will shoot any straggler disobeying these orders. None but reliable men will be selected for the work. O.C. 16th. Notts & Derby Regiment will find one Officer and 54 men, with a proportion of N.C.Os. (See Appendix D). Date and Time of reporting will be communicated later.

7. PRISONERS.

Not more than 10 prisoners should be collected in one place. One man to each 10 will be detailed as Escort; it is however, to be noted, that each man so detailed is a fighting man lost. <u>No prisoners are to be allowed in communication trenches; they must go over the top.</u> Prisoners will be collected at Advanced Bde. H.Q., KNIGHTSBRIDGE BARRACKS, whence they will be escorted by the Provost Establishment of the 16th Sherwoods to Railway Crossing just West of MESNIL at Q.28.c.4.8.

8. COMMUNICATION.

Communication from front to rear will be for by the following means:-
  (a) <u>Telephone.</u> The Battalion Headquarters will be connected with the Brigade by unburied cable. These lines will be liable to brake down.
  Two lines of D1. Cable will be taken forward by the Battalion.

SHEET 3.

(b) Runners. All Battalion and Brigade Runners will wear a Brassard of Blue with a narrow White stripe on the Right arm above the elbow (this will be sewn on) Company Runners will wear the same on the Left arm above the elbow.
4 Battalion Runners will report to Brigade Headquarters for duty at 6 p.m. on the day previous to the operations.
4 Runners per Company will be sent to Battalion Headquarters at 5 p.m. tonight.

(c) Visual. Should other means fail every effort will be made to establish Visual by flag, or disc, shutter or lamp.
There will be two Divisional Visual Stations in 144 Brigade Area near SHAFTESBURY AVENUE.

(d) Aeroplane. During the attack one Aeroplane (distinguishing mark, a broad black band continued on a Streamer on each bottom plane) will be employed as CONTACT PATROL. This Aeroplane will pick up positions of Battalion Headquarters and receive signals by panel from Battalion Headquarters. The signal code for Aeroplane Signalling is attached.

(e) Pigeons. Four trained Pigeoners with one Basket of Pigeons each will accompany the Headquarters of the Battalion.

Note. Men of Company for Third Objective will wear tin discs and carry vigilants and smoke candles on a ratio of one packet to every three men.
Four selected N.C.Os. in each Platoon will carry one flare. They will be used to denote Platoons capture of each object.

9. DRESS AND EQUIPMENT.

Skeleton Marching Order, plus one bandolier extra, 4 Mills Grenades. 2 Sandbags per man. Each Company Bomber, 6 Mills Rifle Grenades in lieu of Mills bombs. Haversacks will be carried in the pack position. Ground Sheets rolled up on the back of the belt. Gas Helmets will be worn in the Alert position. One man in every two will carry a pick and shovel which is to be properly slung on the back. Rear rank only carry these.
No maps of any description showing our own trenches will be taken over but there is no objection to maps showing German system being taken.

10. CARRIAGE OF STORES.

Brigade Carrying Parties will carry forward stores from the Forward Brigade Dumps, to Dumps to be formed at Points 61 and 21 in German Trenches.
Battalion and Company Carrying Parties which have already carried over a proportion of stores with assaulting waves will carry up from these points to their Companies.
Stores to be carried by Carrying Parties with Assaulting Companies.

```
          4 Shovels per man                    1
          6 Picks (two men)                    3
         10 Iron screw stakes (6 per
                                 man)          5
          4 Coils of "B" Wire (1 per man)      4
          6 Boxes of Bombs at 2 per man        3
          2 Coils of Fr. Wire at 1 per
                                 man           2
                                              ──
                                              18
```

Green Rockets will be carried by each Company distributed among the men

SHEET 4.

11. MEDICAL. An extra Medical Officer will be attached to each Assaulting Battalion. These Officers will cross NO MANS LAND with the Third Company of Assaulting Battalions and establish Regimental Aid Posts in Shelters in the German Front Line Trench. They will take with them and erect necessary sign posts to assist casualties to find these posts.

12. SYNCHRONIZATION OF WATCHES. 2nd.Lt. W.N. Birkin will attend at Brigade Headquarters at KNIGHTSBRIDGE BARRACKS at 8.50 p.m. tonight and two hours before Zero.
Company Commanders will attend at Battalion Headquarters at 9.30 p.m. tonight one hour before Zero.
Too much stress cannot be laid on the greatest possible care being observed in getting correct synchronization.

13. DUMPS. O.C. Companies will arrange for Dumps at suitable places and when fixed, will at once inform Bn. H.Q.

14. REPORT CENTRE. Battalion H.Q. will be situated near Junction of POND and VICTORIA STREET at Q.17.c.4.8.

15. Hour of ZERO. The hour of Zero will be notified later.

16. TIME TABLE. Times of sequence of events attached.

17. NOTE. Absolute silence must be maintained during the Assembly and while in the Front Line Trenches.

30.8.1916.
      (sd) T. Thornton. Capt & Adjt.
        17th. Sherwood Foresters.

Copies issued to:-
117th Infantry Brigade.
117th Machine Gun Company.
117th T.M.B.
16th Rifle Brigade.
17th. K.R.R. Corps.
O.C. A.Company.
O.C. B.Company.
O.C. C.Company.
O.C. D.Company.
Lewis Gun Officer.
Signalling Officer.
Officer Commanding.
War Diary. (2)
Office Copy.

ADD Para 2. (e) An R.E. Party of one Officer and 20 men will follow over with Third Company and construct 3 Strong Points at positions to be arranged with O.C. Party.
This Party will assemble with "C" Company.

COPY.   Appendix E.

To Accompany 117th Infantry Brigade Order No.50, dated 29.8.16.

Positions and Quantities of Dumps.

1. S.A.A.

    Distributed in front trenches.   100 boxes
    Junction of CONSTITUTION HILL and KNIGHTSBRIDGE   100   "
        Barracks.
    FORT JACKSON.   100   "
    Divl. Reserve. ACHEUX WOOD (P.8.d.8.8.)

2. Grenades.

    Near junction POND St. – LONG SAP (Q.17.c.4.9.)   5000   "
    Near junction LOUVERCY St. – SLOANE St (Q.17.d.2.2.)   5000   "

    Divl. Depots. No. (1) Q.28.a.7.7.   (2). Q.16.d.0.2.

3. WATER.

        Q.17.d.2.2½.   400 galls.
        Q.17.c.3.7.   400 galls.
        Q.16.d.2.8.   1000 galls.

4. Very Lights.

    FORT JACKSON.   10 boxes.

5. STOKES MORTAR AMMUNITION.

    BUCKINGHAM PALACE.   1000 rds.
    GIPSY HILL.   1000   "
    Q.16.c.9.2½.   2000   "
    Divl. Reserve. (P.8.d.8.8.)

6. Rations.

    Near junction CONSTITUTION HILL & KNIGHTSBRIDGE (Q.16.d.3.7.)
                                                4500.

7. R.E. Stores.

    Left Forward Dump (Q.17.c.3.7.) Right Forward Dump (Q.17.c.4.4.)

    Brigade Dump. (Q.16.c.9.1.) Divisional Dump, ENGLEBELMER
                                                     (Q.25.a.5.8.)

8. Stores.

    The Reserve Brigade have a supply of the follwoing at Pt. 18.c.5.0.

                RATIONS.
                S.A.A.
                GRENADES.
                STOKES MORTAR AMMUNITION.

Time Table to accompany 119th Bde. O.O.50 dated 28.8.16.

Time	Infantry	Artillery
ZERO	Infantry commence crossing parapet	Intense Shrapnel Barrage 150 yards short of German Front Line.
0.00	and getting out into NO MANS LAND	
0.0½		Intense Shrapnel Barrage lifts on to enemy Front Line.
0.01		Heavy Artillery lifts on to German Reserve Line
0.02	Infantry continue advance across NO MANS LAND	Trench Mortars lifts on to German Support Line
0.03	Infantry advance as close as possible to our Barrage	Intense percussion (only) Shrapnel Barrage on German Front Line. Intense gas shell barrage on Station Road. from 60 pm. R. ANCRE to QUARRY (Q.11.a.4.8.)
0.04	Infantry assault German Front Line	Intense Shrapnel Barrage lifts 50 yards, and continues lifting at the rate of 25 yards every 30 seconds until 2nd Barrage Line is reached.
0.10		Heavy French Mortars lifts on to German Reserve Trench Line.
		22. Trench Mortars cease fire.
0.12	Second Companies of assaulting Battalions close up to our Barrage	Heavy Howitzers concentrate on German Reserve Trench
0.13	Second Companies of assaulting Battalions as close as possible to our Barrage	Intense percussion (only) Shrapnel Barrage on German Support Line.
0.14	Infantry assault German Support Line	Intense Shrapnel Barrage lifts 50 yards, reverts to time shrapnel and continues lifting at the rate of 25 yards every 30 seconds until 3rd Barrage Line is reached.
0.33		60 pm Intense gas shell Barrage slows down to a quick rate. Heavy Artillery lifts off German Reserve Line and barrages at Q.17.a & Q5.9.0. Q11.d140.40.115. Q.11.a.45.20.- Q18.a.00.95- Q18.a.95.50. Beaucourt Station and STATION ROAD at a steady rate of fire. Heavy Trench Mortars cease fire.

Time.	Infantry	Artillery
0.35	Kid Companies of assaulting Battalions advance as close as possible to our Barrage	Intense Percussion (only) Shrapnel barrage on German Reserve Line
0.36	Infantry assault German Reserve Line.	Intense Shrapnel barrage lifts 50 yards, uncut 6 time shrapnel and continues lifting at the rate of 25 yards every 30 seconds until the 4th barrage line is reached.
0.51		Intense Shrapnel barrage ceases and is replaced by bursts of intense fire at uncertain intervals.

SECRET.
V Corps.
G.X.7202.

31st. August 1916.

2nd Division.
39th Division.
144th Brigade.
2*th Divisional Arty.
11th Divisional Arty.
Corps Heavy Arty.
G.O.C.,R.A., V Corps.

The Army Commander wishes all ranks to know that the fall of THIEPVAL is of great importance. Troops must be pushed on with the utmost energy and no opportunity of occupying ground vacated by the enemy, within the limits of our barrage, must be allowed to slip.

The Corps Commander is confident that all ranks will do their utmost to ensure the success of the attack of the V Corps, thereby greatly assisting the main operations South of the River ANCRE directed against THIEPVAL.

G.F. Boyd. B.G., G.S.
V Corps.

NOTE: <u>A copy of this Order is NOT tobe carried by anyone taking part in the attack.</u>

2.

SECRET.

39/G.S.S./11/6/2.

Headquarters, 39th Divl. R.A.
  "   39th Divl. R.E.
  "   116th 117th and 118th Bdes.
O.C. 13th Bn Gloucestershire Regt.
Signals.
O.C. 174th Tunnelling Co. R.E.
O.C. No. 3. M.M.G. Battery.
O.C. 4" Stokes Mortar Battery.

In forwarding the above, the Divisional Commander

SHEET 2.

knows well that he can rely with absolute confidence on all ranks doing their utmost to achieve success, and to gain, and hold, their objectives, and that the honour of the Division is safe in their hands.

31st. August 1916.

F.W. Grosset. Lt. Col.
General Staff.
39th Division.

To All Officers Commanding Units,
117th Infy. Bde.

I wish it explained to all ranks that we are taking part in operations of considerable magnitude. Not only is our own division attacking but the 5th Army and the Army on our right. Our own Brigade has the honour to attack capture and hold the extreme left of the British Forces engaged.

It is to be made clear to all ranks that the Rifle and bayonet are the weapons to accomplish this. Although each man is in possession of 2 bombs, they are not for his personal use, except under special circumstances. He has them merely to carry over and create a reserve against the time when the Germans deliver their counter attack against our left flank - Therefore let every man keep them.

I know what the spirit of the Brigade is since I have had the honour of commanding it for nearly five months. I am certain we shall be successful in carrying out our task.

I wish all ranks good luck.

"L" Day.   R.D.F. Oldman. B.G.
                       Comdg. 117 Infy. Bde.

F.4.

Copy of telegram received from Headquarters,
    39th Division, dated 4.9.1916.
_____

"Fifth Corps wires last night a.a.a. Following
"wire received from Reserve Army begins a.a.a.
"The Army Commander wishes you to convey to the
"39th Division his sympathy with them in the
"failure of today's operations a.a.a. His
"confidence in them is unabated and he is sure
"that before long their bravery and perseverance
"will carry them to complete victory a.a.a.
"ends. a.a.a.

F.5.

REPORT on OPERATIONS on Sept. 3. 1916.

The Assembly was complete by 10.12 p.m. 2nd. Sept. and the Assembly in NO MANS LAND was carried out correctly at ZERO hour. No Casualties occured while in the position of assembly. A report was received by me from O.C. "A" Company (the leading Company) at 6 a.m. that the German Front line was taken.

At the same time another message was received stating that heavy casualties had occured and that reinforcements were urgently needed. One Officer and about 20 men succeeded in getting into the German Second Line but being unsupported had to withdraw back to the German First Line. A rough estimate of the casualties which occured by Companies during the Advance into the German Front Line was "A" Company, about 50%.

"B" Company, about 75%.

"C" Company, about 50%.

"D" Company was split up between different waves for the protective flank as previously arranged.

When the Front Line was occupied the right flank in addition to the left was exposed.

The following notes have been collected from N.C.Os. and men who went over.

1. The Dug-Outs and Front Line were all smashed in, and what appeared to have been Dug-outs were made with railwaylines and wood work.

2. The Handle Brush Bomb was used by them with timing mark 5½ secs. it did not appear to outrange ours.

3. All or practically all carrying parties were knocked out.

4. They counter-attacked from both our right and left flanks with bombing parties of about 20-30 men and all in shirt sleeves and over the top.

5. Very little S.A.A. was used, but all the bombs were got rid of the two carrying parties sent up on different occasions with Bombs and S.A.A. did not reach them.

6. The Machine Guns could not be accurately located but fired from both flanks and front.

SHEET 2.

7. All our casualties were nearly all from bombs and shell fire and a certain amount machine gun.

Bombs were thrown at our first wave from their front line.

They barraged their own front line after we got in and NO MANS LAND with 5.9. and Trench Mortars.

8. Their Casualties appeared to be very heavy and the trenches in parts full of dead.

9. There were a good many men in their second line but the party did not stay long enough to see any dug-outs as they were outnumbered.

10. The wire opposite us was not very well cut in places and several men got hung up.

He amused himself in the afternoon by sniping our wounded in NO MANS LAND, this I believe also occured on my right.

The evacuation of the wounded appeared to me to be very bad. At 7.15 after reinforcements had been asked for 2 Companies K.R.R. were ordered to reinforce my front line, part of one of these I believe actually got up but I got back no information to that effect.

4.9.16.
(sd) H. Milward. Lt.Col.
17th. Sherwood Foresters.

117th INFANTRY BRIGADE.

The following are the timings and sequence of events briefly as they occured in the operations on 3.9.16. I had not time to send in this in the other report.

2nd. September.	10.12 p.m.	Assembly reported complete.
3rd. September.	12.10 a.m.	Lanes cut in wire and fire steps completed.
	5.10 a.m.	Assembly and advance in NO MANS LAND.
	6.0. a.m.	German Front Line captured and reinforcements urgently needed received from O.C. "A" Company.
	6.6. a.m.	Reported that German Second Line full of Machine Guns and barrage asked to be put back on German Second Line.
	7.12 a.m.	Information received from Brigade that K.R.R. will reinforce with 2 Companies.
	7.55 a.m.	Two Battalions Reserve, L. Guns sent forward and carrying party of 16th. Sherwood Foresters with S.A.A. and Bombs.
	8.0. a.m.	1 Company K.R.R. reinforced the Front Line.
	9.52 a.m.	Information received from Brigade that the Attack on our right had failed and ordered to hold on at all costs. 16. R.B. will again attack at 10.30 a.m.
	11.35 a.m.	Bgd. informed that unless I can receive reinforcements attack by 16. R.B. must fail.
	1.30 p.m.	2/Lt. Collen sent to GORDON TRENCH to collect what men he could, he reported that he had got about 30.
	1.50 p.m.	All Detachments of Ourselves and 17th. K.R.R. ordered to withdraw to GORDON TRENCH. Information to this effect sent by runner to any Officer of ourselves or 17th. K.R.R. in German Front Line.
	4.45 p.m.	All men possible collected and sent down to KNIGHTSBRIDGE.

5.9.16.

(sd) H. Milward. Lt.Col.
17th. Sherwood Foresters.

Copy of letter received from Headquarters, 39th Division, dated 14.9.1916.

39/38/3.G.

1. The French Forces and the British Fourth and Reserve Armies will attack tomorrow, September 15th., 1916.

2. All ranks should understand that decisive results are hoped for from this battle: the most important that has been fought during the whole course of the War.

    If success crowns the efforts of the Allies in this battle and during the succeeding days, it is expected that a winter campaign will be unnecessary.

3. The General Officer Commanding therefore trusts that all ranks will use their utmost endeavours to achieve a victory and to destroy the enemy at every opportunity.

(Sd) F.W.GOSSET, Lt.Col.,
G.S., 39th Division.

14.9.1916.

-2-

B.M./A.585

To /
Officer Commanding,
    16th Notts & Derby Regt.   16th Rifle Brigade.
    17th   do   do   117th Machine Gun Coy.
    17th K.R.R.Corps.   117th T.M.Battery.

The G.O.C. directs that the above be brought to the notice of all ranks.

CEMaxwell. Captain,
Brigade Major, 117th Brigade.

14.9.1916.

117th Brigade.
39th Division.

1/17th BATTALION

NOTTS & DERBY REGIMENT

OCTOBER 1 9 1 6

Attached:-

Report on Operations 21st October.

Army Form C. 2118

Vol 8

WAR DIARY
INTELLIGENCE SUMMARY

(Erase heading not required.)

17th SHERWOOD FORESTERS (Welbeck Rangers)

Place	Date 1916	Hour	Summary of Events and Information	Remarks and references to Appendices
BERTRANCOURT	Oct. 1st		Routine, Battalion cleaned up, Inspections etc.	4/9/1941
—do—	2nd		Regtl. Battalion 'thou to HEDAUVILLE. To huts and Billets. Map Reference (P. 34 e).	4/9/1941
HEDAUVILLE	3rd		Routine, Inspections. Raining all day.	4/9/1941
—do—	4th		Routine, Inspections. Raining all day.	4/9/1941
—do—	5th		Battalion relieves 6th Royal BERKSHIRE Regt in the THIEPVAL Sector. (Hut Reference R.20. c. 2t. J.2. to R.20 d. 1.2.) "A" Company in front line; "D" Company Coult. attacks company; "B" Company Support Company; "C" Company Reserve Company.	Kelly 8. C 14/9/1941

COMDG. 17th (S) Bn. SHERWOOD FORESTERS.

Army Form C. 2118

WAR DIARY
INTELLIGENCE SUMMARY
(Erase heading not required.)

17th SHERWOOD FORESTERS (Welbeck Rangers)

Place	Date 1916	Hour	Summary of Events and Information	Remarks and references to Appendices
TRENCHES	Oct 6th		Trench Routine. Heavy artillery Shelling on both sides. 2nd LIEUTS. W.N. BIRKIN and M.A. ELLISEN awarded the MILITARY CROSS. Situation normal.	V/G/NM
-do-	7th		Trench Routine. Heavy artillery Shelling on both sides. 2nd Lieut N.F. BARNES joined for duty 4th & 4th October 1916. Congratulatory message from G.O.C. RESERVE ARMY attached as an Appendix and marked	H.I.
		At 6.5 pm	The artillery on both sides became very violent and it was reported that the enemy were attacking our left flank but the same afterwards the Situation became normal about 8 pm. 2nd Lieut D. St G. PETTIGREW wounded.	V/G/NM

Kirkman .... Lt. Colonel,
COMDG. 17th (S) Bn. SHERWOOD FORESTERS.

Army Form C. 2118

WAR DIARY
of
INTELLIGENCE SUMMARY
(Erase heading not required.) 17th SHERWOOD FORESTERS (Welbeck Rays)

(59)

Place	Date 1916	Hour	Summary of Events and Information	Remarks and references to Appendices
TRENCHES	Oct 8th	5.30 am	The enemy made a Bombing attack on our left flank and succeeded in driving 1st & 2nd Bn posts back to HAMMENWERFER and Henry Nose Battery in rear. Front support and Reserve Nos. a bigger crunk. Attack was made a few mts by Inns expelled & for the temporary position he Captured. 13 Prisoners and killed 25 of the enemy including an Officer. Fresh very little Arco. The enemy subject the 110th Regiment of BADEN-BADEN. Rittmeister, a rather Successful Stunt.	
		8.30 am	Normal Situation. Intense Cannonade through out day.	

.... Lt. Colonel,
COMDG. 17th (S) Bn. SHERWOOD FORESTERS.

WAR DIARY
INTELLIGENCE SUMMARY

17th SHERWOOD FORESTERS (Welbeck Rangers)

Army Form C. 2118

Place	Date	Hour	Summary of Events and Information	Remarks and references to Appendices
TRENCHES	Oct. 1916 9th	—	At 4.30 am the Platoon under 2nd Lt C.H. Statham took part in the attack on SCHWABEN REDOUBT in conjunction with the 16th & 15th SHERWOOD FORESTERS. Point 99 was the objective which was secured with great dash and gallantry, our men accounting for a considerable number of the enemy. After remaining there for over an hour 2nd Lt. STATHAM was forced to retire through the sheer weight of numbers and had to attempt to support on the left flank which had failed and that the attempt to attain the objective. The enemy were hunted into their old fire lines and inflicted many casualties. I was afterwards informed by the officer in Command, Lord Cavendish, Mr. Edwin and G.O.C. of the splendid fighting and good leadership of the officer in Command. CAPTAIN & ADJUTANT T. THORNTON, LIEUT & ADJT. T.W. HARRIOT, and 2nd LIEUT. R.S.M. T. Rogers recommended for the Military Cross for devotion to duty and excellent good work in the field 9th Oct. 1916 to Oct. 7 months.	

M.W. Hand, Lt. Colonel,

COMDG. 17th (S) Bn. SHERWOOD FORESTERS.

WAR DIARY
INTELLIGENCE SUMMARY
(Erase heading not required.) 17th SHERWOOD FORESTERS (Welbeck Rangers)

Army Form C. 2118

Place	Date	Hour	Summary of Events and Information	Remarks and references to Appendices
TRENCHES	1916 Oct. 10th		Trench Raids. Situation normal. Intermittent shrapnel on both sides throughout the day, and intense Barrage was placed on our front support lines at 12:30 pm. No report of an attack being delivered by a Brigade on our right on STUFF REDOUBT. The Battalion so relieved by the 1/1 HERTS REGT. and moved into Martinsart at MARTINSART WOODS. (W.C.) 57d. Casualties during period 1st-5th, 5 days 1 officer wounded, 29 other ranks killed, 70 other ranks wounded, 2 other ranks wounded at duty.	/ App 22 / / App 23 /
MARTINSART WOOD.	12th		Routine. Cleaning up and inspection.	
— do —	12th		Routine. Parades under Coy Officers from 7 am to 12:30 pm. Specialists all day. K.C.P. from 2 to 4 pm.	

.... Lt. Colonel,
17th (S) Bn, SHERWOOD FORESTERS.

WAR DIARY / INTELLIGENCE SUMMARY

(Erase heading not required.) 17th SHERWOOD FORESTERS (Welbeck Rangers)

Place	Date 1916	Hour	Summary of Events and Information	Remarks and references to Appendices
MARTINSART WOOD	12. Continued		2nd Lieut L R WATSON and 2nd Lieut C H STATHAM, rejoined from GHANTRY and Depotin to the field. The MILITARY CROSS to No 3.298. Private S. J. SMEATH and No 29370 Private T. COOPER recommended for gallantry and devotion to duty in the field MILITARY MEDAL.	Weather
—do—	13th		Routine Training under Company Officers 6 - 1pm. Specialists all day. Med. Bd. 2 to 4 pm	Weather
—do—	14th		Routine Training under Company Officers to 1pm. Specialists.	Weather
—do—	15th		Stand by ready to move into Trenches at 5 minutes notice.	Weather
—do—	16th		Battalion relieve to Cheshire Regt. in the THIEPVAL (RIVER SECTION (Map Reference 57d. R. 19. C.) Lieut. F. T. CHAFFYN wounded. Situation normal.	Weather

Mu Vincent
Lt. Colonel,
COMDG. 17th (S) Bn. SHERWOOD FORESTERS.

WAR DIARY

INTELLIGENCE SUMMARY

(Erase heading not required.) 17th SHERWOOD FORESTERS (Bellew Range)

Army Form C. 2118

Place	Date	Hour	Summary of Events and Information	Remarks and references to Appendices
TRENCHES	6/6 16th		Situation normal. Feeble Artillery Barrage on our lines at various intervals throughout the day. 63998 Private Murray S.T. SMEATH awarded the MILITARY MEDAL.	Murray
—do—	17th			
—do—	18th		Situation normal. Enemy entered Lo Barrage on all our lines and communications. Captain T. O. KIRREW dangerously wounded. Preparation made to attack the enemy at 2 points.	K/Capt.
—do—	19th		Situation normal. Enemy continue to barrage. Rain falling heavy. Operation proposed postponed.	
—do—	20th		Enemy made an attack on our two advanced points Senson 16 at 4-7. (Map Reference Sheet 57d S.E. R.19.c.) at 5.30 p.m. It was driven off with loss. Our casualties were light. The Battalion was relieved by the 16th RIFLE BRIGADE and 7me to NORTH and SOUTH BLUFFS on the RIVER MOORE	

M Wilkins...............Lt. Colonel,
17th (S) Bn. SHERWOOD FORESTERS

WAR DIARY
INTELLIGENCE SUMMARY

(Erase heading not required.) 17th SHERWOOD FORESTERS (Welbeck Rangers)

Army Form C. 2118

Place	Date 1916	Hour	Summary of Events and Information	Remarks and references to Appendices
TRENCHES	Oct 30th		Troop Reserve R.36. Battalion in Dug outs and dressed Gun Reb. Battalion in BRIGADE SUPPORT. Lieut C.D. HEWAT wounded. Total Casualties during past 4 days. 4 Officers wounded, 17 other ranks Killed, 41 other ranks wounded.	1/Oct/26
	Continued			
AUTHUILLE	31st		Cleaning up. All the Battalion Carrying Parts etc. to front line 4 Lewis Gun Part despatched to SCHWABEN REDOUBT. Near the attack of Points 16 and 38 Troop Offensive R.19 @ S.W.R.K. otted S.M.h.K.R.P. Capt. "A" Company under the Command of Capt.Jn. F.D. COLLEN left on Reel ANCRE OPERATION ORDERS attached see Appendix G. REPORT ON OPERATIONS attacked and hasted BRIGADE REPORT ON OPERATIONS attacked and hasted. 2nd Lieuts W.H. TORNER, T.S. CLIFFORD, P. COATES. wounded. Total Casualties in the foregoing Operation. 3 Officers wounded. 1 Other rank Killed. 12 Other ranks wounded. 47 Other ranks missing.	I.1 I.2 I.3 1/Oct/26

............................Lt. Colonel,
Commg. 17th (S) Bn. SHERWOOD FORESTERS

Army Form C. 2118

WAR DIARY
INTELLIGENCE SUMMARY
(Erase heading not required.) 17th SHERWOOD FORESTERS (Welbeck Rangers)

Instructions regarding War Diaries and Intelligence Summaries are contained in F. S. Regs, Part II. and the Staff Manual respectively. Title Pages will be prepared in manuscript.

Place	Date 1916	Hour	Summary of Events and Information	Remarks and references to Appendices
AUTHUILLE	Oct 22nd		Further Batches carrying to front line, 4 Officers and 175 other ranks attached to 16th RIFLE BRIGADE up to front line.	
		7 pm	Battalion (remainder) move up into old German front line in VILLAGE of THIEPVAL for the night.	/Murray
THIEPVAL	23rd		Battalion line held by 4 north and South groups at AUTHUILLE mine craters by 11 other coys.	/Murray
AUTHUILLE	24th		Battalion move to RIVER CENTRE SUB-SECTION (see map Reference October 16th) relieving 16th RIFLE BRIGADE situation abnormal.	/Murray
TRENCHES	25th		Battalion were relieved by 12th ROYAL SUSSEX situation abnormal. Battalion move to SOUTH side CENTRE TOBRUFS (See map Reference October 30th 1916) That casualties since October 21st 1916 before march killed 12. other ranks wounded, 1 other rank missing. 2nd Lieut L. R. WATSON awarded the MILITARY CROSS for	/Murray

Kink Randle
COMDG. 17th (S) Bn. SHERWOOD FORESTERS.

WAR DIARY
or
INTELLIGENCE SUMMARY

(Erase heading not required.) 17th Bn. SHERWOOD FORESTERS (Welbeck Rangers)

Army Form C. 2118

Place	Date 1916	Hour	Summary of Events and Information	Remarks and references to Appendices
TRENCHES Contium. AUTHUILLE	Octr. 25th		For gallantry and devotion to duty. Baths, horses cleaned up and Company organization.	Minto Currah 11 May 24?
– do –	26th		Battalion move to RIVER CENTRE SUB-SECTION (as per reference Bethel 16.6.1916) relieving 11th ROYAL SUSSEX. Situation normal. Trench routine. Situation normal.	11 May 24? 11 May 24
TRENCHES R2RA – do –	29th		Trench routine. At 4.30 a.m. a small attack was carried out by two Bombing Parties on the enemy Strong Post at (R.19.c.3.8.) a distance from 80 to 100 yards. There was no Artillery Preparation and the enemy thing to be in considerable strength were taken by surprise and suffered little opposition. Our men took the position with great dash and

M. Michael........Lt. Colonel.
COMDG. 17th (S) Bn. SHERWOOD FORESTERS.

Army Form C. 2118

WAR DIARY
INTELLIGENCE SUMMARY

(Erase heading not required.) 17th SHERWOOD FORESTERS (battle of Flers cont)

Instructions regarding War Diaries and Intelligence Summaries are contained in F.S. Regs., Part II. and the Staff Manual respectively. Title Pages will be prepared in manuscript.

Place	Date 1916	Hour	Summary of Events and Information	Remarks and references to Appendices
TRENCHES	Oct 29th		and to relieve the Point considerably. Stretcher bearers worked all [R.19.C.1.b.] the whole next morning, they being killed and wounded. The consolidated and at remaining in our lines the Camerons during next 2 days and 10th and were killed and later and wounded. The Battalion was relieved by the 1st/5th Black Watch and sent to Camp (tents) at SENLIS. A very wet day.	Appx1
SENLIS	30th		Routine. Cleaning up and inspections. A very wet day.	Appx1
—do—	31st		Battalion set on working parties. Lt & Qr. Baking Dr J.P. and 32 rank & file joined.	Appx1

[signature]

17th (S) Bn. SHERWOOD FORESTERS

Reserve Army.
G.A. 31/4/16.

Message from General Officer Commanding Reserve Army.

With the capture of COURCELETTE, STUFF REDOUBT, and the SCHWABEN REDOUBT, the Reserve Army has at last gained complete possession of the POZIERES Ridge and the high ground which dominates the ANCRE Valley from the South.

For three months every trench and every foot of ground has been stubbornly defended by the enemy, but the gallantry and perseverance of our troops has overcome every difficulty. Great sacrifices have been necessary, and much hardship has been undergone. We have won our way by sheer hard fighting from LA BOISSELLE through POZIERES and OVILLERS, MOUQUET Farm and the LIEPZIG Salient, until COURCELETE and THIEPVAL are in our hands, and the enemy has been driven from his last strongholds. At every step our troops have clearly shown their superiority to the Germans as fighting men, and they have now gained a moral ascendancy which will be of incalculable value in the future.

This is a record of which we should all be very proud, and the Commander of the Reserve Army wishes to thank every unit which has taken part in the operations for its share in the final success.

(Signed) **N. MALCOLM,** *Major-General,*
General Staff.

Headquarters, Reserve Army,
1st October, 1916.

1st Printing Co., R.E., 5th Section. 301

COPY.
SECRET.   17th. SHERWOOD FORESTERS.   OPERATION ORDER No. 32.

REFERENCE.   1,5,000   ST. PIERRE DIVION.
                1,20,000   57.d.S.E.

1. **INTENTION.**   It is proposed to capture and hold Points 38 and 16 pushing out a bombing block about 100 yards along MAISEY LANE. Strong points are to be constructed at Points R.19.c.62.90. - R.19.c.35.90. Trench 16 to 38 will be cleared. The second blocks we now hold between Points 45 and 16 and just west of Point 47 will be held as "Supporting Points."

2. **PLAN.**   2 Companies will be utilised "A" Coy. for the 1st. Attack, "B" Company will be held in readiness to consolidate the positions gained.
Barrage will be provided by 117th. L.T.M. Battery with the possible co-operation of artillery. (L.T.M. Barrage programme attached APPENDIX A.)
At <u>Point 47.</u> block 3.Bombing Squads will be ready at ZERO minus 10 minutes at ZERO Plus 12 Minutes GERMAN Block will be rushed and captured. After Seizing this point a "TIN DISC" Signal will be shown to L.T.M. and on the gun ceasing fire to alter range Point 38 will be attacked.
Then 1st. Bombing Party will proceed up trench to FORK R.19.c.30.83.
2nd. Bombing Party will move to R.19.c.4¼.9. until relieved by 3rd. Party when they will move as far forward as the barrage will permit and there make a block in the meantime the 3rd. Party will establish a block at R.19.c.4¼.9.
The bombing party at present holding Block 47 will advance to Point 38 and the present Reserve Block Squad will move to Point 47.
On the capture of Point 38 the consolidation party will move up and make good as per para B. Company.
At <u>Point 16</u> block 3 Bombing Squads will be ready at ZERO Minus 10 Minutes at ZERO plus 12 minutes Point 16 will be taken, after which the leading Squad will move up STORY TRENCH for about 50 yards and there block.
The <u>Second Squad</u> will move 50 yards along trench towards Point 97 and there create a block.
The <u>Third Squad</u> will move down WEST KOYLI about 50 yards and there block.
The bombing post now in position near Point 16 will move up and take over Point 16.

"B" COMPANY.   Will be under the Command of O.C. "A" Company. Two Platoons will take up position near Point 47 and Two Platoons between Points 45 and 16.
For their cover Shell Slits are being dug tonight.
Two parties as under will be told off previously.
<u>Party No.1.</u> consisting of 20 N.C.Os. and men carrying 8 Picks and 12 Shovels will move forward to consolidate Point 16 and also blocks in STORY TRENCH WEST KOYLI TRENCH and TRENCH leading to Point 97. This party will be under the Officer in charge of Operations against Point 16.
<u>Party No. 2.</u> consisting of 20 N.C.Os. and men will be used for consolidations at Point 38 including a "Strong Point" at R.19.c.35.90. This party will be under the Officer in charge of operations against Point 38.
Tools will be carried as in case of Party No. 1.

TRENCH 16   A Clearing Party will proceed from Point 16 to 38. This
to 38.   will be found by A. Company and will move up to point 16 in Advance of consolidation <u>Party No. 1.</u>

SHEET 2.

LEWIS GUNS. At Point 16 one gun will guard the left flank, one gun will watch TRENCH 16 to 38. At Point 47 one gun will protect the right flank. As soon as Points 16 and 38 are made good one gun will proceed to each point.

VICKER'S GUNS. One gun will be in readiness to go forward to Point 38 on consolidation.

MEDICAL ARRANGEMENTS. The Medical Officer will arrange to have all Stretchers and Bearers as far forward as possible.
The Aid Post is situated at R.19.d.0.½.
Wounded will be evacuated via OLD GERMAN Front Line to JOHNSTONE'S POST.

PRISONERS. Will be escorted to Brigade Hd. Qrs.

AEROPLANE. A contact Aeroplane will fly over the Area from ZERO hour. 5 N.C.Os. and men per platoon will be detailed to carry 3 flares each. Flares will be lit by the leading infantry at ZERO plus 1 hour and again at ZERO plus 2 hours.

STORES. A full supply of Mills Bombs Nos. 5 and 23 will be placed at Blocks 16 and 47 before hand in readiness to be carried forward, also consolidation material.
The O.C. "B" Company will detail 10 men at Points 16 and 47 to carry Bombs and material forward as required.

TIME. Watches will be synchronised with Company Commanders at Bn. Hd. Qrs. at a time to be notified later.

18.10.16.   (sd) T. Thornton, Capt & Adjt.
                                  17th. Sherwood Foresters.

APPENDIX A.
Proposed Scheme for STOKES BARRAGE.

	Minutes.	
ZERO.	0.	6 guns concentrating fire as follows. 2 guns on Point 16.
		1 " " Trench 16-38.
		2 " " Point 38.
		1 " " Point 47.
	01.	1 gun operating in Trench 16-38. lifts to R.19.c.3.8½.
	02.	5 guns concentrated on Points 16-47-38. lifts 40 yards every 30 seconds, until final line of Barrage reached viz:- Point 97.- R.19.c.1½.9. - R.19.a.4½.0.

Rate of fire maintained to be 12 rounds per gun per minute, for first 3 minutes, afterwards 3 rounds per gun per minute remainder of operation.
Liaison between bombing parties and Officer Cmdg. T.M.B. to be by runner.
Observation of Progress of Bombing Squads by means of gun observers and Discs.

COPY.   17th. SHERWOOD FORESTERS.

Report on Operations carried out by one Company of the 17th. Sherwood Foresters supported by the 16th. Rifle Brigade on the 21.10.16.

Reference ST. PIERRE DIVION. 1,5000.

OBJECT. To capture and make good Points 16 and 38. R.19.c.

The assaulting party consisted of 2 groups each of 1 Officer 27 N.C.Os. and men and a 3rd. party of 1 Officer and 20 men detailed as follows:-
1 party to seize 16 and then form 3 blocks in the 3rd. Tr. leading from Point 16.
1 party to seize 47 then 38 and block MAISIE LANE and also R.19.c.20.83.
1 party to make good trench running 16 to 38.

The original intention was to assemble as near respective objectives as possible 20 mins. before the time for assault but owing to the bad conditions of the trenches parties were sent up to be at assembly points as short a while as possible. The gauging of this time worked well and undoubtedly saved casualties and contributed to success achieved at point 16,

POINT 16.   The leading squad rushed it, the enemy put up a stubborn fight for 5 minutes and then cleared.
At this point a MG with broken tripod was encountered - probably the work of the STOKES.
The Block party moving up STORY TR found 9 or 10 HUN in a dugout, they were prevented from coming out by a MILLS BOMB which killed one or two and slightly wounded 3 - the guard mounted was afterwards relieved by the Rifle Brigade and prisoners 7 in number then removed.

Blocks were established at R.19.c.$\frac{1}{2}$.7. and R.19.c.0.5$\frac{1}{2}$. and Point 16. consolidated.

Trench 16 to 38 could not be found nor could WEST KOYLI both seem to have been shell obliterated.

STOKES.   Did excellent, accurate work in the fight for Point 16.

POINT 38. Point 47 was rushed and taken, party moved on towards 38 but were knocked badly by shrapnel and MG fire owing to lack of cover, eventually this attempt had to be abandoned and a block was established about 10 to 15 yards in front of 47
Point 38 was strongly held for a time when enemy suddenly left it and soon afterwards a considerable Shrapnel fire was put on 38 to 47. The retirement from 38 was probably for this purpose.

The Machine Gun doing the damage is thought to have fired from about R.19.c.4$\frac{1}{2}$.9$\frac{1}{2}$.   MAISEY LANE.

STOKES.   The guns helping in the Point 38 effort were unlucky and not of such help as those hitting Point 16.

Rifle Brigade.   Captain KENWOOD was of the utmost assistance together with his men.   To this Officer we are greatly indebted.

Artillery - enemy.   More of this was encountered than we expected.

                    (sd) A.P.H. Le Prevost. Capt.
                         17th. Sherwood Foresters.
                         21.10.16.

COPY.   117th INFANTRY BRIGADE.   I.3

Report on OPERATIONS carried out by one Company of the 17th. Notts
and Derby Regiment, supported by the 16th. Rifle Brigade, on the
21st. October 1916.

Reference.   St. PIERRE DIVION, 1/5000 Map.

GENERAL.

The object of this attack was to capture the trenches known as the
POPE'S NOSE, Points 16 and 38, R.19.c.

The difficulty of the operation was greatly increased by the obliter-
ation of trenches caused by the German bombardment during the attack
on the SCHWABEN REDOUBT in the early hours of the morning.

Places of assembly were rendered unrecognisable, and it was almost
impossible to identify the actual points which formed the objective
of the attack.

The conditions were not very favourable for observation owing to a
slight mist, but valuable reports were nevertheless received.

SPECIAL.

(a) Composition of Assaulting Party.

Under Command of Captain LE PREVOST, 17th. NOTTS & DERBY REGIMENT.

Divided into three groups:-
    Two consisting of One Officer, and 27 Other Ranks, each.
    One consisting of One Officer, and 20 Other Ranks.

Intention:-

One party to seize Point 16, and then form three blocks in the three
trenches leading away from that point.

One party to seize Point 45, then Point 38, and block (a) MAISIE LANE
and (b) R.19.c.20.83.

One party to make good the trench running from Point 16 to Point 38.

(b) Assembly.

Owing to the condition of the trenches the time of assembly as originally
fixed was abandoned, and the various parties were sent up so as to
arrive at their assembly points as short a time as possible before
the hour for the assault.

The estimates of time were accurate, and the plan worked well.

(c) Time.

The Operation was timed to commence with a Light Trench Mortar Bombardment at 12.16 p.m. this was begun punctually to the minute.

(d) The Assault.

  (1) Point 16.

    The leading squad rushed in, the enemy fought stubbornly for five
    minutes, and then withdrew.

    A machine gun with a broken tripod was captured here.

    The Block party moving up STORY TRENCH found 9 or 10 of the enemy
    in a dug-out. One or two were killed, three slightly wounded by

SHEET 2.

a Mills Bomb. Seven of them were taken prisoners.

Point 16 was ultimately consolidated and blocks were established at R.19.c.½.7. and R.19.c.0.5½.

(11) Point 38.

Point 47 was first rushed and taken; the party then moved on towards Point 38 but owing to lack of cover were badly hit by Shrapnel and machine gun fire, the latter seeming to come from about R.19.c.4.½.9½. in MAISIE LANE.

Eventually the advance had to be given up, and a block was established ten to fifteen yards beyond Point 47.

Point 38 was strongly held for a time by the enemy, who suddenly retired, probably in order to give their guns opportunity to shell Points 38 and 47.

A considerable volume of shrapnel fire was opened on these points by the German guns soon after their Infantry had withdrawn.

(111) Trench from Point 16 to Point 38.

This could not be identified, nor could WEST K.O.Y.L.I.

(e) Reports.

Many reports of the capture of POPE'S NOSE were received between 1 p.m. and 3 p.m. chiefly from Artillery and Brigade O.P's.

Actual confirmation as to the capture of Points 16 and 47 was received from the O.C. 16th. Rifle Brigade, dispatched at 2.40 p.m. and received here at 3.23 p.m.

(f) Subsequent measures.

Detachments of R.E. and of the 13th Battalion GLOUCESTER Regiment (Pioneers) were sent up immediately on receipt of the above message.

The R.E. were to consolidate Point 16, the Pioneers Point 47, and a new trench was to be constructed on either side of each captured point for a distance of 50 yards.

(g) Stokes Guns.

These were most useful in the Attack., on Point 16. The guns helping in the attack on Point 38 were unlucky.

(h) Enemy Artillery.

The fire encountered from the enemy's artillery was stronger than had been expected in view of our preliminary bombardment, and of the operations carried out on the right.

October 22nd. 1916.

117th Brigade.
39th Division.

1/17th BATTALION

NOTTS & DERBY REGIMENT

NOVEMBER 1 9 1 6

117th Brigade.
39th Division.

1/17th BATTALION

NOTTS & DERBY REGIMENT

NOVEMBER 1 9 1 6

WAR DIARY
INTELLIGENCE SUMMARY

(Erase heading not required.) 17th SHERWOOD FORESTERS (Welbeck Rangers)

Army Form C. 2118

Place	Date 1916	Hour	Summary of Events and Information	Remarks and references to Appendices
SENLIS	1st		Route. 200 other ranks working party remained. 4 Battalion Training under Coy officers.	1/Aug 24/1
—do—	2nd		Routine. Very wet day. General cleaning of Equipment etc.	1/(Aug 24/1)
—do—	3rd		Battalion relieve the 1st Herts Regt in the RIVER CENTRE Sub-Section. Situation normal.	1/(Aug 24/1)
TRENCHES	4th		Situation normal. 2nd Lieut F R BIRCUMSHAW wounded.	1/(Aug 24/1)
—do—	5th		Situation normal 2nd Lieut F.D. Fox killed. Battalion relieved by the 13th Bn ROYAL SUSSEX and move to MARTINSART WOODS. in Authuile.	1/(Aug 24/1)
MARTINSART WOODS	6th		Battalion relieves the 13th Bn ROYAL SUSSEX in the RIVER CENTRE SUB SECTION. Situation normal.	Off 1/75 cont. Aug 9.C

.... Lt. Colonel,
COMDG. 17th (S) Bn. SHERWOOD FORESTERS.

Army Form C. 2118

WAR DIARY
or
INTELLIGENCE SUMMARY

(Erase heading not required.) 17th Sherwood Foresters (Welbeck Rangers)

Instructions regarding War Diaries and Intelligence Summaries are contained in F. S. Regs., Part II. and the Staff Manual respectively. Title Pages will be prepared in manuscript.

(69)

Place	Date 1916	Hour	Summary of Events and Information	Remarks and references to Appendices
TRENCHES	Nov. 7th		Situation normal.	CM 24r century
— do —	8th	8 p.m.	Situation normal. Relieved by 4/5th BLACK WATCH and move to PIONEER ROAD in 9 detachments. Casualties during period of last 2 days — 6 other ranks wounded.	CM 24r not coy OM off autbatt
PIONEER ROAD	9th		Cleaning up and Inspections.	OM off autbatt
— do —	10th		Battalion moved to SENLIS at 1.45 p.m. 1/1 HERTS took over.	CM 24r
SENLIS	11th		Routine — General cleaning of Equipment etc.	CM 24r
— do —	12th		Y DAY — Day spent cleaning Arms & Equipment.	Appx
— do —	13th		Z DAY — At 12.15 a.m. Battalion ordered to move to PAISLEY AVENUE. Arrived at 4.50 a.m. ZERO HOUR — 5.45 a.m. In Divisional Reserve — ready to move at half an hour's notice. M W [signature]	

.... Lt. Colonel,
COMDG. 17th (S) Bn. SHERWOOD FORESTERS

Army Form C. 2118

WAR DIARY
INTELLIGENCE SUMMARY

(Erase heading not required.) 17th (SERV.) Bn. SHERWOOD FORESTERS. (Welbeck Rangers.)

Instructions regarding War Diaries and Intelligence Summaries are contained in F. S. Regs., Part II. and the Staff Manual respectively. Title Pages will be prepared in manuscript.

Place	Date, 1916	Hour	Summary of Events and Information	Remarks and references to Appendices
SENLIS (continued)	Nov 13th		The following parties were detailed from the Battalion. (a.) One officer and 9 men as guard on AVELUY–AUTHUILLE ROAD at southern exit of AUTHUILLE, at 8.45 p.m. Y day. (b.) Two NCOs and 4 men to O.C. TANKS at 118th Infantry Brigade H.Qrs. PAISLEY DUMP at 5.30 am Z day. (c.) One officer to O.C. Tanks to report at 118th Infantry Brigade H.Qrs. at 5.30 p.m. Y day. (d.) Two officers, five NCOs and fifty men to A.D.S at PAISLEY DUMP at Zero hour. (e.) A Liaison Officer and Two cyclist-runners to 117th Brigade H.Qrs NORTH BLUFFS at 4.45 am. At 6.55 am. A. Coy was ordered to report to O.C. 16th B. SHERWOOD FORESTERS at H.Qrs SPEY SIDE At 7.10 am. C.D.& B. Coys were ordered to follow A. Coy to same destination in order mentioned.	

.... Lt. Colonel,
COMDG. 17th (S) Bn. SHERWOOD FORESTERS.

WAR DIARY
INTELLIGENCE SUMMARY

(Erase heading not required.) 17th (SERV.) Bn. SHERWOOD FORESTERS. (Welbeck Rangers)

Army Form C. 2118

Place	Date 1916	Hour	Summary of Events and Information	Remarks and references to Appendices
SENLIS (continued)	Nov 13		At 8.20 a.m. C. Coy. was ordered to the front line to reinforce the 16th Bn. S.F. (276 prisoners already passed back from front line, more to come.) At 8.30 a.m. A Patrol of one platoon of A. Coy under 2/Lt. R.A.F. MEARS was sent over the top of bank at H.Qrs SPEY SIDE and from thence in an easterly direction to get in touch on the right. At 9.15 a.m. A and D Coys were ordered forward to clear dugouts in trenches taken by the 16th Bn. S.F. The H.Qrs of the 16th S.F. moved forward to GERMAN Batt. H.Qrs in ST. PIERRE DIVION. SPEY SIDE H.Qrs taken over by the 17th Bn. S.F.	

.... Lt. Colonel,
COMDG. 17th (S) Bn. SHERWOOD FORESTERS.

Army Form C. 2118

WAR DIARY
INTELLIGENCE SUMMARY

(Erase heading not required.) 17th (SERV.) Bn. SHERWOOD FORESTERS. (Welbeck Rangers)

Place	Date 1916	Hour	Summary of Events and Information	Remarks and references to Appendices
SENLIS (continued)	Nov 13		At 10.15 am. The Patrol that went out at 8.30 am returned. 2nd Lt. MEARS reported he got in touch with the 12th SUSSEX at No. 8 TUNNEL and with the 4/5th BLACK WATCH at point Q 24. d. 8.7. They worked his way forward till he gained touch with the 16th S.F. The BLACK WATCH reported all clear on their right. At 11.10 am Battalion H. Qrs moved forward to GERMAN Batt. H. Qrs in SAINT PIERRE DIVION. Positions gained were consolidated. At 4.45 pm. Coys were warned to move at a moments notice. At 6.40 pm. Companies were rearranged as follows:—	

_____ Lt. Colonel,
Comdg. 17th (S) Bn. SHERWOOD FORESTERS.

Army Form C. 2118

WAR DIARY
INTELLIGENCE SUMMARY

(Erase heading not required.) 17th (SERV.) Bn. SHERWOOD FORESTERS. (Welbeck Rangers)

Instructions regarding War Diaries and Intelligence Summaries are contained in F.S. Regs., Part II. and the Staff Manual respectively. Title Pages will be prepared in manuscript.

(73)

Place	Date	Hour	Summary of Events and Information	Remarks and references to Appendices
SENLIS (continued)	Nov 13th 10/16		A. Company — RIVER LEFT SECTION. (N°10 TUNNEL.) B. — do. — PAISLEY AVENUE. C. — do. — POINT 87–97. (Their present position) D. — do. — MILL ROAD — Q24. c.9.7. (The assembly position of the 16th Bn. S.F.) Batt. H.Qrs. AID POST — SPEY SIDE. Situation remained quiet throughout the night. The whole operations carried out by the Brigade were very successful. Over 700 prisoners, including a Battalion Commander and several officers were captured, more of which were taken by the 16th S.F. The total captured by the Division was nearly 3,000 O.R.'s & 75	

...........Lt. Colonel,
Comdg. 17th (S) Bn. SHERWOOD FORESTERS.

Army Form C. 2118

WAR DIARY
INTELLIGENCE SUMMARY

(Erase heading not required.) 17th (SERV.) Bn. SHERWOOD FORESTERS. (Welbeck Rangers)

Place	Date	Hour	Summary of Events and Information	Remarks and references to Appendices
SPEY SIDE	NOV 14th 1916		At 11.40am Guides were ordered to meet Staff Captain at WARLOY at 3 p.m. At 1.45 p.m. Battalion marched to WARLOY via BOUZINCOURT - SENLIS. No being served en route near PIONEER ROAD. Batt: arrived at WARLOY at 9.15 p.m. and was billeted in tents.	O.H.S.
WARLOY	15th		At 1. am hostile aeroplanes bombed the camp. LIEUT. E.P. RICHARDSON was wounded. At 10.40am Battalion with all Transport and Stores moved to GEZINCOURT via CONTAY - TOUTENCOURT - PUCHEVILLERS - BEAUQUESNE - BEAUVAL. The battalion halted near PUCHEVILLERS while dinner was served.	

........................Lt. Colonel,
COMDG. 17th (S) Bn. SHERWOOD FORESTERS.

WAR DIARY
INTELLIGENCE SUMMARY
(Erase heading not required.) 17th (SERV.) Bn. SHERWOOD FORESTERS. (Notts & Derbys)

Army Form C. 2118

Place	Date	Hour	Summary of Events and Information	Remarks and references to Appendices
WARLOY (continued)	Nov 15th 1916	At 6.45 pm	Battalion arrived at destination and were billeted in barns.	
GEZINCOURT	16th		Routine - cleaning clothes and equipment.	
do	17th	At 9.30 am	Battalion moved to CANDAS when temporary billets (barns) were arranged till battalion entrained for SAINT OMER at 7.50 pm. Frosty and very cold wind.	
ST. OMER	18th	At 6.10 am	Battalion arrived at ST. OMER. At 8.15 am Marched to TETINGHEM arriving there at 9.40 am. Billeted in barns. Day spent cleaning clothes, arms and equipment.	

.... Lt. Colonel,
COMDG. 17th (S) Bn. SHERWOOD FORESTERS.

Army Form C. 2118

WAR DIARY
or
INTELLIGENCE SUMMARY

(Erase heading not required.) 17th (SERV.) Bn. SHERWOOD FORESTERS. (Welbeck Rangers)

Place	Date 1916	Hour	Summary of Events and Information	Remarks and references to Appendices
TETINGHEM	Nov 19th		While staying at this place the battalion is attached to the Second Army Central School of Instruction and will find any parties, working or otherwise, required by them. Routine - cleaning clothes, arms & equipment. Programme of work arranged by C.O. for the week to be carried out under Company arrangements at times stated.	
— do —	20th		Classes arranged for Lewis Gunners & Signallers. At 9.30 am a working Party of two officers and 100 other ranks reports at the School. A further party of the same strength will report at the School at 2 pm.	

J Mulvey Lt. Colonel,
COMDG. 17th (S) Bn. SHERWOOD FORESTERS.

WAR DIARY
INTELLIGENCE SUMMARY

(Erase heading not required.) 17th (SERV.) Bn. SHERWOOD FORESTERS.

Place	Date 1916	Hour	Summary of Events and Information	Remarks and references to Appendices
TETINGHEM (continued)	Nov 20		The remainder of the battalion paraded as per programme of work set out	
do	21st		The Battalion found the following parties which will be attached to the various Schools until the battalion returns to the 39th Division. (a.) One officer + 40 other ranks — Scribing School. Artillery School TILQUES (b.) 44 other ranks — Scribing School. MONT DES CATS. (c.) 15 — do — Trench Mortar School. BERTHEN. (d.) 42 — do — Grenade School TERDEGHEM. A proportion of picks + shovels were taken by each party. Two officers and 75 other ranks reported to the School at 8.35 a.m. for use in their Five course Scheme.	

J W M Armagh ....Lt. Colonel,
COMDG. 17th (S) Bn. SHERWOOD FORESTERS.

WAR DIARY
INTELLIGENCE SUMMARY

(Erase heading not required.) 17th (SERV.) Bn. SHERWOOD FORESTERS. (Welbeck Rangers)

Army Form C. 2118

Place	Date 1916	Hour	Summary of Events and Information	Remarks and references to Appendices
TETINGHEM	Nov. 21st		All the Transport, Specialists, Servants & available bathed during the day at ST. OMER. O.C. Companies (Captains Collen, Wallis, Kerr & Morrell) together with the C.S.Majors (Sisolono, Ferrer, Reid & Stradling) commenced the full course at the School. Lieuts Mears, Bainbow, Hallam Lilley together with 3 N.C.Os per Company commenced the special Course of Bayonet Fighting & Physical Training at the School.	
TETINGHEM	22nd		Battalion provided the same party for the fine Control Scheme to the School as yesterday. A working party consisting of all available men was also sent to the School. Lewis Gunners & Signallers paraded at g.am under	Oct 26

COMDG. 17th (S) Bn. SHERWOOD FORESTERS.

WAR DIARY
or
INTELLIGENCE SUMMARY

(Erase heading not required.) 17th (SERV.) Bn. SHERWOOD FORESTERS. (Welbeck Rangers)

Army Form C. 2118

Place	Date 1916	Hour	Summary of Events and Information	Remarks and references to Appendices
TETINGHEM	Nov 22nd (continued)		Their Instructors as usual. A Regimental Canteen was opened today. Hours 12 noon to 2 pm and 3.30 pm to 7.30 pm daily.	
—do.—	23rd		The available other ranks of the Battalion (about 80) paraded from 9 am to 12.30 pm for Bayonet Fighting, Physical training, Guard Duties, Arms Drill & Company Drill. The following went on Courses (Period of Course 6 days) (a.) Lewis Gun Course at VOLKERINCKHOVE — one other rank (b.) Bombing Course " do " — four other ranks (c.) Elementary Military Engineering & Trench Work at LEDRINGHEM — one officer and nine other ranks. Leave up to 20% per Company was granted upto ST. OMER from 2 pm to 7 pm.	

.... Lt. Colonel,
COMDG. 17th (S.) Bn. SHERWOOD FORESTERS.

WAR DIARY
INTELLIGENCE SUMMARY

Army Form C. 2118

17th /s SHERWOOD FORESTERS (Welbeck Rangers)

Place	Date	Hour	Summary of Events and Information	Remarks and references to Appendices
TETINGHAM	24th		Parties, Working Parties, see available at Training from 9 to 12.30 pm	9/Aug/24
-do-	25th		Parties, Working Parties, as available at Training from 9 to 12.30 pm	9/Aug/24
-do-	26th		Pk. Sunday Voluntary Divine Service	9/Aug/24
-do-	27th		Parties, Working Parties, all available at Training from 9 to 12.30 pm	9/Aug/24
-do-	28th		Parties, Working Parties, all available at Training. C.O. Parade from 10.15 to 12.15 pm	9/Aug/24
-do-	29th		Parties, Working Parties. 150 other ranks Church Pde for Lieut. Gen. Comdt. (Regimental)	9/Aug/24
-do-	30th		Parties, Working parties. Run Jun Cpls	9/Sept/24

.................Lt. Colonel,
COMDG. 17th (S) Bn. SHERWOOD FORESTERS.

117th Brigade.
39th Division.

1/17th BATTALION

NOTTS & DERBY REGIMENT

DECEMBER 1 9 1 6

Army Form C. 2118

WAR DIARY
or
INTELLIGENCE SUMMARY

(Erase heading not required.)

17th Bn SHERWOOD FORESTERS (Welbeck Rangers)

Vol 10

Place	Date 1916	Hour	Summary of Events and Information	Remarks and references to Appendices
TEVERSHAM	Dec 1st		Routine, Working Parties, 100 Lewis gun class.	1/May/24
do	2nd		Routine Working Parties, 100 Lewis gun class	1/May/24
do	3rd		Routine Working Parties, 100 Lewis gun class	1/May/24
do	4th		Routine Working Parties, 100 Lewis gun class	1/May/24
do	5th		Routine Working Parties, 100 Lewis gun class	1/May/24
do	6th		Routine. All available NCOs sent to 2nd Army School for an attack demonstration.	4/May/24
do	7th		Routine Working Parties 100 Lewis Gun Class.	1/May/24
do	8th		Routine, Working Parties, 100 Lewis gun class	1/May/24

APBathurst Major
Lt. Colonel.
Comdg. 17th (S) Bn. SHERWOOD FORESTERS.

10.C

WAR DIARY

INTELLIGENCE SUMMARY

17th (SERV.) Bn. SHERWOOD FORESTERS. (Lieut Col —)

Army Form C. 2118

Place	Date 1916	Hour	Summary of Events and Information	Remarks and references to Appendices
FETTING CAMP	9th Dec.		Routine, genrl. Clean up.	May 24
—do—	10th		Routine, Divine Service.	May 24
—do—	11th		Routine, working parties, 70 hour gun clnr.	May 24
—do—	12th		Routine, working parties, 70 hour gun clnr, working parties	May 24
—do—	13th		Routine, working parties, 70 hour gun clnr, Bathing 50 men	May 24
—do—	14th		Routine, working parties, 70 hour gun clnr, Bathing 53 men	May 24
—do—	15th		Routine, working parties, 70 hour gun clnr, Bathing 67 men	May 24
—do—	16th		Routine, working parties, 70 hour gun clnr, Bathing —	May 24
—do—	17th		Sunday Divine Service	May 24

Blackwood Major
COMDG. 17th (S) Bn. SHERWOOD FORESTERS.

Army Form C. 2118

WAR DIARY
INTELLIGENCE SUMMARY
(Erase heading not required.) 17th (SERV.) Bn. SHERWOOD FORESTERS. (Mellish Range.)

Instructions regarding War Diaries and Intelligence Summaries are contained in F.S. Regs., Part II. and the Staff Manual respectively. Title Pages will be prepared in manuscript.

Place	Date	Hour	Summary of Events and Information	Remarks and references to Appendices
TATTINGHEM	1916 18th		Routine. Working Parties. All available Battalion Parade under C.O. Service	1/Appx 24
–do–	19th		Routine. Working Parties. All available under C.O. being 3rd Army School	1/Appx 24
–do–	20th		Routine. All available under C.O. Bombing in trenches	1/Appx 24
–do–	21st		Routine. Very bad day. Lectures and Lewis Machine Gun under Cover	1/Appx 24
–do–	22nd		The Battalion Paraded at 7.30 am and entrained at ST MOMELIN (meta sauge) for POPERINGHE. detrained at POPERINGHE (head sauge) and entrained at POPERINGHE (head sauge) for ASYLUM STATION, YPRES. marched to CANAL BANK (Map reference) SHEET 28 Squares C.13. and 19. Battalion relieved 1/ CAMBRIDGESHIRE Regt. and became BRIGADE SUPPORT.	1/Appx 24
BOESINGHE	23rd		Routine. Working Parties to front line etc	1/Appx 24

Archerst .... Lt Colonel
COMDG. 17th (S) Bn. SHERWOOD FORESTERS.

1875 Wt. W593/826 1,000,000 4/15 J.B.C. & A. A.D.S.S./Forms/C. 2118.

WAR DIARY
INTELLIGENCE SUMMARY

Army Form C. 2118

Instructions regarding War Diaries and Intelligence Summaries are contained in F.S. Regs., Part II. and the Staff Manual respectively. Title Pages will be prepared in manuscript.

(Erase heading not required.) 17th (SERV.) Bn. SHERWOOD FORESTERS. (Welbeck Rangers)

Place	Date 1916	Hour	Summary of Events and Information	Remarks and references to Appendices
BOESINGHE	Dec 24th		Routine. Working Parties to front line etc.	
—do—	25th		Battalion relieved the 16th RIFLE BRIGADE in the front line holding the line from C.18.b.3½.3½ to CANAL BANK including INKERMAN (SHEET 28) B.C. and D. Companies in the front line, A Company in Support. Relief complete	
		11.15pm	Trench Routine. Situation normal.	
TRENCHES	26th			
—do—	27th		Trench Routine. Situation normal.	
—do—	28th		Trench Routine. Situation normal.	

Ashwood Major
COMDG. 17th (S) Bn. SHERWOOD FORESTERS.

WAR DIARY

INTELLIGENCE SUMMARY

(Erase heading not required.) 17th (SERV.) Bn. SHERWOOD FORESTERS. (Welbeck Rangers)

Place	Date 1916	Hour	Summary of Events and Information	Remarks and references to Appendices
TRENCHES	Dec 29		Trench Routine, Situation Normal. Battalion relieved by the 16th Rifle Brigade. Relief complete 5.30 p.m. Battalion move to BRIGADE SUPPORT. (RIGHT SECTOR) "A" and "B" Companies Dug out CANAL BANK. Bn. Hd. Qrs. "C" and "D" Companies to CHATEAU des TROIS TOURS. (SHEET 28. B 28. Central.)	MBurton Capt.
BRIELEN	30th		Bathing and Working Parties.	NCaptny
–do–	31st		Bathing and Working Parties.	NCaptny

Prevost Major
COMDG. 17th (S) Bn. SHERWOOD FORESTERS.

Army Form C. 2118

WAR DIARY
INTELLIGENCE SUMMARY

(Erase heading not required.) 17th (SERV.) Bn. SHERWOOD FORESTERS.

Vol X (Welbeck Rangers)

Instructions regarding War Diaries and Intelligence Summaries are contained in F. S. Regs., Part II. and the Staff Manual respectively. Title Pages will be prepared in manuscript.

Place	Date	Hour	Summary of Events and Information	Remarks and references to Appendices
BRIELEN	1917 JAN. 1st		Routine. Battalion moves up to Trenches relieving 14th Bn SHERWOOD FORESTERS in the RIGHT SUB-SECTION of the CENTRE SECTOR. Battalion from (SHEET 28. C 14 a.e.d) A B C Companies in front line. D Company in support at LANCASHIRE FARM. Relief Completed 5.15 pm	1/1/17
TRENCHES	2nd		Trench Routine. Situation normal.	2/1/17
-do-	3rd		Trench Routine. Situation normal.	3/1/17
-do-	4th		Trench Routine. Situation normal. 2nd Lieut F.D. HAXXXM wounded	4/1/17
-do-	5th		Trench Routine. Situation normal. Battalion relieved by 14th Bn SHERWOOD FORESTERS. Battalion went to BRIGADE SUPPORT. Battalion Hd (8H A & B Companies) CHATEAU de TROIS TOUR. C & D Companies to CANAL BANK. Relief Completed 5.15 pm.	5/1/17

[signed] Lt Colonel,
COMDG. 17th (S) Bn. SHERWOOD FORESTERS.

Army Form C. 2118

WAR DIARY
INTELLIGENCE SUMMARY

(Erase heading not required.) 17th (SERV.) Bn. SHERWOOD FORESTERS (Welbeck Rangers)

Instructions regarding War Diaries and Intelligence Summaries are contained in F. S. Regs., Part II. and the Staff Manual respectively. Title Pages will be prepared in manuscript.

Place	Date 1917	Hour	Summary of Events and Information	Remarks and references to Appendices
BRIELEN	Jany 6th		Routine, Cleaning up, Bathing, Working Parties.	Mapping
-do-	7th		Routine, Cleaning up, Bathing, Working Parties.	1/Map 24
-do-	8th		Routine, Cleaning up, Working Parties.	1/Map 24
-do-	9th		Routine, Battalion relieves 16th Sherwood Foresters in the same sector as on January 1st 1917. Relief complete 4.45 pm B Company in support. A C & D Companies in front line. 2nd Lieut. F. D. WAKHAM wounded.	1/Map 24
TRENCHES	10th		Trench Routine, Situation normal.	1/Map 24
-do-	11th		Trench Routine, Situation normal.	1/Map 24

K. Wunh Lt. Colonel
COMDG. 17th (S) Bn. SHERWOOD FORESTERS.

Army Form C. 2118

WAR DIARY
or
INTELLIGENCE SUMMARY

(Erase heading not required.) 17th (SERV.) Bn. SHERWOOD FORESTERS (Wellesley Rangers)

Instructions regarding War Diaries and Intelligence Summaries are contained in F.S. Regs, Part II. and the Staff Manual respectively. Title Pages will be prepared in manuscript.

Place	Date 1917	Hour	Summary of Events and Information	Remarks and references to Appendices
TRENCHES	Jan. 12th		Trench Routine. Situation normal. Battalion relieved by the 16th SHERWOOD FORESTERS and two A Coy BANK Relief complete with A + B Companies in Canal BANK Relief complete at 9 pm. That casualties in the area 1 officer and 3 other ranks wounded. Battalion now Brigade Support.	1 Coy 7/41
BRIELEN	13th		Cleaning up. Battalion moved to P Camp (A.15.d.5.0) being relieved by 14th ROYAL WELSH FUSILIERS. Battalion arrived in Camp at 8.0 pm	1 Coy 7/41
VOX-VRIE	14th		Battalion moved to "C" CAMP (A.30.a. 1.4.) arrive about 12 noon.	1 Coy 7/41
C.CAMP	15th		Cleaning up and inspections.	1 Coy 7/41
—do—	16th		Xmas Day for Battalion.	1 Coy 7/41

(Signed) ....
COMDG. 17th (S. Bn. SHERWOOD FORESTERS

WAR DIARY
INTELLIGENCE SUMMARY

(Erase heading not required.) 17th (SERV.) Bn. SHERWOOD FORESTERS. (Welbeck Rangers)

Army Form C. 2118.

Place	Date 1917	Hour	Summary of Events and Information	Remarks and references to Appendices
"C" Camp.	17th		Routine Company Training under Company Officers to 12.30pm. adv. Battalion Programme issued. Weather bad.	1/Sep 1917
—do—	18th		Routine, Company Training under Company Officers to 12.30pm adv. Battalion Programme issued.	1/Sep 1917
—do—	19th		Routine, Company Training under Company Officers to 12.30pm adv. Battalion Programme issued.	1/Sep 1917
—do—	20th		Routine, Company Training under Company Officers to 12.30pm adv. Battalion Programme issued. 1st Battalion Cross-Country run at 12 noon. Distance 9½ miles.	1/Sep 1917
—do—	21st		Sunday Divine Service. Inspection of Camp by C.O.	1/Sep 1917

Lt. Colonel,
17th (S) Bn. SHERWOOD FORESTERS.

WAR DIARY
INTELLIGENCE SUMMARY

(Erase heading not required.)

Army Form C. 2118.

17th (SERV) Bn. SHERWOOD FORESTERS (Welbeck Rangers)

Place	Date 1917	Hour	Summary of Events and Information	Remarks and references to Appendices
"C" CAMP	Jan 22nd		Routine Battalion Parades under Coy Officers until 12.30 p.m. and Battalion Programme issued. Battalion Bathed in the afternoon.	M/4787
—do—	23rd		Routine Battalion Parade under Coy Officers until 12.30 p.m. and Battalion Programme issued. An Battalion Corn Guard Run Durham Light Infantry.	M/4787
—do—	24th		Relief Battalion relieved 1 Kent Regt in the Canal Bank at (I.1.F.) relief complete 8 p.m. Battalion became L/1 Brigade Support.	M/4787
KAAIE	25th		Battalion relieved by 16th Bn Sherwood Foresters. Lt. Battalion move into the line LEFT SUB SECTION, WIELTJE SECTOR. Holding the line from C 29 a 4.1. to C 28 a.4.8. with WIELTJE as a strong point. "B" Coy Right front, "D" Coy left front. Company "A" Coy left support, "C" Coy Reserve Coy. Bn Hd Qrs St JEAN.	M/4787

COMDG 17th (S) Bn SHERWOOD FORESTERS.

Lt. Colonel.

Army Form C. 2118.

WAR DIARY
INTELLIGENCE SUMMARY

(Erase heading not required.) 17th (SERV.) Bn. SHERWOOD FORESTERS. (Welbeck Rangers)

Place	Date 1917	Hour	Summary of Events and Information	Remarks and references to Appendices
TRENCHES	Jan 26th		Trench Routine. Situation normal. 2 Other ranks wounded.	
-do-	27th		Trench Routine. Situation normal.	
-do-	28th		Trench Routine. Situation normal. "C" Coy relieve "B" Coy. "A" Coy relieve "D" Company in the front line.	
-do-	29th		Trench Routine. Situation normal.	
-do-	30th		Trench Routine. Situation normal. Battalion relieved by the 16th Bn. SHERWOOD FORESTERS. Relief complete 1.30 a.m. 31.1.17. Battalion move to Brigade Support in Canal Bank. See 24th January 1917.	
KAAIE	31st		Routine. Cleaning up. Battalion all out working parties to front line.	

K. Howard
Lt. Colonel,
Comdg. 17th (G) Bn. SHERWOOD FORESTERS.

WAR DIARY
INTELLIGENCE SUMMARY

17th (SERV) Bn. SHERWOOD FORESTERS (Welbeck Rangers)

Place	Date 1917	Hour	Summary of Events and Information	Remarks and references to Appendices
KAAIE	Feb 1st		Routine cleaning up. Battalion out working Parties to front line all night.	1/2 (Arty)
—do—	2nd		Ditto, cleaning up Battalion on working Parties to front line all night.	1/2 (Arty)
—do—	3rd		Ditto. Battalion relieves 12th Royal Sussex in the Right Sub-section of the Railwood Sector (I. 11. 6.) 'B' Coy Right Front Coy. 'D' Coy Left Front Coy. "A" Coy Support Coy. 'C' Coy Right Support Coy. Relief Complete 11. 30 p.m.	1/3 (Arty)
TRENCHES	4th		Trench Routine. Lieut Colonel H.M. Milward invalided. Situation normal. Major N. Houghton 16/ Sherwood Foresters assumed command of Battalion. 2.30	1/4 (Arty)
—do—	5th		Trench Routine. Situation normal.	1/5 (Arty) 12.C J.D.

N. Houghton Major
O.C. 17th Bn. Sherwood Foresters

Army Form C. 2118.

WAR DIARY

INTELLIGENCE SUMMARY

(Erase heading not required.)

17TH (SERV) Bn. SHERWOOD FORESTERS. (Welbeck Rangers)

Place	Date 1917	Hour	Summary of Events and Information	Remarks and references to Appendices
TRENCHES	Feb. 6th		Trench Routine. Sunken Road Battalion relieved by 17th Bn K.R.R Corps relief complete 8.15pm. Battalion moves to ÉCOLE (I.9.c.) and become BRIGADE SUPPORT to Right Battalion. Had casualties during this tour 2 other ranks killed, one officer wounded, 2 other ranks wounded.	Appx 1
YPRES	7th		Cleaning up, Routine, Working Parties to Front line & Rowe Keep.	Appx 2
do	8th		Routine. Company training under Coy officer before 1pm. Working Parties to front line at night.	Appx 3
do	9th		Routine. Company training under Coy Officer before 1pm. Battalion relieves 17th K.R.R Corps in the Right Sub Sector RAILWAY WOOD SECTOR. See diagram appended 5pm February 1917. A Coy Right front Company, "C" Company Left front Company "D" "B" Coys Rfts.	

Army Form C. 2118.

WAR DIARY
INTELLIGENCE SUMMARY

(Erase heading not required.) 17th (SERV.) Bn. SHERWOOD FORESTERS (Welbeck Rangers)

Instructions regarding War Diaries and Intelligence Summaries are contained in F. S. Regs., Part II. and the Staff Manual respectively. Title Pages will be prepared in manuscript.

Place	Date 1917	Hour	Summary of Events and Information	Remarks and references to Appendices
YPRES. (Continued)	Feb 9th		Right Support Coy. "C" Company 17th K.R.R. Corps attacked. Left front Coy.	1/ Appx 764
TRENCHES		10h.	Trench Patrols. Situation normal. Heard from Battalion headquarters in front line in account of its intended trench shelling.	1/16 Appx 764
— do —		11h.	Trench Patrols. Situation normal.	1/ Appx 764
— do —		12h.	Trench Patrols. Situation normal. A learn Prisoner brought. Whilst he was on patrol in Donham by N°. 3124 & Pte A. Henshaw who was on listening Post a very heavy fear & heavy attacked the whole of the enemy patrol which consisted of one Battalion relieved by 17th K.R.R. Corps and have to ECOIVRE see disposition 6th February 1917. The Casualties during the tour was 1 Other Rank Killed 16 Other Ranks Wounded.	1/ Appx 764

Signature
Lt. Col.
Comdg. 17th (S) Bn. SHERWOOD FORESTERS.

Army Form C. 2118.

WAR DIARY
INTELLIGENCE SUMMARY

(Erase heading not required.) 17th (SERV) Bn. SHERWOOD FORESTERS. (Mullers & Payer)

Place	Date 1917	Hour	Summary of Events and Information	Remarks and references to Appendices
YPRES.	Feb. 13th		Routine. Clearing up. Llew Ser Classes. Physical training and working parties to front line.	1/Apy 1
-do-	14th		Routine. Working parties to front line. Bombing accident while at Rifle Grenade practice. Lieut. P. Barr wounded. 8 O.R. wounded.	1/Apx 2
-do-	15th		Routine. Working parties to front line. Battalion relieved by 1/Liverpool Regt. 'A' & 'D' Company move to CANAL BANK at (C.I.g.) and are attached to 14th Bn. ROYAL WELSH FUSILIERS. Strength 5 officers 192 other ranks. 3 Lewis Guns. 'B' & 'C' Company move to the night to the RAMPARTS YPRES. and (I.8.a.) Bn. H.Q. and Hm to O.C.M.P. (A.15.d.5.0.). Battle Casualties. 1st 3 days 5 other ranks wounded.	4/Sept 2,1
VOX. VRIE.	16th		Routine. Clearing up. 'A' & 'C' Companies move to CANAL BANK about (I.I.L.P.) strength 6 officers 150 other ranks, and are attached to 113th and 114th Infantry Brigades.	1/Apx 4

M.Forsythe Lt. Colonel
17th (S) Bn. SHERWOOD FOREST Regt

Army Form C. 2118.

WAR DIARY
INTELLIGENCE SUMMARY

(Erase heading not required.)

17th (SERV.) Bn. SHERWOOD FORESTERS (Welbeck Rangers)

Place	Date 1917	Hour	Summary of Events and Information	Remarks and references to Appendices
VOX, VRIE	Feb 17th		Rather cloudy up. Draft of 134 Mr rank & file	Apps 1
—do—	18th		Divine Service. Inspection of Camp.	Apps 2
—do—	19th		Battalion Training under Coy Officers with Specialist Classes. Parties 'B' and 'D' Coys sent return to Headquarters.	Apps 3
—do—	20th		Battalion Training under Coy Officers with Specialist Classes. Routes.	Apps 4
—do—	21st		Battalion Training under Coy Officers with Specialist Classes. Parties 'A' and 'C' Coys sent return to Headquarters.	Apps 5
—do—	22nd		Battalion Training under Coy Officers with Specialist Classes. Routes.	Apps 6
—do—	23rd		Battalion Training under Coy Officers with Specialist Classes. Routes. No 31418 Pte A. HENSHAW awarded Military Medal for Gallantry and Devotion to Duty.	Apps 7

J.W. Webb
Major
17th (S) Bn. SHERWOOD FORESTERS.

Army Form C. 2118.

WAR DIARY
INTELLIGENCE SUMMARY
(Erase heading not required.)

17th (SERV.) Bn. SHERWOOD FORESTERS. (Welbeck Rangers)

Place	Date 1917	Hour	Summary of Events and Information	Remarks and references to Appendices
VOX-VRIE	February 24th		Battalion Training under Coy Officers with Special Classes. Routine.	
—do—	25th		Divine Service. Battalion Cross Country Run. Route.	
—do—	26th		Organization. 1 Draft to Coy. Battalion rec'd 6 furloughs to PoPERINGHE. Route.	
			STATION and entrain. 1 Detrain at the ASYLUM, YPRES and relieve the 13th Durham N.L.I. Infantry on the Right Sub. Sector of the Reft. Sector HOOGE. "A" "B" "C" Coys in the trenches and "D" Coy in Support. 10th C.R.P.B. Division "A" Coy Support A Coy "B" Coy, "A" in line "D" Coy Close Support. Relief Complete 11 p.m.	
TRENCHES	27th		Trench Routine. Situation normal.	
—do—	28th		Trench Routine. Situation normal.	

17th (2) Bn. SHERWOOD FORESTERS.

WAR DIARY
or
INTELLIGENCE SUMMARY

(Erase heading not required.) 17th (SERV.) Bn. SHERWOOD FORESTERS (Welbeck Rangers)

Army Form C. 2118.

Vol / 3

Place	Date	Hour	Summary of Events and Information	Remarks and references to Appendices
TRENCHES	1917 Wed 1st		Trench Routine. Situation normal.	Maps
— do —	2nd		Trench Routine. Situation normal.	
— do —	3rd		Trench Routine. Situation normal.	
— do —	4th		Trench Routine. Situation normal. Battalion relieved by 11th Bn K.R.R. Corps, and moved to "L. BARRACKS" YPRES. Relief and move to BRIGADE RESERVE. Relief complete 9.50 p.m. Casualties during the tour. 4 Other ranks wounded. Brigadier General R.D.F. OLDMAN traced General of 117th Infantry Brigade. Other fanfare of any unusual authorities.	
YPRES 5th			Cleaning up Routine, 3 Other Ranks wounded. Inter Battalion futboll matches	

COMMG. 17th (S) Bn. SHERWOOD FORESTERS

13.C

Army Form C. 2118.

WAR DIARY
or
INTELLIGENCE SUMMARY

(Erase heading not required.) 7th (SERV.) Bn. SHERWOOD FORESTERS. (The Robt Foresters)

Instructions regarding War Diaries and Intelligence Summaries are contained in F.S. Regs., Part II. and the Staff Manual respectively. Title Pages will be prepared in manuscript.

Place	Date 1917	Hour	Summary of Events and Information	Remarks and references to Appendices
YPRES	March 6th		Routine. 3 Companies working in front line.	March
—do—	7th		Routine. 3 Companies working in front line.	March
—do—	8th		Routine. 3 Companies working in front line. Major A.M. McPHERSON wounded organising the Battalion this day.	March
—do—	9th		Routine. 3 Companies working in front line.	March
—do—	10th		Routine. Battalion relieved by 1/1 HERTS Regt and moved to ST. LAWRENCE CAMP. (G.II.c.) relieve complete 6 a.m.	March
ST LAWRENCE CAMP	11th		Divine Service. Routine.	March
—do—	12th		Routine. Training under Coy officers into 1 pm. Lecture by Platoon all day. Brig Gen G.H. ARMITAGE D.S.O. assumed command of the 117th Infantry Brigade vice 9th March 1917.	March

Atwood Lt Colonel
COMDG. 17th (s) Bn. SHERWOOD FORESTERS.

WAR DIARY or INTELLIGENCE SUMMARY

Army Form C. 2118.

(Erase heading not required.) 17th (SERV.) Bn. SHERWOOD FORESTERS (Welbeck Rangers)

Place	Date 1917	Hour	Summary of Events and Information	Remarks and references to Appendices
SLAUGHTER CAMP	13th		Routine Training under Company Officers until 1 pm. Footbath 1 pm - 4 pm by Platoons.	A/Capt 244
-do-	14th		Routine Training under Company Officers until 1 pm. Footbath 1 pm - 4 pm by Platoons.	A/Capt 244
-do-	15th		Routine Training under Company Officers until 1 pm. Relieved the H/5 BLACK WATCH in the LEFT SECTOR HUDGE. See 24th February 1917. Relief complete 1 a.m. 16/2/17. 'A' Coy front line Company 'D' Coy Close Support, 'B' Coy Support Company, 'C' Coy Reserve Coy.	A/Capt 244
TRENCHES	16th		Trench Routine. Situation normal. 2 Lieut A. RANGDALE & 2nd Lieut G.W. TURNPENNEY wounded at duty.	A/Capt 244
-do-	17th		Trench Routine. Situation normal.	A/Capt 244
-do-	18th		Trench Routine. Situation normal.	A/Capt 244

Rutherford
Lt Colonel
COMDG. 17th (S) Bn. SHERWOOD FORESTERS

WAR DIARY
INTELLIGENCE SUMMARY

Army Form C. 2118

(Erase heading not required.) 17th (SERV.) Bn. SHERWOOD FORESTERS. (Welbeck Rangers)

Place	Date 1917	Hour	Summary of Events and Information	Remarks and references to Appendices
TRENCHES	19th		Trench Routine. Situation normal.	1 Copy 24
-do-	20th.		Trench Routine. Situation normal. Minor Operation carried out without result. Operation order attached to appendices marked K.1.	K.1. 1 Copy 24
-do-	21st		Trench Routine. Situation normal. Battalion relieved by the 17th K.R.R.C. relief complete 9.10 p.m. Battalion move to The Barracks YPRES and became BRIGADE SUPPORT. Total casualties during tour 2 officer wounded 3 other ranks killed, 3 other ranks wounded. A Company attached to 17th K.R.R.C. in the line owing to that Battalion being weak in numbers.	1 Sept 24
YPRES	22nd		Routine. Cleaning up, Battalion all on working in front line etc.	1 Sept 24
-do-	23rd		Routine. Battalion all on working in front line etc.	1 Copy 24

Ashehurst
Lt. Colonel
COMDG. 17th (S) Bn. SHERWOOD FORESTERS

WAR DIARY
INTELLIGENCE SUMMARY

(Erase heading not required.) 17th (SERV.) Bn. SHERWOOD FORESTERS. (Welbeck Rangers)

Army Form C. 2118

Place	Date 1917	Hour	Summary of Events and Information	Remarks and references to Appendices
YPRES	March 24th		Routine, working parties all day & night. "B" Company relieve "A" Company in RITZ STREET & front line. "A" Coy to Bn H.Qrs.	1/Copy 24
—do—	25th		Routine, working parties all day & night to front line. Sunday. Divine Service.	1/Copy 25
—do—	26th		Routine, working parties all day & night to front line.	1/Copy 26
—do—	27th		Routine, working parties all day & night to front line.	1/Copy 27
—do—	28th		Routine. Battalion relieved by 1/1 HERTS Regt. relief complete 4.0 am. Battalion move to (Corps) Reserve at MONTREAL CAMP.	
MONTREAL CAMP	29th		(H.Q. 1 & 2 Coy.) Casualties during (Brigade Reserve & other reliefs) 2 O.R. wounded. Routine. 'B' Company rejoin Battalion. Party from attached to 1st K.R.R.C. 3 officers 98 O.R. weekly Coy officers & 100 men working party under "B.M.O." Bathing. attached	1/Copy 28, 1/Copy 29

Army Form C. 2118

WAR DIARY
INTELLIGENCE SUMMARY

(Erase heading not required.) 17th (SERV.) Bn. SHERWOOD FORESTERS. (Welbeck Rangers)

103

Place	Date 1917	Hour	Summary of Events and Information	Remarks and references to Appendices
MONTREAL CAMP	March 30th		Routine Training under Coy. Officers. Bathing. 180 working party under R.E.	1 Appx 44
—do—	31st		Routine Training under Coy Officers. 120 Working Party.	1 Appx 44

Retreat
.... Lt. Colonel,
COMDG. 17th (S) Bn. SHERWOOD FORESTERS.

Army Form C. 2118

WAR DIARY
INTELLIGENCE SUMMARY

(Erase heading not required) 11th (SERV.) Bn. SHERWOOD FORESTERS (Nottts & Derby)

Place	Date 1917	Hour	Summary of Events and Information	Remarks and references to Appendices
MONTREAL CAMP	April 1st		Routine. Divine Service.	Y of Y Maps attd
—do—	2nd		Routine. Training under Coy officers, before 10m. working Parties.	W Carthy
—do—	3rd		Routine. Training under Coy officers before 1 pm. working Parties. Battalion move to Barracks YPRES. See March Order 31/3/17	W Carthy
YPRES	4th		relieving 1/6 CHESHIRE Regt. Battalion became BRIGADE RESERVE, relief complete 11.10 pm. Routine. Battalion all out working in front line and vicinity.	Maps Atts 1 Reg Atty
—do—	5th		Routine. Battalion all out working in front line and vicinity.	Maps Atts

14. C

WAR DIARY

INTELLIGENCE SUMMARY

Army Form C. 2118

(105) 17th (Serv.) Bn. SHERWOOD FORESTERS. (Welbeck Rangers)

Place	Date 1917	Hour	Summary of Events and Information	Remarks and references to Appendices
YPRES	April 6th		Routine. Working parties to front line, "B" Company 100 strong Ypres into front line. MAPLE COPSE and STAFFORD STREET to the right Sub Section. and are attached to the 16th Bn. SHERWOOD FORESTERS for tactical purposes.	1 Casualty
–do–	7th		Routine. Working parties to front line and weather.	1 Casualty
–do–	8th		Routine. Working parties to front line and weather. 20 men to "E" Coy. Res 16th April 1917	1 Casualty
–do–	9th		Routine. Working parties to front line and weather. 2nd Lieut G.W. TURNPENNEY wounded. Battalion Headquarters moved into RAMPARTS YPRES.	1 Casualty
–do–	10th		Routine. Working parties to front line and weather.	1 Wounded (Officer)

WAR DIARY
INTELLIGENCE SUMMARY

(Erase heading not required.) 17th (SERV) Bn. SHERWOOD FORESTERS. (Welbeck Rangers)

Army Form C. 2118

Place	Date 1917	Hour	Summary of Events and Information	Remarks and references to Appendices
YPRES	April 11th		Routine. Working Parties. Front line and vicinity. A/s 11.36 Pte MARKS STACK recommended for D.C.M. for Gallantry and devotion to duty. During the enemy bombardment on the front line, 9th/10th April 1917, Pte Stack went out alone under the enemy's shell and machine gun fire and repaired the telephone wire from the front line forward sunken lorry (the sole line of infantry keeping communication from the front line and Bn. H.Q. (Advisory) awarded the Military Medal for gallantry in re-establishing communication). Battalion relieved by 11th Bn Royal Sussex & relief complete 10.30pm. Battalion went to St Lawrence Camp (G.11.c). Total Casualties during past 8 days: 1 Officer wounded, 10 O.R killed, 7 O.Ranks wounded.	1(App 161)
ST LAWRENCE CAMP	12th		Routine. Cleaning up. 150 working Party to front line.	1(App 64)
—do—	13th		Battalion move to BOLLEZEELE entraining at POPERINGHE at 6.10 am detraining at ESQUELBECQ thence by march route	

1875 Wt. W593/826 1,000,000 4/15 J.B.C. &A. A.D.S.S./Forms/C. 2118.

WAR DIARY
or
INTELLIGENCE SUMMARY

(Erase heading not required.) 17th (Serv.) Bn. SHERWOOD FORESTERS. (Welbeck Rangers)

Army Form C. 2118

Place	Date 1917	Hour	Summary of Events and Information	Remarks and references to Appendices
ST JANS CAPPEL CAMP	13th		to BOLLEZEELE, 1st Line Transport by Road, very scattered Billets	1/Capt Adj
BOLLEZEELE	14th		Route, Physical Training before breakfast. Cleaning up during the day. Companies billeted & mixed away.	1/Capt Adj
-do-	15th		Sunday. Divine Service Cancelled owing to enclosures needed.	1/Capt Adj
-do-	16th		Route. Coy. Training under Coy Officers. New Organization in the Training of Platoon for offensive action. Training to be progressive. Hours of work 6.30 a.m. to 8 p.m. with lectures in the evening.	1/Capt Adj
-do-	17th		Route. Same as for the 16th April 1917.	1/Capt Adj
-do-	18th		Route. Same as for the 17th April 1917.	1/Capt Adj

J.P.Becket Lt. Colonel
COMDG. 17th (S) Bn. SHERWOOD FORESTERS.

Army Form C. 2118

WAR DIARY
or
INTELLIGENCE SUMMARY

(Erase heading not required.) 7th (SERV.) Bn. SHERWOOD FORESTERS. (Welbeck Rangers)

Place	Date 1917	Hour	Summary of Events and Information	Remarks and references to Appendices
BONZÉELE	April 19th		Routine. Same as for 16th April 1917. No 11366 L.Cpl. C.SLACK awarded a bar to the MILITARY MEDAL for gallantry and devotion to duty.	May 24 [Appdx]
do	20th		Routine. Same as for 16th April 1917.	[Appdx] May 24
do	21st		Routine. Same as for 16th April 1917.	[Appdx] May 24
do	22nd		Sunday. Battalion took part in Brigade Parade for Divine Service in marching order.	May 24 [Appdx]
do	23rd		Routine. Company Training. Coys. under Coy officer. Musketry. Organizing attack and attack Practice. 2nd & 3rd Coys 8.30am to 12pm. Lecture in the evening.	History May 24
do	24th		Routine. Same as for 23rd April 1917. Much interest taken in Cricket Pulling Scheme	May 24 [Appdx]

B.W. Roberts Lt. Colonel
7th (S) Bn. SHERWOOD FORESTERS.

Army Form C. 2118

WAR DIARY
or
INTELLIGENCE SUMMARY
(Erase heading not required.) 17th (SERV.) Bn. SHERWOOD FORESTERS. (Welbeck Rangers)

Place	Date 1917	Hour	Summary of Events and Information	Remarks and references to Appendices
BOEZEELE	April 25th		Radio. Battalion practises attack in new Organized Defensive in Training Area in the presence of General Sir. H. C. O. PLUMER GCMG ADC etc.	1 Copy att!
—do—	26th		Entire Attack Practise on Training Area and a Company Training under Coy Officers.	1 Copy att!
—do—	27th		Battalion parade 9 am and move to "Y" Camp (F.25.a.) SHEET 27. entraining at ESQUERDEES and detraining at POPERINGHE and thence by March Route to Camp. Transport by road.	
Y CAMP	28th		Ratns. 500 all ranks at work on Railway Construction work "A" Camp. To Battalion "lire by march for-ing Battalion in "A" Camp (SHEET 28. H.1. d.7.0.) Route to "A" CAMP	
"A" CAMP	29th		Ratns. 500 all ranks at work on Railway Construction work 30 other ranks under R.E. A Coy Training with Specialists.	

W. G. Briggs? Lt. Colonel
DDMDB. 17th (S) Bn. SHERWOOD FORESTERS.

ought to be prepared in manuscript.

WAR DIARY
or
INTELLIGENCE SUMMARY

(Erase heading not required.) 17th (SERV) Bn. SHERWOOD FORESTERS. (Welbeck Rangers)

Army Form C. 2118

Place	Date 1917	Hour	Summary of Events and Information	Remarks and references to Appendices
"A" COMPANY	April 30th		Posting 3 Corporal working on Railway Construction. Remainder "A" Company under the Command of Capt. W.S. HOLDEN Marched to ST. MOMELIN for training under Camp COMMANDANT 2nd ARMY. STRENGTH 5 officers 169 other ranks.	W.Guess

..................Lt. Colonel,
OOMDG. 17th (S) Bn. SHERWOOD FORESTERS.

WAR DIARY
INTELLIGENCE SUMMARY

Army Form C. 2118

17 Nov 17
Feb 1 5
(Railway Ranger)

15 (Serv.) Bn. SHERWOOD FORESTERS

Place	Date 1917	Hour	Summary of Events and Information	Remarks and references to Appendices
"A" Camp	May 1st		Further 3 Companies working on Railway Construction work. Special Training. Battalion moves to "C" Camp. Map reference (Sheet 28. A. 30 Central)	1 Apl 24
"C" Camp	2nd		Routine. 3 Companies working on Railway Construction work. Special Training. (350 men)	1 Apl 24
—do—	3rd		Routine. 3 Companies working on Railway Construction work. Special Training. (410 men)	1 Apl 24
—do—	4th		Routine. 3 Companies working on Railway Construction work. Special Training. (410 men)	1 Apl 24
—do—	5th		Routine. 3 Companies working on Railway Construction work. Special Training. (410 men)	1 Apl 24
—do—	6th		Sunday. Routine. 3 Companies working on Railway Construction work. Special Training. (410 men)	15. 1 Apl 24

COMDG. 17th (S) Bn. SHERWOOD FORESTERS.
Lt. Colonel,

Army Form C. 2118

WAR DIARY
or
INTELLIGENCE SUMMARY

(Erase heading not required) 23th (SERV.) Bn. SHERWOOD FORESTERS. (Welbeck Rangers)

Instructions regarding War Diaries and Intelligence Summaries are contained in F. S. Regs, Part II. and the Staff Manual respectively. Title Pages will be prepared in manuscript.

(17)

Place	Date 1917	Hour	Summary of Events and Information	Remarks and references to Appendices
C. CAMP	May 7th		Routine. 3 Companies working on Railway Construction work (410 men). Specialist Training.	1 (App A1)
—do—	8th		Routine. 3 Companies working on Railway Construction work (410 men). Specialist Training.	1 (App A1)
—do—	9th		Routine. 3 Companies working on Railway Construction work (410 men). Specialist Training.	1 (App A1)
—do—	10th		Routine. 3 Companies working on Railway Construction work (410 men). Specialist Training.	1 (App A1)
—do—	11th		Routine. 3 Companies working on Railway Construction work (410 men). Specialist Training.	1 (App A1)
—do—	12th		Routine. 3 Companies working on Railway Construction work (410 men). Specialist Training.	1 (App A1)

BTC?.West............Lt. Colonel.
COMDG. 17th (S) Bn. SHERWOOD FORESTERS.

WAR DIARY
or
INTELLIGENCE SUMMARY

(Erase heading not required.) 17th (SERV.) Bn. SHERWOOD FORESTERS. (Welbeck Rangers)

Army Form C. 2118

Place	Date	Hour	Summary of Events and Information	Remarks and references to Appendices
"C" CAMP	MAY 9/17 13th		Routine. 3 Corporal working on Railway Construction Work. (±10 men) Specialist training.	Appx aa
—do—	14th		Routine. 3 Corporal working on Railway Construction Work. (±10 men) Specialist training.	Appxbb
—do—	15th		Routine. 3 Corporal working on Railway Construction Work. (±10 men) Cease work at 12 mn. "A" Company return the Battalion at 10.0 pm. ST MOMELIN Battalion entrain at BRANDHOEK for the ASYLUM YPRES at 10.30 pm and relieved 1st HERTS REGT in the HILL TOP SECTOR, LEFT Battalion, MAP REFERENCE, SHEET 28. C 21 and 15. 2nd/1st Battalion Head quarters at LA BELLE ALLIANCE. "C" Company LEFT FRONT COMPANY, "B" COMPANY RIGHT FRONT COMPANY. "A" COMPANY LEFT SUPPORT COMPANY "D" COMPANY RIGHT SUPPORT COMPANY Relief complete at 3. 5 am 16.5.17.	Appxcc

E.W. Ellicock Lt. Colonel,

COMDG. 17th (S) Bn. SHERWOOD FORESTERS.

WAR DIARY

INTELLIGENCE SUMMARY

(Erase heading not required) 11th (SERV.) Bn. SHERWOOD FORESTERS. (Nottshc Regt.)

Army Form C. 2118

Instructions regarding War Diaries and Intelligence Summaries are contained in F.S. Regs., Part II. and the Staff Manual respectively. Title Pages will be prepared in manuscript.

Place	Date	Hour	Summary of Events and Information	Remarks and references to Appendices
TRENCHES	MAY 16th 1917		Trench Routine. Situation normal.	
-do-	17th		Trench Routine. Situation normal.	
-do-	18th		Trench Routine. Situation normal. About 8.45 p.m. after a steady barrage on our front line all day, the enemy's artillery suddenly opened up an intense barrage on our front line in Right Section at the junction with Battalion on our Right. S.O.S. Signals were sent up from Left Company Right Company and Battalion on our Right. Our artillery were prompt in opening up, and silenced the enemy after about 20 minutes. It appeared that the enemy contemplated a raid and of course the heavy blanket stopped it. In our afternoon...	

Lt. Colonel,
COMDG. 11TH BN. SHERWOOD FORESTERS.

WAR DIARY

INTELLIGENCE SUMMARY

(Erase heading not required.) 17th (SERV.) Bn. SHERWOOD FORESTERS. (Welbeck Rangers)

Army Form C. 2118

Instructions regarding War Diaries and Intelligence Summaries are contained in F. S. Regs., Part II. and the Staff Manual respectively. Title Pages will be prepared in manuscript.

Place	Date 1917	Hour	Summary of Events and Information	Remarks and references to Appendices
Trenches	May 18th On Km		Reported to bn rendered the Division in our immediate Rgt. Although the enemy was intense, it was very inaccurate. Our Casualties were light 1 OR killed 10 OR wounded. Retaliation was normal about 10 p.m.	1 Appdx
—do—	19th		Trench Routine. Situation normal. A Coy Relieved "C" Coy in front line. "D" Coy Relieved "B" Coy in front line. Dispositions: Right front Company "D" Coy, Left front Coy "A" Coy. Regt'l Support Coy "B" Coy. Left Support Coy "C" Coy.	1 Appdx
—do—	20th		Trench Routine. Situation normal.	1 Appdx
—do—	21st		Trench Routine. Situation normal.	1 Appdx
—do—	22nd		Trench Routine. Situation normal.	1 Appdx

.................Lt. Colonel,
SHERWOOD FORESTERS.

WAR DIARY
or
INTELLIGENCE SUMMARY

Army Form C. 2118

(Erase heading not required.) 7th (SERV.) Bn. SHERWOOD FORESTERS. (Welbeck Rangers)

Place	Date 1917	Hour	Summary of Events and Information	Remarks and references to Appendices
TRENCHES	MAY 23rd		French Routine. Situation Normal. Battalion relieved by the 16/Bn. SHERWOOD FORESTERS and moved to BRIGADE SUPPORT. LEFT BATTALION on the CANAL BANK. Map reference, SHEET 28.C.25. Relief Complete 11.50 p.m. Three Casualties during tour: 1 officer slightly wounded at duty, 1 other rank killed, 3 other ranks wounded.	Appx 1
CANAL BANK	24th		Cleaning up. Routine. Battalion working full strength in front line. etc.	Appx 2
–do–	25th		Routine. Battalion full strength working in front line and vicinity.	Appx 3
–do–	26th		Routine. Battalion full strength, working in front line and vicinity.	Appx 4
–do–	27th		Routine. Battalion full strength, working in front line and vicinity.	Appx 5

B.C. Prescott .... Lt. Colonel,
Commdg. 17th (S) Bn. SHERWOOD FORESTERS.

Army Form C. 2118.

WAR DIARY
INTELLIGENCE SUMMARY

(Erase heading not required.) 17th (SERV.) Bn. SHERWOOD FORESTERS. (Welbeck Rangers)

Place	Date 1917	Hour	Summary of Events and Information	Remarks and references to Appendices
CANAL BANK	MAY 28th		Routine. Battalion at full Strength working in front line and reserve.	
do	29th		Routine. Battalion at full Strength working in first line and reserve.	
do	30th		Routine. Battalion at full Strength working in front line and reserve.	
do	31st		Routine. 1 Coy. + 1 Section working in front line and reserve. Total Casualties during the 8 days 11 Other ranks wounded. a) 10 Embarked and 2 Platoons) B Coy Bivouacy with 13th Welsh return 13th Bn. Hambilin 10S.1 in do WIETJE SECTOR map reference (See 25th January 1917) A Coy FRONT Cg. B Coy SUPPORT Cg. C Coy. (2 Platoons) RIVER BANK TRENCH. Reserve 2 Platoons D Coy and 1 Section 1 D. Coy MOVE 2" CAMP (See 1st MAY 1917).	

A. Becket, Lt. Colonel,
COMDG. 17th (S) Bn. SHERWOOD FORESTERS.

WAR DIARY
INTELLIGENCE SUMMARY

Army Form C. 2118.

17th (SERV.) Bn. SHERWOOD FORESTERS (Welbeck Rangers)

Place	Date	Hour	Summary of Events and Information	Remarks and references to Appendices
TRENCHES	Nov 1st		Trench Routine. Situation normal. At 3 am 8" Special Coy R.E. discharged 500 gas Drums from projectors. This is a specially dangerous gas and of a secret nature the whole operation was highly successful, the wind being very favourable to our side. Intention of operation attached as an Appendix and marked Ins 1.	Nov 14/41 Ins 1
do	2nd		Trench Routine. Situation normal. Enemy Artillery very active. Our Artillery very intense. The trenches of Anthony Bryn were the place daily hit on the front and by the right and left of Poelcapelle. 2/Lieut F.S. WILLIAMS encountered an enemy patrol in NO MANS LAND about 1 am estimated strength about 15 strong. his party created it & he found them on their & stand up" when no Field enemy replied in good	

F. Hucknall Lt. Colonel,
Comdg. 17th (S) Bn. SHERWOOD FORESTERS.

WAR DIARY
INTELLIGENCE SUMMARY
(17th (SERV.) Bn. SHERWOOD FORESTERS.) (Welbeck Rangers)

Army Form C. 2118.

Place	Date	Hour	Summary of Events and Information	Remarks and references to Appendices
TRENCHES	MAY 2nd 1917 continued		replied "How many are you?" Lieut WILLIAMS replied about 40 and sent two men on an order saying "One Company to the Right and another to the Left". The Bluff Sec. 2 nosed the enemy retiring quickly being by the kept rushed with them Bombing indiscriminate shooting from both sides prevailed and it was thought by his comrades that one of the enemy was hit but carried away by his comrades. Returns who searched afterwards had only an enemy hand grenade discovered.	Moved
—do—	3rd		Trench Routine. Our Artillery (acting the role of Red Army Group) Independent to be from 3 pm to 3.30 am. Smoke Barrage was also included with the operation. Retaliation from the enemy was slight at the time but increased	

.... Lt. Colonel,
COMDG. 17th (S) Bn. SHERWOOD FORESTERS.

WAR DIARY or INTELLIGENCE SUMMARY

Army Form C. 2118.

(Erase heading not required.) 17th (SERV.) Bn. SHERWOOD FORESTERS. (Welbeck Rangers)

Place	Date 1917	Hour	Summary of Events and Information	Remarks and references to Appendices
TRENCHES	MAY 3rd Continued.		in violence during the next 12 hours. The enemy paid particular attention to Battalion headquarters at ST JEAN getting two direct hits towards midnight. He put but very inconsiderable numbers of extra men into Fanghu or Phosphorus Shell Trench & he divamphir of all the troops.	1st May
do	4th		Trench Routine. Yesterday One Transport man severely shelled One man killed at 10:45. the enemy shelled St JEAN and Battalion headquarters with 4.10 very calibre shells. Very accurate Shooting retaliation by our heavy artillery asked for. The french routine.	WRS a/4/17
do	5th		afternoon all the artillery on 2nd ARMY front had a practice barrage from 3 pm to 3:10 pm.	

G.CW.F.O. 17th (S) Bn. SHERWOOD FORESTERS.
.... Lt. Colonel

Army Form C. 2118.

WAR DIARY
INTELLIGENCE SUMMARY
(Erase heading not required.)

17th (SERV.) Bn. SHERWOOD FORESTERS (Welbeck Rangers)

Instructions regarding War Diaries and Intelligence Summaries are contained in F.S. Regs., Part II. and the Staff Manual respectively. Title Pages will be prepared in manuscript.

Place	Date 1917	Hour	Summary of Events and Information	Remarks and references to Appendices
Trenches	JUNE 6		Trench Routine - St Jean again heavily shelled. Practice barrage on our front.	WDS 4/day
- do -	7	3.10 a.m.	Great offensive on our right commenced. Terrific fire put up. Explosion 2 mines early job at St Jean. MESSINES RIDGE captured. 7000 prisoners.	WDS 2/day
- do -	8		Quiet on our front. Trench Routine.	
- do -		2.45 a.m - 3.15 a.m	Terrific bombardment. Trench Routine. Relieved by 16th Bn SHERWOOD FORESTERS	WDS 2/day
			ST JEAN. Bn proceeded to "O" Camp.	
		10.20 p.m	RELIEF COMPLETE. Special for operation carried out (A 30 Central).	
			on our immediate left front & on our own front	
'O'Camp	9		Settled in Camp. 150 men on working parties. Remainder - cleaning up and training programme. Good news re the offensive on Messines Ridge.	WDS 2/day

K. Mulvaney Lt. Colonel,
COMDG. 17th (S) Bn SHERWOOD FORESTERS

Army Form C. 2118.

WAR DIARY
or
INTELLIGENCE SUMMARY
(Erase heading not required.)

17th (SERV.) Bn. SHERWOOD FORESTERS. (Welbeck Rangers)

Place	Date	Hour	Summary of Events and Information	Remarks and references to Appendices
"O" Camp	June 17 10th		Working parties for R.G. Artillery – making furzbins. Strength of Bn. 25. 9 officers 400 other ranks. Lt. Col. N. M. Milward D.S.O. He assumed command of the Bn. this day	
O. Camp	11th		Repeat of yesterdays working parties. Remainder of Bn. training.	
O. Camp	12th		Repeat of yesterdays working parties. Remainder of Bn. training.	
O. Camp	13th		Working parties – 2 Officers 100 other ranks. Remainder of Bn. on parade under Training Programme.	
O. Camp	14th		Working party – 2 Officers 100 O.R. – Bn. training under Training programme. 280 ORs talk to 2/Lt. J.N. Le Patrol left Bn RRC to take over command of 17th Bn Lx. R.R.C. 75	
O. Camp	15th		Working party 1 officer, 50 ORs. Remainder of Bn. under programme of training. Lewis Gun went up to 16 Severely Wded. Take over from 11th Bn R. Sussex Regt	

N.M. Milward Lt. Col.
Comdg. 17th Bn Sherwood Foresters.

Army Form C. 2118.

WAR DIARY
INTELLIGENCE SUMMARY
(Erase heading not required.)

17th (SERV.) Bn. SHERWOOD FORESTERS. (Weather Proper)

Instructions regarding War Diaries and Intelligence Summaries are contained in F. S. Regs., Part II. and the Staff Manual respectively. Title Pages will be prepared in manuscript.

Place	Date 1917	Hour	Summary of Events and Information	Remarks and references to Appendices
"O" CAMP	JUNE 16th		Routine Inspection. Battalion relieve the 11th Bn. ROYAL SUSSEX Regt. in the HILL TOP SECTOR (map reference SHEET 28. C 15-11.) relief complete 12.50 am 17. 6.17. RIGHT FRONT COMPANY "D" COMPANY, LEFT FRONT COMPANY, "C" COMPANY, RIGHT SUPPORT COMPANY, "B" COMPANY, LEFT SUPPORT COMPANY, "A" COMPANY.	Monday
TRENCHES	17th		TRENCH ROUTINE. At 2.45 am an Enemy Patrol of 6 approached our/one Post. Sgt ROBERTS with 3 men attacked the Party and Captured 2 Prisoners, (unwounded) belonging to the 26nd Division. a very worthy achievement. N° 11201 SERGT. W. ROBERTS, D.C.M. Recommended for Medal on date/ "76186 La Corp R. HANNAH, M. MEDAL Strength for Gallantry "26705 Pte A. MURPHY, M MEDAL and attention to duty in the field.	1. 12 am 26

J Michael........Lt. Colonel,
COMDG. 17th (S.) Bn. SHERWOOD FORESTERS.

2449 Wt. W14957/M90 750,000 1/16 J.B.C. & A. Forms/C.2118/12.

Army Form C. 2118.

WAR DIARY
INTELLIGENCE SUMMARY

(Erase heading not required.) 17th (SERV.) Bn. SHERWOOD FORESTERS. (Nottingham Rangers)

Instructions regarding War Diaries and Intelligence Summaries are contained in F.S. Regs., Part II. and the Staff Manual respectively. Title Pages will be prepared in manuscript.

Place	Date	Hour	Summary of Events and Information	Remarks and references to Appendices
TRENCHES S	June 1917 18th		Trench Routine, very little shell fire from enemy during day but heavy at times. Pvts [?] & [?] no reply from our artillery. Lieut H. BATCHENER wounded at duty.	Mar 241
—do—	19th		Trench Routine. The enemy seem to be chary to keep up his trench defs. keep all ability [?]. Our artillery does not seem to answer. Lieut E. RAMSDALE severely wounded.	Mar 241
—do—	20th		Trench Routine. Enlive Mdoss [?] to our line, by the enemy. Our Grenades are joining Lieut N. L. DEXTER wounded at duty.	Mar 241
—do—	21st		Trench Routine. The enemy plastered our No Man's Land. The enemy plastered our line very persistent in the Holdings of Mulroy Square and Keel [?] in withdrawn from the front from heavy shelling. Capt H. Crowder [?]	Mar 241

COMDG. 17th (S) Bn. SHERWOOD FORESTERS.

Army Form C. 2118.

WAR DIARY
INTELLIGENCE SUMMARY

(Erase heading not required.) 17th (SERV.) Bn. SHERWOOD FORESTERS. (Welbeck Rangers)

Instructions regarding War Diaries and Intelligence Summaries are contained in F. S. Regs., Part II. and the Staff Manual respectively. Title Pages will be prepared in manuscript.

Place	Date	Hour	Summary of Events and Information	Remarks and references to Appendices
Trenches Oatlow	Thur 21st (Sept 1917)		Are heavy to day with a greater proportion of gas shells than usual.	1 Sept 24?
—do—	22nd		Trench Routine. Same pressure by Hostile Artillery, but Artillery are a little more quiet to day. "C" Company LEFT FRONT COMPANY are relieved by 2 Companies of 5th GORDON HIGHLANDERS. and move to:— 2 Platoon IRISH FARM, 2 Platoon CANAL BANK, the remaining 3 Companies remain in support on the 16th Inst night.	1 Sept 24?
—do—	23rd		Trench Routine. Enemy Artillery now marked than other days, very intense throughout the night. Annable very heavy.	1 Sept 24?

[signature]
Lt. Colonel,
Comdg. 17TH (S) Bn. SHERWOOD FORESTERS.

Army Form C. 2118.

WAR DIARY
or
INTELLIGENCE SUMMARY

(Erase heading not required.) 17th (SERV.) Bn. SHERWOOD FORESTERS. (Welbeck Rangers)

Instructions regarding War Diaries and Intelligence Summaries are contained in F. S. Regs., Part II. and the Staff Manual respectively. Title Pages will be prepared in manuscript.

Place	Date 1917	Hour	Summary of Events and Information	Remarks and references to Appendices
TRENCHES	JUNE 2nd		Trench Routine. Same procedure by both Artilleries as the previous few days. An hostile aeroplane was brought down by M.G. and machine gun at 4.35 pm it fell close to our lines. Battalion relieved by the 16th Bn SHERWOOD FORESTERS and moved to CANAL BANK (Map Reference Sheet 28. C 25) Relief Complete 12.30am 3/6/17. Total Casualties during Relief 8 days. Officers wounded 3, Killed Other Ranks 10, wounded Other Ranks 45. Total 58.	[illegible]
CANAL BANK	3rd		Routine. Battalion Cleaning up. Battalion at full Strength now all ought working in OHMEN'S 3 Craters A B & D digging in Trench "HORNBY TRENCH" M.27/28/30/6/10 Cpl R HANNAH and No. 24305 Pte A MURPHY awarded the MILITARY MEDAL for gallantry and devotion to duty at the 17th June 1917.	[illegible]

[signature] Lt Colonel,
17th (SERV.) Bn. SHERWOOD FORESTERS.

Army Form C. 2118.

WAR DIARY
INTELLIGENCE SUMMARY

(Erase heading not required.) 17th (SERV.) Bn. SHERWOOD FORESTERS. (Welbeck Rangers)

Instructions regarding War Diaries and Intelligence Summaries are contained in F. S. Regs., Part II. and the Staff Manual respectively. Title Pages will be prepared in manuscript.

Place	Date 1917	Hour	Summary of Events and Information	Remarks and references to Appendices
CANAL BANK	JUNE 26th		Rubin. Battalion at full strength working in front line and vicinity during all hours of darkness.	1/Appdx
—do—	27th		Rubin. Battalion at full strength working in front line and vicinity during all hours of darkness.	1/Appdx
—do—	28th		Rubin. Battalion at full strength working in front line and vicinity during all hours of darkness.	1/Appdx
—do—	29th		Rubin. Battalion at full strength working in front line and vicinity during all hours of darkness.	1/Appdx
—do—	30th		Rubin. A very wet day. Battalion relieved by the 11/HANTS ("37" and moved into Divisional Reserve under Canvas at "C" CAMP (Map Reference SHEET 28 A, 30 central)	1/Appdx

Comdg. 17th (S) Bn. SHERWOOD FORESTERS.
Lt. Colonel,

Army Form C. 2118.

WAR DIARY
or
INTELLIGENCE SUMMARY

(Erase heading not required.) 17th (SERV.) Bn. SHERWOOD FORESTERS. (Mellish Bn. 6th)

Instructions regarding War Diaries and Intelligence Summaries are contained in F. S. Regs., Part II. and the Staff Manual respectively. Title Pages will be prepared in manuscript.

Place	Date	Hour	Summary of Events and Information	Remarks and references to Appendices
CANAL BANK	JUNE 1917 30th continued		Bn Casualties during past 6 days in CANAL BANK. 1 Officer wounded. 6 Other O.R. killed. 16 Other ranks wounded.	Mar 141

K Mitchell, Lt. Colonel,
Comdg. 17th (S) Bn. SHERWOOD FORESTERS.

COPY.

11th Bn., R.Suss.R.	116th M.G.Company.	G.126.
12th Bn., R.Suss.R.	116th L.T.M.Bty.	
13th Bn., R.Suss.R.	17th Notts & Derby.	
14th Bn., Hants.R.		

1. "Q" Special Company R.E. will discharge 500 gas drums from Projectors at Zero hour on 1st June.

2. Targets :-
   CALL SUPPORT from its junction with CALL LANE to C.23.c.4.7.
   CALL RESERVE from C.23.c.9.6. to C.23.a.45.05.
   CAMBRAI RESERVE from C.23.d.0.0. to C.23.c.77.30.

3. The following precautions will be observed by all Troops and Working Parties :-
   (a) Posts in the front line between NEW JOHN STREET and ARMYTAGE TRENCH will be moved to Trench C.29.9.
   (b) Posts in MONMOUTH TRENCH will be moved into ADMIRAL TRENCH.
   (c) NEW JOHN STREET and BILGE TRENCH South of WIELTJE ROAD will be cleared.
   (d) ARMYTAGE TRENCH South of WIELTJE - ST.JULIEN ROAD will be cleared.
   (e) Sentries will be placed on all exits to WIELTJE Dugouts.
   (f) Above moves will be completed by Zero hour and trenches will be re-occupied at Zero plus 5.

4. O.C.17th Notts & Derby will arrange to accomodate the 40 men of "Q" Special Company R.E. (employed in discharging the gas drums) in the WIELTJE Dugouts from Zero onwards in case of hostile retaliation.

5. 39th Divisional Artillery will co-operate as follows:-
   (a) At Zero to Zero plus 5, 18 prs. and 4"5"" Howitzers open fire on CAMPHOR LANE and CALIFORNIA DRIVE.

6. Zero hour will be 3 a.m. 1st June 1917.

7. It is essential that all reliefs in the line are completed by 2.30 a.m. 1st June.

8. "Gas Alert" precautions will be observed from 10 p.m. to 3.30 a.m.

9. Should the weather conditions not permit of discharge, a Code message "BORDER" will be sent out to all recipients of this order.

10. Arrangements regarding Synchronization of Watches will be notified later.

11. A C K N O W L E D G E.

31.5.17.

J.G.W.Lord, Captain,
Brigade Major,
116th Infantry Brigade.

Army Form C. 2118.

WAR DIARY
INTELLIGENCE SUMMARY

(Erase heading not required.) 17th (SERV) Bn. SHERWOOD FORESTERS.

Instructions regarding War Diaries and Intelligence Summaries are contained in F. S. Regs., Part II. and the Staff Manual respectively. Title Pages will be prepared in manuscript.

Vol 17

Place	Date 1917	Hour	Summary of Events and Information	Remarks and references to Appendices
"C" CAMP Fily	1st		Battalion move by Route March to POPERINGHE STATION and entrain for WATTEN. In 2 Parties. R.H.Q. "B" & "C" Coys move by 1st Train. "A" & "D" Coys move by 2nd Train. Route by march Route to MOULLE (Map reference SHEET 27. Q. 11. c.) first line Transport by Road taking 2 days. Battalion in Billets.	(App.1)
MOULLE	2nd		Routine. Battalion cleaning up. Inspections.	(App.2)
—do—	3rd		Routine. Battalion commences Training in X 2 Area from 8 to 2 pm. A Coy musketry on B. Range. from 2 to 6 pm. Training Area Boundaries SHEET 27. MINDAL, INGLINGHEM, CQ. DIFQUES, MORINGHEM, BARKINGHEM.	(App.3)
—do—	4th		Routine. 2 Corporals digging on TASQUES Area. 2 Corporals Training from 8 to 2. 4 pm. X 2 Area.	(App.4)

Richmond
Lt. Colonel
COMDG. 17th (S) Bn. SHERWOOD FORESTERS.

WAR DIARY

INTELLIGENCE SUMMARY

(Erase heading not required.) 17th (SERV.) Bn. SHERWOOD FORESTERS. (hellie of Cuppes)

Army Form C. 2118.

Place	Date 1917	Hour	Summary of Events and Information	Remarks and references to Appendices
MEULLE	July 5th		Routine Battalion Training in X 2 AREA from 11 to 6 pm. Specialist Classes in Billets in the morning.	1/30 July 17
-do-	6th		Routine Battalion digging from 9 to 6 pm in TR 9/58 Area. No 11201 Sgt. W. ROBERTS awarded the Distinguished Conduct Medal for gallantry and devotion to duty. Specialist Classes in Billets from 9 to 11.30 am.	1/31 July 17
-do-	7th		Routine Battalion exercise in TR 9/8 S area from 1.15 to 5.15 pm. Battalion attack.	1/31 July 17
-do-	8th		Sunday. Raining, very hot day. Divine Service Cancelled.	1/00 July 17

Hubbard Lt. Colonel,
COMDG. 17th (S) Bn. SHERWOOD FORESTERS.

WAR DIARY
INTELLIGENCE SUMMARY

(Erase heading not required.) 17th (SERV.) Bn. SHERWOOD FORESTERS.

(Mulley Rupert)

Army Form C. 2118.

Place	Date	Hour	Summary of Events and Information	Remarks and references to Appendices
MOVILLE	July 9th 1917		Routine Training in Area at TIRQUES. Attack Practice. 8 am to 2 pm.	May 24/1
—do—	10th		Routine Training in Area at TIRQUES, Attack Practice 8 am to 2 pm.	May 24/1
—do—	11th		Routine Training in Area at TIRQUES. Attack Practice 8am to 2 pm.	May 24/1
—do—	12th		Routine. Bathing in Canal.	May 24/1
—do—	13th		Routine. Battalion Parade at 12.30 am for BRIGADE ATTACK at Dawn in conjunction with 11th Infantry Brigade in TIRQUES Area Operation Cancelled 6.30 am.	May 24/1

Michael ....Lt. Colonel
COMDG. 17th (S) Bn. SHERWOOD FORESTERS.

Army Form C. 2118.

WAR DIARY
INTELLIGENCE SUMMARY

(Erase heading not required.) 17th (SERV.) Bn. SHERWOOD FORESTERS. (Mellech Rogen)

(32) Instructions regarding War Diaries and Intelligence Summaries are contained in F. S. Regs., Part II and the Staff Manual respectively. Title Pages will be prepared in manuscript.

Place	Date 1917	Hour	Summary of Events and Information	Remarks and references to Appendices
MOULLE	JULY 14th		Entire Battalion Parade at 8.0 am for Divisional attack Scheme on TILQUES Area. Operation ceased at 3.30 pm.	Manay
—do—	15th		Sunday. Brigade Divine Service. Address by the Bishop of Khartoum.	Manay
—do—	16th		Entire Parades under Company officers. Platoon and Specialist Training. Bathing 300 men.	Manay
—do—	17th		Entire Battalion at Rickety Range. Battalion fired 30 rounds per man, also Lewis Gun testing in following attack by C.O. to all ranks.	Manay

J Mulvany Lt. Colonel
COMDG. 17th (S) Bn. SHERWOOD FORESTERS.

WAR DIARY
INTELLIGENCE SUMMARY

Army Form C. 2118.

(Erase heading not required.) 17th (SERV.) Bn. SHERWOOD FORESTERS (Mellé ? (Cambrai))

Place	Date	Hour	Summary of Events and Information	Remarks and references to Appendices
MOURKÉ	July 18th 1917		Routine, Battalion under Coy officers. Platoon and Specialist Training.	Appx A.S.1
—do—	19th		Routine Battalion under Coy officers. Platoon and Specialist Training.	Appx A.S.1
—do—	20th		Routine. Battalion took part in a Brigade Decare attack on TIRQUES area Operation concluded about 8 am. First line transport move for four days to Camp at "A" 30 (SHEET 28). Ration for the "ng U" GENINKHOUDT.	Appx A
—do—	21st		Battalion move by Busses to A 30 Camp (SHEET 28). Started 1.15 pm arrived 2 am 22nd inst. Battalion bivouac in a very bad field.	Appx A
—do—	22nd		Sunday, Routine Battalion clearing up.	Appx A

................Lt. Colonel,
COMDG. 17th (S) Bn. SHERWOOD FORESTERS

Army Form C. 2118.

WAR DIARY
INTELLIGENCE SUMMARY
(Erase heading not required)

(13th) (SERV.) Bn. SHERWOOD FORESTERS. (Welbeck Rangers)

Place	Date 1917	Hour	Summary of Events and Information	Remarks and references to Appendices
Bivouac A.30 Central	July 23rd		Routine. Company training under Coy. Officers from 9 to 12.30 pm	Maps
—do—	24th		Routine. Company training under Coy. Officers from 9 to 12.30 pm	Maps
—do—	25th		Routine. Company training under Coy. Officers from 9 to 12.30 pm. 200 men working on front line at night.	Maps
—do—	26th		Routine. Company training under Coy. Officers from 9 to 12.30 pm	Maps
—do—	27th		Routine. Company training under Coy. Officers from 9 to 12.30 pm	Maps
—do—	28th		Routine. Company training under Coy. Officers from 9 to 12.30 pm	Maps
—do—	29th		Routine. Battalion testing and drawing Sks. etc. for forthcoming operations at 8.30 pm. Battalion moved to CANAL BANK (Wipers sector) Map referred (SHEET 28 C.25.d.)	Maps

COMDG. 17th (S) Bn. SHERWOOD FORESTERS.
Lt. Colonel.

SECRET.   17th. Bn. SHERWOOD FORESTERS.

AMENDMENTS to OPERATION ORDER No. 43.

TANKS.   5. After last line add, "O.C. Companies will detail parties to move 100 yards in front of the Tanks when seen to clear any wounded from their track."

FLARES.   11. After last line add "Every man should carry a match box on which to strike Flares if the striking apparatus fails. An ordinary safety match box is suitable."

PRISONERS.   13. After last line add "No escort will consist of less than 3 Other Ranks."

APPENDIX   15. Delete, "Wirecutters (short) 50.
"B".   "Wirecutters (long) 50.
                           "Hedging Gloves   200."

                    (sd) T. Thornton. Capt & Adjt.
                         17th. Sherwood Foresters.
27.7.17.

Copies to the same Recipients as Operation Order No. 43.

M 1

SECRET.   17th. Bn. SHERWOOD FORESTERS.
         AMENDMENTS to OPERATION ORDER NO. 43.

Para. 8.   After (e) add "(ee). 3 RED DISCS. Am broken down."
Para. 14.   After Line 4. add "au Prisoners will be sent to
                 Battalion Headquarters."
                 Delete. Line 4. "Prisoners will be used as Stretcher
26.7.19.   Bearers.(sd) T. Thornton. Capt & Adjt.
                         17th. Sherwood Foresters.

         Copies to the same Recipients as Operation Order NO. 43.

WAR DIARY
INTELLIGENCE SUMMARY

Army Form C. 2118.

(Erase heading not required.) 17th (SERV.) Bn. SHERWOOD FORESTERS. (Nottingham)

Place	Date	Hour	Summary of Events and Information	Remarks and references to Appendices
CANAL BANK	JULY 30th 1917		"Y" Day. Orders issued prior to attack on "Z" day at 10.20 p.m. the Battalion move up to place of assembly in the HILL TOP SECTOR (map reference SHEET 28. C 31.b.)	May 141
HILL TOP SECTOR TRENCHES	31/7		ASSEMBLY Completed at 1.15 am "Z" day. No casualties caused whilst the Battalion was under Rifle & Machine Gun fire. Zero hour at 3.50 am the 8th ARMY Corps which our Division 39th are forming attack, the enemy's front line and to a depth of from 1½ to 3 miles. The following appendices give the detailed account sent in account account of the operation.	M.T. 14 ? S.F. 3

Murhead
.... Lt. Colonel.
COMDG. 17th (S) Bn. SHERWOOD FORESTERS.

M 1

SECRET.   7th. Bn. SHERWOOD FORESTERS.   OPERATION ORDER No. 43.

Reference Trench Map, ST. JULIEN 28. N.W. 2. 1. 10,000.

NOTE. In these Orders the day of Attack is referred to as "Z" day throughout.

INTENTION. 1. The Battalion will attack the KITCHENER SYSTEM and secure the crossings of the STEENBEEK.

OBJECTIVES. 2. (a) C.17.a.4.75.6.00. to C.10.d.7.50.2.00. (BLACK LINE).
(b) C.11.c.8.00.2.75. to C.11.c.3.25.7.50. - (ADVANCED BLACK LINE).
(c) C.11.b.9.50.1.75. to C.11.b.3.00.7.50. (DOTTED GREEN LINE).

PLAN. 3. (a) The Battalion will advance from the Position of assembly in Artillery formation in the following order. O.C. Companies will arrange and communicate to all ranks the exact bearing of their line of advance.
A. and C. front Companies in 2 lines of Platoons at deploying interval and 75 yards distance, followed by B. and D. Companies at deploying interval and 75 yards distance (a distance of 150 yards will be maintained between the leading 2 Companies and the rear 2 Companies).
On arrival at the BLUE LINE the Platoons of A. and C. Companies will advance straight through the captured position and deploy to the left on a bearing of 323° at 6 paces interval behind the protective barrage.
B. and D. Companies will still remain in the same formation keeping the same distance.
THE 1st. WAVE of A. and C. Companies will then advance behind the barrage (as per Appendix "A") and attack and consolidate the BLACK LINE.
THE 2nd. WAVE of A. and C. Companies will then advance through and just beyond KITCHENER'S WOOD and dig the advanced BLACK LINE behind the protective barrage.
O.C. A. and C. Companies will detail parties to mop up in dugouts that may be in their Section in KITCHENER'S WOOD.
As consolidation progresses O.C. A. and C. Companies will push forward their BLACK LINE Platoons to the ADVANCED BLACK LINE which will be made the main line of resistance.
B. and D. Companies will follow up A. and C. Companies and remain West of CANOE TRENCH until it is time for them to move forward.
O.C. A. Company will leave one clearing up party at OBLONG FARM, they will rejoin their Company.
O.C. B. and D. Companies will detail a reconnoitring patrol of 1 Officer and 2 N.C.Os. each to go forward with the REAR WAVE of the leading 2 Companies to reconnoitre the lines of advance etc., to the ADVANCED BLACK LINE.

(b) THE LEADING WAVE of B. and D. Companies will then advance through the ADVANCED BLACK LINE behind the barrage (as per Appendix "A") on to the DOTTED GREEN LINE. (The line of the STEENBEEK at the same time securing all crossings in their Sector).
The DOTTED GREEN LINE will be held as an Out-Post Line until troops passing through them have consolidated the next Line in Front.

- 2 -

THE REAR 2 PLATOONS of B. Company will advance up to and as close to the protective barrage as possible ready to occupy the Strong Points ALBERTA and HUPP HOLLOW directly it lifts. These 2 Platoons will act independently of the First Wave of B. and D. Companies who will be advancing on the STEENBEEK
THE REAR 2 PLATOONS of D. Company will remain on the BLACK LINE IN SUPPORT.

MACHINE GUNS.

(c) (1) The 117th Machine Gun Company will detail one section, less one detachment, for the defence of the BLUE LINE; one section, less one detachment, for the defence of the DOTTED BLACK LINE, and two detachments for the defence of the crossings of the STEENBEEK.

(2) Detachments will assemble and go forward in rear of the last wave allotted to the Objective they have been detailed to defend. They will be preceded by Scouts, and will not enter any trench until it has been mopped up.

(3) Two Sections, 117th Machine Gun Company, will carry out a Machine Gun Barrage under Divisional Orders. Details of this, and Corps Machine Gun Barrages, are being issued separately.

TRENCH MORTAR BATTERY.

(d) (1) One Section, 117th Trench Mortar Battery, will accompany the second wave of the attack, and take up positions in the enemy front line prepared to support the advance to the BLUE and DOTTED BLUE LINES.
After the capture of the BLACK LINE this Section will move forward and take up defensive positions to cover the DOTTED BLACK LINE.

(2) One Section will accompany the fourth wave of the attack, and will take up positions in the BLUE LINE to cover consolidation, and support any further advance. Two guns from this section will be sent up at the discretion of O.C. 117th Trench Mortar Battery, when the crossings of the STEENBEEK have been captured to cover these crossings.

ASSEMBLY. 4. (a) The Battalion will move up from the CANAL BANK by Platoons, by cross-country routes within the Brigade Area as far as the Junction of BUFFS Road and FINCH Street, thence by Communication trenches or over-land routes to Assembly positions. Over-land routes will be reconnoitred on X/Y night, and assemble in the following formation :-
A. and C. Companies in Artillery formation (lines of Platoons) in front of BILGE TRENCH.
A. Company on the Right.
B. and D. Companies respectively behind A. and C. Companies in Artillery formation (lines of Platoons) in and behind BILGE TRENCH.

(b) Assembly will be complete by ZERO Minus 3 hours.
The Battalion will not reach the line of BILGE TRENCH before 11 p.m.

ARTILLERY. 5. (a) The rate of barrage will be 100 yards in 4 minutes throughout.

(b) The creeping barrage will be Shrapnel 50% on graze.
The various lifts are shewn in APPENDIX "A".

- 3 -

  (c) It will lift off the German Front Line, the BLUE LINE and the BLACK LINE at the same time, on the whole Army Front, to allow each of these Objectives to be carried simultaneously.
  (d) The following information will be sent to Battalion Headquarters about all Hostile guns captured :-
   (1) Map reference.
   (2) Number and apparent condition of guns.
   (3) Ammunition available at gun position.
  (e) No captured gun will be damaged unless there is a danger of it being recaptured or taken away by the enemy, in this case a written order will be sent by the Battalion Commander concerned to the nearest L.T.M. Detachment to send up a Destruction Party from his Detachment.

R.E. 6. 1 Section 234 Company R.E. will move forward after the capture of the DOTTED GREEN LINE to assist in constructing the Strong Point at ALBERTA. The Officer in charge of this party will report to the Commanding Officer at CANOE TRENCH.

TIMINGS. 7. See APPENDIX "A".

TANKS. 8. (a) 2 Tanks will accompany the Battalion and assist in the destruction of the BLACK LINE, they will cross the DOTTED BLUE LINE at Zero plus 1 hr. 15 minutes, they will also accompany the Infantry down to the DOTTED GREEN LINE.
  (b) Infantry will not wait for Tanks or follow close behind them.
  (c) Each Tank working with the Brigade will have the letter "G" and a number painted on the back.
  (d) The location and number of any Tank becoming derelict will be immediately sent to Battalion Headquarters.
  (e) All Ranks will know the following Signals :-
   RED DISC. Wire uncut (i.e. DANGER).
   GREEN DISC. Wire cut. (i.e. SAFE).
   RED DISC   )
    and   ) Have reached my Objective.
   GREEN DISC.)

   RED DISC.)
   WHITE DISC.) Enemy is in dugouts.
   RED DISC.)
  (f) Attention is directed to "Tank coloured Disc and Light Code" (Second Edition) recently issued.
  (g) The approximate routes to be followed by the Tanks are shown on the Map issued.

TRAFFIC. 9. (a) The following Trenches will be used for IN and OUT Traffic from X/Y night inclusive as follows:-
   IN. CONEY Street.
      GOWTHORPE Road.
      DIGGLES Street.
      CLARK Street.
   OUT. FINCH Street (common to both Brigades).
      GILLson Street.

  (b) Runners will be allowed to use any Trench in either direction.

- 4 -

DRESS and EQUIPMENT.

10. Fighting Order, water bottles filled. All water bottles will be filled by Zero.
Every man will carry the following :-
(1) 1 pair Socks.
  Towel and Soap.
  Canteen.
  One complete day's rations.
  Iron rations.
  Waterproof sheet.
  Box Respirator (in the alert position)
  P.H. Helmet (the best method is to carry this
         Over the shoulder and under the belt
         without crossing the chest)
  1 Waterbottle (filled). (Two if desired).
  Haversack.
  Entrenching Tool.
  4 Sandbags on the belt in front and not behind.
  2 Mills Grenades)   Except Runners, M.G.Coy.
  2 Flares   )   and T. Mortar Batty.
(2) Lewis Guns will be carried slung to prevent Lewis Gunners being picked out by enemy snipers.
No maps of any description showing our trenches will be taken over.
O.C. Companies should be in possession of a map giving barrage lines and times of lifts of the portions of the enemy's lines they are assaulting but great care must be exercised that these maps do not fall into the enemy's hands.
The following Distinguishing Marks will be worn by Companies :-
BLACK LINE PLATOONS - Black and White ribbon on Left shoulder.
ADVANCED BLACK LINE PLATOONS. Black Ribbon on Left shoulder.
DOTTED GREEN LINE PLATOONS. Green Ribbon on Left shoulder.
ALBERTA and HUGEL HOLLOW STRONG POINT PLATOONS. Green Ribbon on Right shoulder.
TWO SUPPORT PLAT'NS. ("D" Company) NIL.
All Officers will wear men's jackets and waterproof sheets in the battle, and no raincoats are to be taken.
Platoon Commanders to carry rifles and bayonets.
No Officers to carry Sticks.
Packs will be stored at the present Quartermaster's Stores.

STORES etc.

11. MILLS NO. 23. 4 man loads (10 per Rifle Bombing Section)
RIFLE GRENADE CUPS. 1 per man of Rifle Bombing Section.
             1 per 2 buckets of Rifle Bombing Section.
M.S.K. BOMBS. 4 per Bombing Section.
NOTE:- If bombs No. 23 MK. 11 are issued for both 1 & 2 every man could carry 5 rods in right breast pockets 5 blanks in section of a bandolier sewn on to outside of right breast pocket and there would thus be a reserve of rifle grenades.
S.A.A. LEWIS GUNS. 20 Drums per gun.
1" VERY LIGHTS.   12 per Company for Signalling.
                    50 per Battalion Headquarters.
VERY LIGHT PISTOLS 1". 6 per Company and 2 for Battalion Headquarters.
1½" VERY LIGHT. S.O.S. 6 per Company, 12 per Battalion Headquarters.
PISTOLS VERY LIGHT 1½". 1 per Company and 2 per Battalion Headquarters.
1" VERY-LIGHTS RED. 24 per Battalion Headquarters.

- 5 -

	SHOVELS.	50% of every Platoon will carry shovels with a proportion of picks.
	1 TRENCH BOARD.	Each Platoon for DOTTED GREEN LINE.
	AUTHORISED STORES.	All authorised Stores as per Establishment will be carried.

FLARES. 12. Flares will be lit (by leading Troops only) when called for by the Aeroplane. This call will be a succession of "A's" on the Klaxon or one White Very Light.
Troops will be particularly on the look-out for these signals on reaching each successive Objective.
Flares are to be lit at the bottom of trenches and shell holes. Flares which can be seen by the enemy Ground Observers form excellent ranging marks for his Artillery.

DUMPS. 13. (a) Stores will be issued from Advanced Brigade Dumps at any time on the signature of any Officer in the Brigade.
Os.C. 17th. Sherwood Foresters and 16th Rifle Brigade will form their own Battalion Dumps in CANOE TRENCH as required from the Advanced Brigade Dumps at FUILTUR and CIVILISATION Farms until the Brigade Dump has been established at OBLONG FARM.
(b) The following are the map references of the dumps and Headquarters known to exist in the enemy's lines:-
Battalion Headquarters   - ALBERTA, C.11.a.
Dumps   - CANOE TRENCH, C.17.a.00.75
                          - ALBERTA, C.11.d.00.64

LIAISON. 14. (1) 1. OBLONG FARM.
2. Southern corner of KITCHENER'S WOOD.
3. Building at C.11.b.4.0.
4. Tramway Junction in CANOE TRENCH, C.10.d.7.3.
5. HEDGE Junction at N.E. edge of KITCHENER'S WOOD C.11.c.15.65.
(2) O.C. Companies will arrange liaison with Companies on their flanks.
(3) Capt. W.S. Holden will report as LIAISON Officer to Brigade Headquarters at ZERO Minus 2 hours.
(4) 2nd.Lt. M.A. Ellissen will report to O.C. 14th Hants at ZERO Minus 3 hours.
These Officers will take their Servants with them to act as Runners.

MEDICAL. 15. (1) The Regimental Aid Post for all Battalions will be at the Battalion Headquarters C.21.b.3.2.
(2) As soon as the BLUE LINE is captured Lieut. N.S. Temple will select a site for Forward R.A.P.S. in or near the BLUE LINE.
(3) As soon as the BLACK LINE is captured Medical Officers of the GREEN LINE Battalions will go forward and occupy their Forward R.A.P'S.
(4) No Medical Officer is to leave the R.A.P. The Medical Officers of GREEN LINE Battalions will not leave their Forward R.A.P's. when once they have occupied them.
(5) All wounded cases requiring treatment are to be brought to M.O's. and on no account will any M.O. leave his Aid Post to visit any case.

- 6. -

PRISONERS. 16. All arms will be removed at once. Documents will be taken from Officers only.
Escorts will be 5 men for 100 prisoners.
Prisoners will be used as Stretcher Bearers.

S.O.S. 17. The Fifth Army is issuing a special S.O.S. Signal which bursts into two Red and two Green balls. This will be the S.O.S. Signal from ZERO on the whole Army Front.

COMMUNICATION. 18. (a) Positions of Brigade Forward Station "A".
    (1) Before ZERO - BILGE TRENCH at approx. C.21.b.65.10.
    (2) Brigade F.S. "A" advances in rear of A. and B. Battalions to KULTUR FARM - C.16.c.70.30.
    (c) Brigade F.S. "A" advances in rear of C. and D. Battalions to OBLONG FARM - C.16.b.50.20.

(b) Positions of Brigade Forward Station "B".
    (1) Before ZERO - IRISH FARM at approx. C.27.a.15.60.
    (2) Brigade F.S. "B" advances at ZERO plus 5 hrs. to ALBERTA Farm C.11.c.90.60., calling at OBLONG FARM en route.

(c) Brigade H.Q.
    (1) Before ZERO - HILL TOP Dugouts C.21.d.10.90.
    (2) Brigade H.Q. advances in rear of C. and D. Battalions to OBLONG FARM.

(d) Signallers and Runners distributed as follows ;-
  (1)

Unit.	Signallers.	Runners.
Platoon H.Q.	-	2
Company H.Q.	2	4
Battalion H.Q.	11	18

  (2) Communications will be maintained as follows:-
    (a) Between Platoon and Company - By Runner to Company H.Q.
    (b) Between Company and Battalion - By Runner or Visual to Battalion Forward Command Post or to Brigade Forward Stations. By Power Buzzer and Amplifier.
    (c) Between Battalion and Brigade - By Runner and Runner Relay Post, Visual, Telephone from Battalion F.C.P. to Brigade F.S. Power Buzzer and Amplifier, Pigeons.
    (d) Between Infantry and Aeroplanes - Visual, Flares Ground Shutter etc., Klaxon Horn.
    (e) Runners will carry their messages in the top right hand pocket. Runner Casualties will be searched for Messages.

SYNCHRONISATION 19. O.C. Companies will synchronise watches at Battalion
OF WATCHES. Headquarters at a time to be notified later.

REPORT CENTRES. 20. (1) Headquarters will be as follows from "Y/Z" night:-
  Brigade Headquarters.   C.21.d.15.85. HILL TOP Tunnels, Dugout 29.
  16th Sherwood Foresters. C.21.b.4.2. Junction of BILGE and CONEY Street.
  17th Sherwood Foresters. C.21.b.15.85. HILL TOP Tunnels, Dugout 49.

17th K.R.Rif.C.	C.15.c.8.3., Junction of BELLINGHAM Trench & DIGGLES St.
16th Rifle Brigade.	C.21.a.95.50. Junction of BILGE and GILLSON Street.
117th Machine Gun Coy.	C.21.d.15.85. HILL TOP Tunnels with Brigade Headquarters.
117th Trench Mortar Batty.	C.21.b.4.2. Junction of BILGE & CONEY St., with O.C. 16th Sher. Foresters.

~~(8)~~ On "A" day.
(2) On "Z" day.

(a) ZERO. HILL TOP Dugouts C.21.d.10.85.
(b) After ZERO German Front Line C.22.a.1.2. (approx)
(c) On occupation of BLUE LINE C.16.c.9.8. (approx)
(d) CANOE TRENCH C.16.b.75.80.

A large Notice will mark Battalion Headquarters.

~~ZERO~~
HOUR OF ZERO. 21. The hour of ZERO will be notified later.

NOTE. Assembly will be carried out in silence and will be complete by a time to be notified later. After that time there will be no movement of any kind in the trenches. No wave will leave its assembly trenches before ZERO.
Report of Assembly complete to Battalion Headquarters immediately on assembly.

ACKNOWLEDGE.

25th July 1917.
(sd) T. Thornton. Capt & Adjt.
17th. Sherwood Foresters.

Copies to:-

117th Infantry Brigade.	1
16th Sherwood Foresters.	1
16th Rifle Brigade.	1
14th Hants.	1
Commanding Officer.	1
O.C. A.B.C.D. & H.Q. Companies.	1
Signalling Officer.	1
Medical Officer.	1
Adjutant.	1
War Diary.	2
Office Copy.	1

REPORT on OPERATIONS on
----------- 31st July 1917. -----------

3.15 a.m.   The assembly of the Battalion was complete and was carried out without any casualties, although promiscuous shelling went on the whole time including gas shells.

3.50 a.m.   The advance commenced to our front line and across "No Man's Land" following up the assaulting Battalion of the front German System, this was crossed before the German barrage came down.

During the advance 2 Platoons of the Right Assaulting Company and the Right Rear Company slightly lost direction owing to there being a wood very similar to Kitchener's on their right front, but these were readjusted at the position of deployment.

4.16 a.m.   Blue Line reached without opposition and assaulting Companies deployed behind the protective barrage.

Slight casualties were incurred at this position owing to the short and high bursting of our protective barrage.

5.13 a.m.   The advance on the Black Line behind barrage commenced. Slight opposition was met with by two enemy machine guns in the vicinity of Oblong Farm, these were at once engaged by our rifle men on a flank who covered by two Lewis guns, assaulted and killed the garrison.

The advance was continued until temporarily held up by machine guns and snipers from Canoe Trench, the two assaulting Companies at once sending out Lewis gunners on their flanks and by their fire effectively stopped the enemy machine guns firing.

5.33 a.m.   Under cover of the Lewis guns and barrage Canoe Trench was then captured. All the enemy were killed with the exception of one; it being found that several had been hit by our Lewis guns, the remainder who resisted being bayoneted.

The advance was then continued by the Second Wave through Kitchener's Wood to the Dotted Black Line. Several prisoners and three enemy machine guns being taken in the Wood.

On arrival on the Eastern side of the Wood at the Dotted Black Line two enemy machine guns opened on us from Alberta, these were engaged with our Lewis guns, rifle grenadiers, and Stokes guns and with the assistance of two tanks which opened fire at close range. We drove the enemy into concrete dug-outs, our riflemen then worked round and when the protective barrage lifted assaulted and captured the farm, the garrison surrendering.

Consolidation was then proceeded with. I would here like to mention the Tank Commander of G.47. who did excellent work.

The total captures up to this point were 120 Prisoners including 2 Officers, 4 Machine guns and one Anti-Tank gun.

2.

6.50 a.m. The Dotted Green Line Companies and Hugel Hollow Platoon formed up behind protective barrage.

7.30 a.m. Advance behind protective barrage began.
Very little resistance was met with during this advance but several prisoners being taken from Hugel Hollow and concrete dug-outs to the North East of Alberta including machine guns.

7.55 a.m. The Steenbeek was reached and advanced over and consolidation commenced on the Eastern side.
At this point heavy rifle and machine gun fire was opened on us from the enemy on the ridge in front causing several casualties, and several shells from our own batteries were dropped into the line that we were now consolidating, the enemy's fire being replied to by our riflemen and Lewis Guns.
Total number of prisoners taken up to this point by the Dotted Green Line Companies was 137 and 3 machine guns making a total of 257 prisoners, 7 machine guns and one Anti-Tank gun.

10.15 a.m. The 118th Infantry Brigade passed through us and rather late for the barrage but were held up after going about 250 yards by rifle and machine gun fire from both flanks. About an hour after reaching their position they began to retire, being followed up by small parties of the enemy, and very heavy and machine gun fire from both flanks.
We succeeded in stopping the enemy's advance by Lewis gun and rifle fire and inflicted heavy losses on him, some of the enemy only being stopped when within about 12 yards from our position.
Several of 118th Infantry Brigade were then rallied and took up a position in our line.

---o---

During the next 4 days in which we remained in occupation of the positions won, the enemy were very active with his snipers and machine guns. Great execution was done by all ranks sniping, One Officer alone claiming 34 victims. It being practically impossible to move about during the day and very great credit is due to the runners of these Companies, although suffering heavy casualties nearly always succeeded in getting messages through.
Communications throughout from front to rear were extremely difficult owing to the nature of the ground and climatic conditions.
Our barrage throughout was good but at times was very apt to burst too short and too high, and I consider that the Barrage put up for the 118th Infantry Brigade and our own protective barrage being much too weak at that long range.
I also consider that the pauses before the advance on the Dotted Green Line and especially on the Solid Green Line were too long the enemy being given time to appreciate the situation and if demoralized reform.
The Battalion on my right were never up on the East side of the Steenbeek, in fact, from where they did get to, when the 118th Infantry Brigade withdrew, they also withdrew to the Dotted Black Line thereby leaving my right flank very much in the air, but dispositions were made to meet any contingency from a South Easterly

direction and a protective flank formed.

The Battalion on my right was afterwards told to advance and did so, but not far enough to be of much assistance, however, we were always in communication with them from Alberta. I was in close touch with the Battalion on my left throughout and also Brigade Headquarters.

I would like to add that the behaviour of the Officers, Non-Commissioned Officers and men under the awful climatic conditions was exemplary throughout.

In conclusion the work done by the First Line Transport who never failed to get the rations up to the Battalion although suffering heavy casualties in men and animals, was excellent.

My total casualties during the operations and the following days of occupation of the captured position :-

Killed in Action.	2 Officers.
Wounded.	5 Officers.
Wounded, at duty.	2 Officers.
Killed in Action.	43 Other Ranks.
Died of Wounds.	3 do
Wounded.	208 do
Missing.	12 do
Gassed.	8 do
Shell Shock.	1 do
Wounded, at duty.	3 do
Hospital.	32. do

Lt.Col.,

7th August 1917.   Cmdg. 17th. Sherwood Foresters.

APPENDIX "A".

TIME TABLE.

TIME	ACTIONS BY COMPANIES etc.
ZERO.	Advance into NO MAN'S LAND.
ZERO plus 6 mins.	Arrival in NO MAN'S LAND.
ZERO plus 18 mins.	Arrival GERMAN FRONT LINE.
ZERO plus 26 mins.	Advance to BLUE LINE and form up behind Protective barrage.
ZERO plus 1 hr. 23 mins.	Advance behind barrage to BLACK LINE commences.
ZERO plus 1 hr. 43 mins.	Assault of BLACK LINE.
ZERO plus 1 hr. 47 mins.	Advance on ADVANCED BLACK LINE.
ZERO plus 2 hrs. 5 mins.	Consolidation of ADVANCED BLACK LINE behind Protective barrage.
ZERO plus 3 hrs.	ALBERTA and HUGEL HOLLOW Platoons form up behind Protective barrage followed by dotted GREEN LINE Platoons.
ZERO plus 3 hrs. 40 mins.	ALBERTA assaulted followed by HUGEL HOLLOW, DOTTED GREEN LINE Platoons advance.
ZERO plus 4 hrs. 5 mins.	DOTTED GREEN LINE reached.
ZERO plus 4 hrs. 13 mins.	Protective barrage in front of DOTTED GREEN LINE.
ZERO plus 6 hrs. 58 mins.	Protective barrage lifts, 116th Infantry Brigade pass through Brigade.
N.B.	Protective barrages will become intense for eight minutes before lifting.

APPENDIX "B".

BRIGADE and ADVANCED BRIGADE DUMPS.

Material.	Brigade Dump, C.21.c.8.8.	LEFT Adv.Bde. Dump, C.21.b.1.9.	RIGHT Adv.B Dump, C.21.b.8.33.
Mills No.5 H.G.	5,000	3,000) or No23(3,000	
		)Mark 11(	
Mills No.23 R.G.	1,000	3,000) 6,000 (3,000	
Hales No.20 R.G.	1,000	---	---
S.A.A.	500,000	50,000 for Rifles	50,000
		25,000 for L.G's.	25,000
Stokes 3" T.M. Ammn.	1,000	---	---
"P" Grenades.	500	---	---
1" White Very Lights.	1,000	---	---
S.O.S. Signals.	200	---	---
Picks.	100	---	---
Shovels.	300	---	---
Wirecutters - short.	50	---	---
Wirecutters - long.	50	---	---
Hedging Gloves.	200	---	---
Sandbags.	10,000	---	---
Barbed Wire, Coils.	200	---	---
Plain Wire, Coils.	5	---	---
Pickets, screw, long.	100	---	---
" " short.	200	---	---
" wood, 5 ft.	200	---	---
Direction Boards.	50	---	---
Tracing Tape, Coils.	50	---	---
Spun yarn, Coils.	10	---	---
Mauls.	5	---	---
Hammers.	10	---	---
Saws, hand.	10	---	---
" cross cut.	5	---	---
Axes, hand.		---	---
" felling.	5	---	---
Billhooks.	20	---	---
Rope, 1½" for Yukon Packs.	2,000 ft.	---	---

17th. Bn. SHERWOOD FORESTERS.

CASUALTIES.

KILLED IN ACTION. 2nd.Lt. T.W. Betts.   31.7.17.
                   2nd.Lt. F.P. Waterson.   31.7.17.

WOUNDED.   2nd.Lt. A.S. Beck.   31.7.17.
                   2nd.Lt. J.E. Neal.   31.7.17.
                   Revd.   P.T. Hutchinson.   1.8.17. (Attached Wesleyan
                                                              Chaplain)
                   2nd.Lt. W.G. Lilley.   31.7.17.
                   2nd.Lt. B.V. Hughes.   1.8.17.

WOUNDED, AT DUTY. Capt & Adjt. T. Thornton.
                                    M.C.   31.7.17.
                   Capt. J.W.J. Miller.   31.7.17.

KILLED IN ACTION.   Headquarter Company.
27146. Pte. Watts   J.T.   38710. Pte. Clarke   F.
                             A. Company.
  5157. Sgt. Smith   A.   235076. Pte. Harper   A.E.H.
235062. Pte. Branner   H.   235060. Pte. Haynes   G.W.
 18494. Pte. Bowman   W.   235087. Pte. Moody   J.
235067. Pte. Colkin   F.   71578. Pte. Smith   W.G.
 76160. Pte. Duncan   J.T.   61054. Pte. Smith   J.
 31351. Pte. Francis (1.8.17) G.
                             B. Company.
  5049. Sgt. Harrison C.   29305. Pte. Hardy   E.
 70337. L/Cpl. Forman E.W.   38196. Pte. Mitson   W.
 70478. L/Cpl. Johnstone J.   60543. Pte. Wright   E.H.
 70032. L/Cpl. Robinson W.   31101. CQMS. Thompson   J.
 70380. L/Cpl. Wheatley T.
                             C. Company.
 70224. Pte. Bishop   J.   53285. Pte. Parkin   J.
 38764. Pte. Hargreaves(2.8.17)W.H. 235182. Pte. Sherry G. (1.8.17)
 76214. Pte. Lewis   W.   235191. Pte. Whitworth   S.
                             D. Company.
 71076. Cpl. Phillips W.   37035. Pte. Johnson   H.S.
 46688. L/Cpl. Hingley H.   38590. Pte. Kenyon   W.A.
 21748. L/Cpl. Lowe   J.   21086. Pte. Layhe   C.W.
  3812. Pte. Burke   E.   70351. Pte. Money   W.
 71490. Pte. Cox   G.   48099. Pte. Newbold   A.
 76159. Pte. Edmund   J.   30989. Pte. Neep   H.
 76160. Pte. Ewen   G.   70021. Pte. Perry   J.

DIED OF WOUNDS.

Headquarter Company.
28893. Pte. Sheldon J.R. (3.8.17)

B. Company.
65893. Pte. Salt H.G. (3.8.17)

D. Company.
43005. Pte. Wright J. (1.8.17)   6067-3. Pte. Woodward G.W. (4.8.17)

WOUNDED.

Headquarter Company.
26910.	Sgt.	Beresford	J.E.	47224.	Pte. Chamberlain	S.
27155.	RQMS.	Smith	C.	40292.	Pte. Mason	A.C.
27307.	Cpl.	Hickling	J.	46391.	Pte. Cross	P.A.
28918.	Pte.	Copley	E.	31140.	Pte. Jackson	G.H.

A. Company.
30788.	Sgt.	Summers	J.	33854.	Pte. Jackson	R.
6853.	Sgt.	Peet	E.E.	48152.	Pte. Lane	G.H.
19975.	L/Sgt.	Shaw	F.	60483.	Pte. Lunt	G.
27140.	Cpl.	Bostock	E.	51608.	Pte. Markham	F.
5943.	Cpl.	Griffiths	T.	48455.	Pte. Moody	J.
53077.	Cpl.	Fotheringham	F.	49313.	Pte. Oswin	J.W.
27186.	L/Cpl.	Berry	W.	32491.	Pte. Punter	F.
27290.	L/Cpl.	Deverill	A.	33593.	Pte. Payne	F.
31179.	L/Cpl.	Hearn	A.	11606.	Pte. Reynolds	G.
70213.	Pte.	Andrews	G.	70037.	Pte. Robinson	F.
235061.	Pte.	Buxton	W.H.	18786.	Pte. Smedley	J.
50617.	Pte.	Curtis	J.	31384.	Pte. Stone	H.
31481.	Pte.	Drury	G.	75315.	Pte. Simpkin	H.E.
235070.	Pte.	Davis	F.	70390.	Pte. Smith	D.A.
18649.	Pte.	Eyre	A.	49477.	Pte. Tatton	G.H.
27404.	Pte.	Flint	F.	71572.	Pte. Turner	F.P.
6021.	Pte.	Fletcher	L.	235096.	Pte. Todd	C.
50189.	Pte.	Frakes	W.H.	76415.	Pte. Welbourne	W.
71564.	Pte.	Haslam	C.	33689.	Pte. Whitemarsh	E.
76398.	Pte.	Hampson	T.	60736.	Pte. Wilson	A.T.
76397.	Pte.	Howcroft	F.	235099.	Pte. Wright	G.
76400.	Pte.	Heron	T.	57508.	Pte. Wilson	T.
235082.	Pte.	Hukin	D.	235090.	Pte. White	G.W.
76199.	Pte.	Jeffrey	J.			

B. Company.
29088.	CSM.	Williams	D.	76399.	Pte. Henks	H.W.
27097.	Sgt.	Chappell	L.	31362.	Pte. Hamilton	J.E.
306 68.	Sgt.	Woolley	A.W.	4054.	Pte. Jones	R.
13305.	Cpl.	Dilkes	W.	38673.	Pte. Jeavons	J.
53712.	Cpl.	Stainton	W.	52836.	Pte. King	W.
13189.	L/Cpl.	Hobster	M.	76383.	Pte. Law	F.
18415.	L/Cpl.	Hardy	J.	4630.	Pte. Leafe	G.
76346.	L/Cpl.	Yull	J.	49394.	Pte. Mills	F.
71465.	Pte.	Aspinal	F.	65345.	Pte. Mourne	A.H.
71569.	Pte.	Anthony	W.	29597.	Pte. Porter	J.
43871.	Pte.	Bell	G.H.	25659.	Pte. Phillips	H.
27360.	Pte.	Brittain	S.	43717.	Pte. Plowright	C.
19937.	Pte.	Buck	A.E.	58454.	Pte. Pritchett	C.H.
30549.	Pte.	Burley	A.	70020.	Pte. Robinson	W.A.
19755.	Pte.	Buckingham	J.	70160.	Pte. Rigden	H.
70218.	Pte.	Barber	A.E.	65150.	Pte. Roderick	T.
31488.	Pte.	Broughton	S.	6600.	Pte. Reader	J.
70215.	Pte.	Bates	J.H.	14509.	Pte. Sharpley	J.C.
28436.	Pte.	Bacon	M.	45939.	Pte. Turner	A.E.
65364.	Pte.	Critchley	A.	58267.	Pte. Verdy	H.
76494.	Pte.	Crawford	D.R.	25931.	Pte. Walker	

&.

15785.	Pte.	Cook	J.	3641.	Pte.	Rowley	A.
73087.	Pte.	Coombes	R.C.	22651.	Pte.	Whiteman	R.
60991.	Pte.	Calow	F.W.	19671.	Pte.	Wood	J.
31748.	Pte.	Copland	R.	61954.	Pte.	Walker	J.E.
80047.	Pte.	Dean	H.H.	11798.	Pte.	Woodward	G.
78588.	Pte.	Ensden	W.	35748.	Pte.	Woolley	G.C.
30334.	Pte.	Etches	C.C.	46348.	Pte.	Webster	H.
85020.	Pte.	Edwards	H.	30469.	Pte.	Peel	F.
28085.	Pte.	Flint	W.				
51685.	Pte.	Goodwin	W.				
70340.	Pte.	Garner	E.				

C. Company.

24927.	Sgt.	Golding	J.	1901.	Pte.	Heron	T.H.
70259.	Cpl.	Fenton	J.	70423.	Pte.	Maltby	J.H.
38437.	L/Cpl.	d'Hoogh	H.	19547.	Pte.	Martin	L.
76186.	L/Cpl.	Hannah	R.	22809.	Pte.	Milner	K.
80197.	L/Cpl.	Harrod	P.	98108.	Pte.	McKenzie	H.
11366.	L/Cpl.	Slack	G.	49762.	Pte.	Matthews	L.
99967.	Pte.	Allen	G.	36495.	Pte.	Mellor	B.
36750.	Pte.	Adams	G.	67117.	Pte.	Merritt	O.
6358.	Pte.	Ball	T.	13737.	Pte.	Neal	M.
16069.	Pte.	Crossley	K.	935173.	Pte.	Perry	W.H.
18098.	Pte.	Edwards	W.	935125.	Pte.	Prescott	J.
43909.	Pte.	Fenton	W.	235176.	Pte.	Parker	A.
76163.	Pte.	Fraser	J.B.	80948.	Pte.	Stafford	G.
18495.	Pte.	Green	J.	65898.	Pte.	Stanley	A.
65873.	Pte.	Hallam	A.	70049.	Pte.	Streets	A.
65632.	Pte.	Holmes	W.	935185.	Pte.	Shaw	J.
24425.	Pte.	Hinton	E.	70097.	Pte.	Thomson	C.H.
61017.	Pte.	Hooker	R.C.	65651.	Pte.	Tebbett	D.
65859.	Pte.	Jaggers	F.	935188.	Pte.	Tunnicliffe	T.
13761.	Pte.	Jenkins	J.	35370.	Pte.	Wild	A.
76409.	Pte.	King	C.W.	3748.	Pte.	Wells	S.
65381.	Pte.	Long	G.E.	65861.	Pte.	Wright	T.

D. Company.

13870.	CSM.	Lee	S.C.	44489.	Pte.	Findon	G.E.
30471.	Sgt.	Hewitt	W.	73390.	Pte.	Greaves	G.
18398.	Cpl.	Gresnley	K.	15381.	Pte.	Green	J.
97168.	Cpl.	Hurden	G.	34766.	Pte.	Guildford	H.
60737.	Cpl.	Walker	E.	76390.	Pte.	Hughes	H.M.
13155.	Cpl.	Gellie	A.	76191.	Pte.	Hendry	A.
36219.	L/Cpl.	Haywood	D.	71474.	Pte.	Harrihill	J.T.
30546.	L/Cpl.	Rawson	A.	935164.	Pte.	Joynson	J.H.
87401.	L/Cpl.	Radford	A.	935166.	Pte.	Jones	R.
50629.	L/Cpl.	Godson	A.	935171.	Pte.	Hoyston	J.J.
36495.	L/Cpl.	Dolby	G.	40319.	Pte.	Nobbs	T.
3514.	L/Cpl.	Burton	J.	64518.	Pte.	Organ	D.
30961.	L/Cpl.	Bowden	L.	70093.	Pte.	Pawlest	T.
31883.	L/Cpl.	Lender	H.	935173.	Pte.	Podley	W.
18748.	L/Cpl.	Davies	G.	935180.	Pte.	Rigby	D.
19409.	L/Cpl.	Scarlett	G.	50184.	Pte.	Sootney	F.
71466.	Pte.	Arnold	W.	84597.	Pte.	Shaw	J.H.
71469.	Pte.	Anderson	F.	70048.	Pte.	Spruce	R.G.
31137.	Pte.	Broadhead	H.	935187.	Pte.	Toft	J.T.
71476.	Pte.	Bowler	J.	81341.	Pte.	Wilkinson	J.
71479.	Pte.	Burnett	M.	935199.	Pte.	Watkiss	W.
71484.	Pte.	Bod	T.E.	71493.	Pte.	Clayton	A.
43667.	Pte.	Brittle	J.	31887.	Pte.	Blood	G.W.
13764.	Pte.	Chesham	H.	43770.	Pte.	Garside	J.S.
70386.	Pte.	Deacon	F.H.				

Copy.

Fifth Army.
G.A. 657/275.

2nd August, 1917.

II Corps.
V Corps.
VIII Corps.
XIV Corps.
XVIII Corps.
XIX Corps.
5th Bde. R.F.C.
Adv. Tanks.
O.C. Spl. Coys. R.E.
O.C. A.A. Group.

----

1. The Army Comdr. wishes to offer his heartiest congratulations to the troops under his command on the success gained by them on July 31st.

2. For a fortnight prior to the attack the enemy has maintained a heavy and continuous Arty. fire, including an unprecedented use of H.V. guns against back areas, and a new form of gas shell, all of which caused severe casualties.
Despite this and the fact that the forward area was dominated by the enemy at all points, the necessary Prepartions for the battle were completed and the difficult forward march and assembly of nine Divs. successfully carried out and the assault launched. This alone constitutes a performance of which the Army may well be proud.

3. As a result of the battle the enemy has once again been driven by the 1st French Army and ourselves from the whole of his front system on a front of about 8 miles, and we are now firmly established in or beyond his second line on a front of 7 miles.

4. We have already captured 5 448 prisoners, including 125 Officers. Up to date the capture of 8 guns, 10 T.M's and 36 machine guns has been reported.

5. In addition we have inflicted extremely heavy casualties on the enemy. Owing to losses during our preliminary bombardment he was forced to bring up 6 fresh Divisions. Since then 3 more Divs. have been withdrawn shattered.
Thus, in a fortnight, we have disposed of 7 or 8 Divs. and severely handled 10 more, several of which must be shortly withdrawn.

6. The Second Army on our right and the 1st French Army on our left have been as successful as ourselves. The French captures to date number 157 prisoners, and 3 guns. The Second Army have also taken 390 prisoners and several machine guns.

7. Despite the weather on the day of the battle we shot down 5 enemy machines and 1 balloon, losing only one machine ourselves.

(sd) R.T. COLLINS, Lt-Colonel,
for Major-General, G.S.

17th. Bn. SHERWOOD FORESTERS.

CASUALTIES.

Attached 117th L.T.M. Battery.

76149.	Pte.	Dyer	M.	Wounded	31.7.17.
27186.	Pte.	Pepper	C.	"	"
54304.	Pte.	Wilmot	J.	"	"
65287.	Pte.	Dewsbury	J.	"	"
70080.	Pte.	Buxton	H.	Missing	"

Attached 117th Brigade H.Q.

11569.	Cpl.	Addington	J.	Wounded	31.7.17.
71573.	Pte.	Stanhope	J.	"	"
5659.	Pte.	Holmes	A.	"	"
28087.	Pte.	Ward	H.W.	"	"
76156.	Pte.	Ewen	D.	"	"
25565.	Pte.	Blagg	A.E.	Missing	"

Attached 117th Machine Gun Company.

36099.	Pte.	Roberts	J.	Wounded	1.8.17.
29326.	Pte.	Bannister	J.	"	"
70281.	Pte.	Bailey	L.	"	31.7.17.
32308.	Pte.	Edis	F.	"	"
30983.	Pte.	Heeley	G.	"	"
54880.	Pte.	Lockley	G.D.	Killed in Action	"
45357.	Pte.	Booth	A.	"	"
32066.	Pte.	Scott	W.	"	"

XVIII CORPS.

ORDER OF THE DAY.

The Field Marshal Commanding-in-Chief today called upon me for the purpose of congratulating the XVIIIth Corps and the 39th and 51st. Divisions upon their successful operations yesterday.

These operations resulted in the defeat of several hostile divisions, the capture by this Corps of 1763 prisoners and the death of a large number of other Germans.

Success was due to the gallantry and endurance of the Officers and the troops, to the precision with which they carried out their fighting programme from start to finish and to the admirable manner in which the Field and Heavy Artillery performed their allotted tasks.
I wish to add my own appreciation of the zeal and energy displayed by all ranks throughout the period of training previous to the 3rd BATTLE OF YPRES.

1st August 1917.

Ivor Maxse. Lieutenant General,
Commanding XVIII Corps.

M.4.

S P E C I A L   O R D E R
BY
MAJOR-GENERAL G.J.CUTHBERT, C.B., C.M.G., COMMANDING 39th DIVISION.

August 20th 1917.

39th Division -   I have been ordered to proceed to England to take up the Command of a Division there, and, in bidding you farewell, I wish to thank all ranks most sincerely for your invarying gallantry, good conduct and soldierly spirit, which has made the whole period of my Command one of intense pride and pleasure - You have never failed to give of your best, willingly, cheerfully and fully ; either when training, in battle, or when holding the line - Rest you have never known, but your good spirit and great fighting qualities have successfully carried you through all fatigue, dangers, and difficulties - Memories of your victories on the ANCRE, at SCHWABEN REDOUBT, at STUFF TRENCH, and at ST. PIERRE DIVION, together with the recent third battle of YPRES, will always remain my proudest recollections, and I know that in future, as in the past, your one thought will always be for the honour and good name of the Division and the Blue-and-White badge - Goodbye-

(SD) G.CUTHBERT,
Major-General,
Commanding 39th Division.

Army Form C. 2118.

WAR DIARY
or
INTELLIGENCE SUMMARY

(Erase heading not required.) 17th (SERV.) Bn. SHERWOOD FORESTERS. (Welbeck Rangers)

37 1/A 1/8

18.C

Place	Date	Hour	Summary of Events and Information	Remarks and references to Appendices
TRENCHES STEENBEEK	Aug 6/17 19		Yesterday the enemy all help to at Mrs M of the Battalion. Greatest day we [have] had on [platoon], the heaviest. No enemy offered much to head toil of this 2 years a rest of [miles]. 91 was a twice test and worthy of the SHERWOOD FORESTERS Record. The day is very bad, and the ground fell wet and mud. We have seemed to [advance] of the STEENBEEK (Map Reference SHEET 2 C 11 b 9 1 to C 11 b 3 7) and have dug in. The enemy is [preparing] to [counter] attack. The Battalion is quite prepared to resist to end. The Battalion Staff Worked hard work. The enemy [forn] the counter attack that are expected much to [find] shots shelling in where the hard is worth. The Battalion are splendid and though to the top by getting more NCOs such a [dirty] condition.	M (Guerry) M(Guerry)

Cmdg. 17th (S) Bn. SHERWOOD FORESTERS

Lt. Colonel,

WAR DIARY
or
INTELLIGENCE SUMMARY

Army Form C. 2118.

(Erase heading not required.) 17th (SERV.) Bn. SHERWOOD FORESTERS (Notts & Derby)

Place	Date	Hour	Summary of Events and Information	Remarks and references to Appendices
TRENCHES ST PIERRE DIVION	3rd		The Battalion then held the ground won. The Grenadier Guards are being had also that captured had moved up. One Company Sherwood in Lancaster Regiment on the right of the Battalion. Relieved at night by Lancashires. Battalion moved back to Clairfaye Farm Huts and bus met to convey Battalion to Raincheval arriving at about 3 a.m. (one man missing and 12 wounded Casualties.)	M.W.H.
-do-	4th		The Battalion then held the Bn. formed up and was conveyed in Lorries to Perdu part where they had breakfast and the returned by way of CAMBRIDGE STREET to Camp at lone tree Camp. Reveillé Roll Call Breakfast at 10 a.m. the Battalion left to march (exception of the Lewis Gun (Corps) Refreshers & one left in 8th Corps) to the Railhead & Hon. (Corps Refreshers Sheet 57 C 15 d and C 22 a.)	M.W.H

J. W. Howard Lt. Colonel,
COMDG. 17th (S) Bn. SHERWOOD FORESTERS.

WAR DIARY
INTELLIGENCE SUMMARY

(Erase heading not required.)

17th (SERV.) Bn. SHERWOOD FORESTERS.

Army Form C. 2118.

Instructions regarding War Diaries and Intelligence Summaries are contained in F.S. Regs., Part II. and the Staff Manual respectively. Title Pages will be prepared in manuscript.

Place	Date	Hour	Summary of Events and Information	Remarks and references to Appendices
OLD GERMAN FRONT LINE	Aug 5/17		Majority) Battalion did not (Minority) get much sleep, being as they had not been exhausted, but they took time and an inch of ground captured now. The enemy are shelling us very much in the position. We are relieved to-day at 5.30 pm by 4/7th BERKS REGT. and move to CANAL BANK Hut Top Sector. (see 29th July 1917.)	
CANAL BANK	6th		Relief Battalion being changing & cleaning of all Clothing available. Battalion is in a comfy Camp, bathing and cleaning up arms.	
—do—	7th		Battalion marched by Route March, Rail and Motor Bus to LE ROUKLOSHILLE. (Map Reference Sheet 29. X.1.a.3.3.) Commenced 5.45 am arrived 11.30 am. Battalion in Tents.	

COMDG. 17th (S) Bn. SHERWOOD FORESTERS

Army Form C. 2118.

WAR DIARY
or
INTELLIGENCE SUMMARY

(Erase heading not required.) 17th (SERV.) Bn. SHERWOOD FORESTERS. *(12th Page)*

Place	Date 1917	Hour	Summary of Events and Information	Remarks and references to Appendices
LE POURRES AIRE -Captured	Aug 28th Captured		Official Entrance to British. The Battalion was at rest at the Blort it to bury from Country.	Y/Aug 28
-do-	-do-		Police Employed. Cleaning and washing and employing. I Captain I Battalion G.O. Put in Brigade Order for speech by Divisional General. Lyn Pres 9 Guthrie OB CMG has Push Div! was sleep to the Bagine sent thin on he was they first of are open to join the 17th Duty in Division. The Division is for the formed for the V Army to the 2nd Army under General (PLUMER and I york Corps under Lieut Genl [Sir T HYLWYND]	V/Aug 28
-do-	-do-	9h	Police Retain Cleaning up, Writing and enjoying day. another kit of Australia Reinforcements who had left 0.1.7 joined the Battalion during the afternoon. 3 J. J/8/17 were attached. See in appendices and numbers	N 1

.... Lt. Colonel
COMDG. 17th (8) Bn. SHERWOOD FORESTERS.

Army Form C. 2118.

WAR DIARY
INTELLIGENCE SUMMARY

(Erase heading not required) 17th (SERV.) Bn. SHERWOOD FORESTERS. (Welbeck Rangers)

Place	Date	Hour	Summary of Events and Information	Remarks and references to Appendices
LE ROUKLOS MINE Continued	Aug 9th		**MILITARY MEDAL** 18441 Pte BUTLER. T.S., 72357 Pte PORTER. F.A., 204316 Cpl DICKENSON. H., 27165 L.Cpl BERRY. W., 5134 Pte BULLOCK.G.W., 21372 Pte HEARDEN. H., 45560 Cpl SMITH. F.H., 20964 Sgt KOWBRIDGE. H., 32576 Pte MANE. F.H., 47275. Pte ALLWOOD. T. 28203 Cpl BOYDEN. W., 51168 Pte MARKHAM. F., 76392 Pte HENTY F.E. 31679 Pte WHARTON. W., 32117 Sgt ADAMS. H., 7203. Pte STEELE. H. 28009 Pte THOMAS. R, 3857 Cpl FOWLER T., 35656. Pte BRENNEN H., 60624 L.Cpl TURNER. W., 15513 Pte BRITTON. W., 71587 Pte RUDD. J.H. 24744 Pte EDWARDS. T. **BAR TO MILITARY MEDAL** 5171 Pte. SWALES. T.W.	Nominal
-do-	-10th-		Routine Batchelor 10th Para to a BRIGADE Parade for the General commanded General PLUMER the Corps Commander. Lieut-Col SURT. HOSKINS the Bn's BDR. Gen'l. The Army Commander inspected the Brigade. Men a form turn out.	Nominal

COMDG. 17th (S) Bn. SHERWOOD FORESTERS.

Army Form C. 2118.

WAR DIARY
or
INTELLIGENCE SUMMARY

(Erase heading not required.) 17th (SERV.) Bn. SHERWOOD FORESTERS. (William Rayford)

Place	Date	Hour	Summary of Events and Information	Remarks and references to Appendices
LE ROUKLOY HILL 9R continued.	Any 1917		The following Officers, W.O's N.C.O's and Men have been recognised for [illegible] [illegible] to the Field of duty in gallantry and devotion to duty. As action 31/7/17 to 7/8/17. DISTINGUISHED SERVICE ORDER. Captain & Adjt T. THORNTON. MILITARY CROSS Captain F A CORKER, Captain TWT MILNER, Captain N.R. TURNER, 2nd Lieut S.B.V. HUGHES, 2nd Lieut F.S. WILLIAMS, 2nd Lieut W.E. ELSE, 2nd Lieut M.E. DISNEY, Lieut N.A. DEXTER, 27155 8 H.Sgt. S. SMITH. DISTINGUISHED CONDUCT MEDAL. 43740 Pte HAQUE S. 70231 L/Sgt CLOWNEY J.H. 11143 Sgt BLACKHOUSE R. 28216 Pte COPLEY E. 58162 Pte VARDY E. 27937 Cpl HERRING J. 9391 C.S.M. FISHER A. 32253 L/Cpl HASTINGS A. MILITARY MEDAL 7309 L/Cpl DUNCAN. R.G. 18169 Pte JENKINSON S. 20123 Pte. ELSTON. S.	

[signature] Lt. Colonel
Comdg. 17th (S) Bn. SHERWOOD FORESTERS.

Army Form C. 2118.

WAR DIARY
INTELLIGENCE SUMMARY

(Erase heading not required) 17th (SERV.) Bn. SHERWOOD FORESTERS. (Bullock, Report)

Instructions regarding War Diaries and Intelligence Summaries are contained in F.S. Regs., Part II. and the Staff Manual respectively. Title Pages will be prepared in manuscript.

Place	Date 1917	Hour	Summary of Events and Information	Remarks and references to Appendices
LE ROUKLOS- HILLE	Aug 11th	11 a.m.	Routine Training under Company Commanders, duty Classes, Specialists Training with Specialist Officers. P.N. 12.30 p.m.	1/Mar 241
do	12th		Sunday. Divine Service 10.30 a.m. Specialist Classes cancelled. Specialist officers remained for 5th Army Commanders Congratulatory remarks to G.H.G. K.O.B. marshes and attached authorities S.R.U.s, on P.G.H.G.H. K.O.B.	1/Mar 24) Q.2
do	13th		Routine. Specialist Classes 7 to 11 a.m. Battalion moves by march Routs and Bus to RIDGEWOOD Map reference (Sheet 28. N.5 a) Battalion in Dugouts and Tents. We relieve 13th ROYAL SUSSEX Regt.	1/Mar 244
RIDGE WOOD	14th		Routine. The Battalion relieve the 3rd ROYAL FUSILIERS and become Support Battalion to W. KLIEN ZILLEBEKE SECTOR	1/Mar 244

.... Lt Colonel
COMDG. 17th (S) Bn. SHERWOOD FORESTERS

Army Form C. 2118.

WAR DIARY
INTELLIGENCE SUMMARY

(Erase heading not required.) 17th (SERV.) Bn. SHERWOOD FORESTERS. (Welbeck Rangers)

Place	Date	Hour	Summary of Events and Information	Remarks and references to Appendices
RIDGE WOOD	Aug 14th 1917		Map Reference (Sheet 28 I 3+) Battalion still in and about RHINE WOOD in German Dug-outs etc.	[illegible]
Continued				
TRENCHES	15th		Relieve Battalion Carrying R.E. material and supporting Bermondsey Hostile artillery intense.	[illegible]
do	16th		Relieve Trench Artillery [illegible] 2 Companies Carrying by day & night 2 Companies sheltering all night in the Salient Rue.	[illegible]
do	17th		Relieve Battalion relieve 16th SHERWOOD FORESTER'S in the front line Left Sub Section KLEIN ZILLEBEKE SECTOR Map Reference. (Sheet 28 J. I. 36.) "A" Coy Right front Coy, "C" Company Left front Company "D" Coy Left Support Coy.	[illegible]

.... Lt. Colonel
COMDG. 17th (S) Bn. SHERWOOD FORESTERS.

Army Form C. 2118.

WAR DIARY
or
INTELLIGENCE SUMMARY

(Erase heading not required.) 7th (SERV.) Bn. SHERWOOD FORESTERS (Nlbbis)

Place	Date	Hour	Summary of Events and Information	Remarks and references to Appendices
TRENCHES	Aug 17th 1917		"B" Company Regt. Support Company.	Map ref 41
Cinnamon	—do— 18th		Rather Active Artillery leny Active. 2/Lieut R.W. CLARK killed. Lieut W.E. BOSWORTH wounded at duty.	Map ref 41
—do—	—do— 19th		Rather Active Artillery leny Active. Battalion relieved by 11 H&LI Regt. relief Complete 11.35 pm on being reld relief taking into Consideration the old French line. Battalion move to Camp at RIDGE WOOD. Map reference See August 17th 1917. Casualties during Past 3 days 1 officer killed 1 officer wounded, 5 other ranks killed 16 other ranks wounded.	Map ref 41

J. M. Marsland Lt. Colonel,
COMDG. 17th (S) Bn. SHERWOOD FORESTERS.

2449 Wt. W14957/Mgo 750,000 1/16 J.B.C. & A. Forms/C.2118/12.

WAR DIARY
INTELLIGENCE SUMMARY

(Erase heading not required) 17th (Serv.) Bn. SHERWOOD FORESTERS (Welbeck Rangers)

Army Form C. 2118.

Place	Date	Hour	Summary of Events and Information	Remarks and references to Appendices
RIDGE WOOD	1917 Aug 20th		Routine. Battalion cleaning up and inspection. Major General E. FEETHAM C.B. C.M.G. assumed Command 39th Divsion to day vice Major General Sir T. CUTHBERT C.B. C.M.G. to England. Special Order by Major Gen CUTHBERT attached in appendice — do — Commander of II ARMY — do —	*[illegible]* P.1 P.2
— do —	21st		Routine. Battalion training under Company Officers. Specialists Classes. Working Parties.	*[illegible]*
— do —	22nd		Routine. Battalion training under Company Officers. Specialists Classes. Working Parties.	*[illegible]*

[signature]
COMDG. 17th (S) Bn. SHERWOOD FORESTERS .... Lt. Colonel.

Army Form C. 2118.

WAR DIARY
INTELLIGENCE SUMMARY

(Erase heading not required.) 17th (SERV.) Bn. SHERWOOD FORESTERS.

Instructions regarding War Diaries and Intelligence Summaries are contained in F. S. Regs., Part II. and the Staff Manual respectively. Title Pages will be prepared in manuscript.

Place	Date 1917	Hour	Summary of Events and Information	Remarks and references to Appendices
RIDGE WOOD	Aug 23rd		Routine Battalion training under Company Heads. Specialists Classes. Working Parties. Battalion relieved the 13th Royal Sussex Regt. at BOIS CONFLUENT hut reference SHEET 28. (O.L.E.) relief complete 6.45pm. Battalion then in BRIGADE SUPPORT to my 1st Battalion with HOLLEBEKE SECTOR.	Appx 23/1 Appx 23/1
BOIS CONFLUENT	24th		Routine, Specialists Classes, Working Parties & enemy being quiet	Appx 24/1
-do-	25th		Routine, Specialists Classes. Working Parties to front line, day & night.	Appx 25/1
-do-	26th		Routine, Specialists Classes, Working Parties to front line, day & night.	Appx 26/1

.... Lt. Colonel,
COMDG. 17th (S) Bn. SHERWOOD FORESTERS

Army Form C. 2118.

WAR DIARY
INTELLIGENCE SUMMARY
(Erase heading not required.) 17th (SERV.) Bn. SHERWOOD FORESTERS. (Welbeck Rangers)

Place	Date 1917	Hour	Summary of Events and Information	Remarks and references to Appendices
BOIS CONFLUENT	Aug 29th		Routine Inspection of all Lewis Guns & Cooking Pots etc by C.O. The weather was fine during the day but heavy rain fell and thunderstorm Br[ig]. Gen. Wollen inspected Huts etc. To Battalion relieve the 10 K.R. SHERWOOD FORESTERS in the Right Sub-Section of the HOLLEBEKE SECTOR maps reference (SHEET 28 0.11.z & 0.12.a.) "B" Coy Reg Ut Front Ln, "D" Coy left front line "A" Coy Support Coy "C" Coy Reserve Coy Relief Complete 12.5 am 29/8/17	Map Ref
TRENCHES	30th		Artie Situation Quiet. A very Bad Saty front line shelled these Huts around pond & bruis.	Map ref
-do-	31st		Artie. Situation Quiet. A Coy harassed shelling of notes artillery in the support area. Z" Battalion to relieve by the 10th Bn. York & Lancasters. Brigade Major to	Map Ref

17th (S) Bn. SHERWOOD FORESTERS.

Army Form C. 2118.

WAR DIARY
INTELLIGENCE SUMMARY

of 17th (SERV.) Bn. SHERWOOD FORESTERS.

(Welbeck Paget)

Place	Date 1917	Hour	Summary of Events and Information	Remarks and references to Appendices
TRENCHER	Aug 29th		CHIPPEWA CAMP Map Reference (M.6a47) Relief by March Route and Patris arriving about 3 am 30/4/17. This Coy to be a key post one. Relief Complete 10.45 am.	Map ref
Ankwel?				War Diary
CHIPPEWA CAMP	30th		Ranks cleaning up and Inspections.	
— do —	31st		Ranks Coys under the Coy Officer for training. Special Speeches under Specialist Officers. Instr by Bn O/r eng at and O Coy Emperor in Musketry under by Lt Emeij Bn Musk Officer	War Diary

COMDR. 17th (S) Bn. SHERWOOD FORESTERS

COPY.

ROUTE ORDERS
by
Brigadier General G.A. ARMYTAGE, D.S.O.
Commanding 117th Infantry Brigade.

August 12th 1917.

SPECIAL ORDER. 1010. The Commander of the Fifth Army wishes to thank all ranks of the 39th Division for their splendid work on July 31st 1917. Practically all objectives were taken and the Division has every right to be proud of its achievements on that day.

         X   XX   X

D.H. Cohen, Capt., for Captain,
Brigade Major,
117th Infantry Brigade.

12.8.17.

Army Form C. 2118.

WAR DIARY
or
INTELLIGENCE SUMMARY

(Erase heading not required.) 17th (SERV.) Bn. SHERWOOD FORESTERS.

Place	Date	Hour	Summary of Events and Information	Remarks and references to Appendices
CHIPPENHAM CAMP	Sept 1917 /31		Routine of training under "Specialist" training minor Company, Street, Sheperd's under "Specialist officer" Inspection of C & D Companies by hatching dress by the C.O. The following have been awarded the Military Medal for gallantry and devotion to duty in the 31.7.1917. 11646 A.C.S.M. Ribackhouse. 70231. Sgt. T.W. Olney. 70954 Sgt. H. Lowbridge. 27307. Cpl. T. Hickling. 9391. A/C.S.M. A. Fisher. 20946. Cpl. J. Dickenson. 73094. Cpl. R.G. Duncan. 32253. R.Cpl. A. Hastings. 60674. L/Cpl. W. Turner. 28293. L/Cpl. W. Boyden. 27185. R/Cpl. E. Berry. 70357. L/Cpl. F. Porter. 43740. Pte. S. Hague. 56663. " E. Vardy. 18157. " S. Tenkinson. 20422. " G. Elston. 18441. " J.S. Butler. 3566 " F. White. 47275. " T. Allwood. 20392. " F.F. Henry. 15513. " W. Britton. 24744. " T. Edwards.	

Army Form C. 2118.

WAR DIARY
INTELLIGENCE SUMMARY
(Erase heading not required) 7th (SERV.) Bn. SHERWOOD FORESTERS. (Matthew Carroll)

Instructions regarding War Diaries and Intelligence Summaries are contained in F. S. Regs., Part II. and the Staff Manual respectively. Title Pages will be prepared in manuscript.

Place	Date	Hour	Summary of Events and Information	Remarks and references to Appendices
CHIPPAWA CAMP (Ontario)	Sept 1st 1917		No. 31679 Pte W. WHARTON Pte 49394 Pte W.F. ALLCOCK Reed on a splendid record and a fitting memorial for the Battalion (2nd) Month the 31st August 1917.	N(att.24)
do	2nd		Sunday. Parke Divine Service. The Battalion's 3 days left ruts are at No9 Distributing Point on the firsts of the Shield GREEN & CHESAPEAKE (Regimental Colours) fulfilling BLACK + GREEN.	N(att.24)
do	3rd		Route Companies Training under Company Officers. Specialists under Specialists Officers. The following men is awarded the Distinguished Conduct Medal for gallantry and devotion to duty on the 31.7.17. No 28218 Private E COPLEY.	N(att.24)

Lt. Colonel
SHERWOOD FORESTERS

WAR DIARY
INTELLIGENCE SUMMARY

(Erase heading not required.) 17th (SERV.) Bn. SHERWOOD FORESTERS. (Welbeck Rangers)

Army Form C. 2118.

Place	Date 1916	Hour	Summary of Events and Information	Remarks and references to Appendices
CHIPPEWA CAMP.	Sept 4th		Routine. Battalion Parade under C.O. for Arm Drill. One hour. Battalion Parade at 2.30 p.m. and move by Route march to STEENVOORDE AREA. Battalion billeted in Camp etc. Very Scattered. But Ref. Map reference Sheet 27 K 25. C. 8. 8. Further heavy rain in lieu of march. Feel N.n. in Good Marching Condition though of Wet Trenches.	
STEEN-VOORDE	5th		Routine. Battalion Cleaning up and Inspections.	
—do—	6th		Routine. Route marching before Breakfast. Training by Companies under Company Officers, Specialists under Specialist Officers. Special Parade from C in C. SIR Douglas HAIG to Sir Hubert GOUGH on bad work operation attacking hay harvest	Q 1

Army Form C. 2118.

WAR DIARY
or
INTELLIGENCE SUMMARY

(Erase heading not required.) 17th (SERV) Bn. SHERWOOD FORESTERS (Nottingham Regt)

Place	Date 1917	Hour	Summary of Events and Information	Remarks and references to Appendices
STEEN-VOORDE	Sept 7th		Anti aircraft gun practice. Training for Company under Coy Officers. Specialist sub-classes (Specialist Officers). Battalion sports in the afternoon. Major A.D.H.E. PREVOST (Second in Command) acting Lieut Colonel to 17th K R R CORPS. in the Brigade attended the DISTINGUISHED SERVICE ORDER for gallantry and devotion to duty.	Harvey
—do—	8th		Route Training or Training Area in the vicinity of BUS de BEAUFORDE (Sheet 27 K 33-34) under the Company Officers.	Harvey
—do—	9th		Brigade Sports. Today for the second time in succession the Battalion won the Sports Trophy awarded for most Points. Prior to the sports, Maj-Gen E FEETHAM C.B. C.M.G presented Medal Ribbons to N.C.O's & men since July 3, 31	

2449 Wt. W14957/M90 750,000 1/16 J.B.C. & A. Forms/C.2118/12.

Army Form C. 2118.

WAR DIARY
~~INTELLIGENCE~~ SUMMARY

(Erase heading not required.)

17th (SERV) Bn. SHERWOOD FORESTERS. (Welbeck Rangers)

Place	Date 1917	Hour	Summary of Events and Information	Remarks and references to Appendices
STEEN-VOORDE	Sept 10th		Routine. Training on Training Area in the vicinity of BOIS de BEAUVOORDE (Sheet 27 K 33-34) under the Army Officer.	M. Loff
—do—	11th		Routine. Training on Training Area in the vicinity of BOIS de BEAUVOORDE (Sheet 27 K 33-34) under the Cmdy Officer.	Relief
—do—	12th		The Battalion relieved the 12th ROYAL SUSSEX REGT in the SHREWSBURY FOREST SECTOR. Moved by Bus. Battalion becoming (L 29 d) Bayside Support.	
TRENCHES	13th		Routine. Battalion on carrying party all night. Accommodation very bad.	
—do—	14th		Routine. Carrying parties. Situation Quiet.	
—do—	15th		Enemy shell fire very heavy in retaliation for our Barrages (Ruettes) 7 killed 11 wounded.) Batt relieved by 13th ROYAL SUSSEX R/r moved to bivouacs at N 9 b.	
N 9 b	16th		Routine. Cleaning up.	

COPY.   B.M./A.

                                              General Headquarters,
                                              British Army in the Field.
O.A. 800/18.   1st October 1917.

General Sir Hubert Gough, K.C.B., K.C.V.O.

        I desire to assure you and the Army under your Command,
that although recent bad weather conditions have hampered progress and
imposed great hardships on the troops, their efforts have nevertheless
already produced more important results.

        Tactically tactical, positions of most importance
covering a wide front have been won in spite of the most determined
resistance on the part of the enemy.

        When it is remembered with this is the degree to which the
enemy's powers of resistance are being used up, and the rapidity
with which his reserves are being exhausted, it will be seen that
far more has been accomplished than is apparent even from the
extent of territory already gained.

        In addition to the fact that the enemy has found it
necessary already to employ a large proportion of the whole of his
forces on the Western Front, in his attempts to stop our advance,
it is becoming evident that the drain on him in power is
outstripping his resources.

        For him everything is at stake in this battle. Failure to
stop our progress will shake the confidence of his Army, the trust
in it of the civil population of Germany, and the faith of his
Allies. With this knowledge he has concentrated his best troops to
oppose us and is throwing them into the battle at a rate which he
has not the means to continue for very long.

        In conveying to you personally, to your Staff, to the
Commanders and Staffs serving under you, and to your troops my
congratulations on all they have already accomplished, please
assure them that the prospect for the future is good, and that
their steady courage and determination in spite of bad weather
and great hardships have gone much towards bringing us nearer to
final victory.

                                              D. HAIG.
                                              Field-Marshal.

SECRET. 17th Bn. SHERWOOD FORESTERS. OPERATION ORDER No. 51.

Reference: Sheet 28 and Trench Maps.

INFORMATION. 1. (a) The enemy are holding the general line JEHU TRENCH — GREENBUG FARM by a series of posts with a strong point at J.25.d.3.9.
(b) This front is reported held by parts of the 395th Infy. Regt. and the 6th R.I.R. each with one Battalion in the front line, one Battalion in support in the valley of the BASSEVILLEBEEK, and one Battalion in reserve in the WARNETON LINE.
(c) The dividing line between these Battalions is an East and West line 100 yards S. of the northern edge of BULGAR WOOD.
(d) Both regiments belong to the 9th Reserve Division which is of Prussian-Polish extraction, but has always fought well. It has been in the line since about August 25th.

OBJECTIVE. 2. The Battalion will capture and consolidate the RED LINE between J.31.b.9.50.2.50. and J.26.c.4.25.9.50.

PLAN. 3. (a) The Battalion will advance from position of assembly on a Company Front in the following order :- A. Company, C. Company, D. Company., B. Company following in Support, on the following Compass Bearings,
A. Company, 116° M.
C. Company, 124° M.
D. Company, 112° M
(b) Front Line Companies in the following formations:-

1st. WAVE. Skirmishing platoon extended in two ranks to about 6 paces and covering the Company front.

2nd. WAVE. Two platoons following at a distance of about 20 paces in lines of half platoons in file at deploying interval.

3rd. WAVE. One platoon in line of half platoons in file at 50 paces distance and deploying interval.
N.B.
All Company Waves in line and working approximately by the left flank.

SUPPORT COMPANY. Will follow the Centre Company at 50 paces distance and in line of platoons in file and at deploying interval.
This Company remains and consolidates on the line J.31.b.3.50.6.00, to J.25.d.7.50.4.00.

(c) MACHINE GUNS. 2 Sections will accompany the Battalion and take up a position for the defence of the RED LINE.

(d) TRENCH MORTARS. 2 Mortars will accompany the Battalion and take up a position in the RED LINE and on the capture of the GREEN LINE will move forward there.

ASSEMBLY. 4.(a) The Battalion will assemble on tapes and white pegs on a bearing of 220° m. from the left. in the same formation as for the attack but closed up so that the depth, from front to rear, is not more than 75 yards and will be completed by ZERO — 2 hours.

2.

Platoon Commanders of the 1st. Two Waves will be given white finger posts which they will place in the ground showing their direction of advance at each halt, and carefully check by Compass.

(b) <u>MACHINE GUNS and TRENCH MORTARS</u>, allotted to the Battalion will assemble in the interval between the Battalion and the Battalion on our left.

(c) The Battalion will advance at ZERO: rear lines will halt when clear of enemy Barrage to get proper attacking distances.

BOUNDARIES.　5.　RIGHT FRONT COMPANY – J.31.d.8.75.8.00. inclusive to J.25.c.9.0. exclusive.
CENTRE COMPANY – J.25.C.9.0. inclusive to J.25.c.9.75.2.75.inclusive.
LEFT FRONT COMPANY – J.25.x.9.7.50. exclusive to J.25.d.1.5. inclusive.

RESERVES.　6.　No portion of the BLUE LINE Battalions will be employed to capture the RED LINE unless the original attack on it fails. In the event of an enemy attack after the capture of the BLUE LINE O.C. 16th Sherwood Foresters will have a direct call on 2 Companies of the Battalion i.e., B. and C. Companies. These Companies on the capture of the BLUE LINE will reconnoitre the routes. The remaining 2 Companies remaining in occupation of the RED LINE.

CONSOLIDATION.　7.　(a) Each objective will be consolidated by the construction of a shell hole position. The shell holes occupied by each platoon will be connected together, and the whole line wired.
(b) All captured enemy dugouts will be cleared and garrisoned.

ARTILLERY.　8.　(a) At ZERO the Creeping Barrage will open 150 yards beyond our present front line.
(b) It will lift (100 yards in each case) as follows :–
(i) Zero plus 3.
(ii) Zero plus 7.
(iii) Zero plus 11.
(iv) Zero plus 17 and every 6 minutes until it reaches the DOTTED RED (Protective Barrage) LINE.
(v) Zero plus 1 hour 20 mins. and every 8 minutes until it reaches the DOTTED BLUE (Protective Barrage) LINE.
(vi) Zero plus 3 hours 52 mins. and every 8 minutes until reaching the DOTTED GREEN (Protective Barrage) LINE.
(c) The arrival of the Barrage at each of these lines will be shewn by the firing of a proportion of Smoke Shell.
(d) A proportion of the Field Artillery will fire a rolling barrage behind the creeping barrage, and will put down a Smoke Screen along the ZANVOORDE Ridge.
(e) There will be a Field Artillery Liaison Officer for all Battalions at the Left Battn. H.Q. in the RAVINE from 12 noon on the day before the Attack. He will go forward to Battn. H.Q. at N.W. corner of BULGAR WOOD before 3 p.m. on Attack Day.

3.

R.E.

9. (a) A small party of engineers from the 227th Field Coy. R.E. will accompany each Company H.Q. carrying mobile charges for the destruction of the doors of enemy dugouts.
(b) The following strong points will be constructed on the night of the Attack Day by the 227th Field Coy. R.E. for the defence of the RED LINE.
 (i) At WELBECK GRANGE.
 (ii) At J.26.c.3.0.
 (iii) At J.26.a.4.0.

DISTINGUISHING MARKS.

10. (a) The Brigade Forward Party will wear white tape on their right shoulder straps.
(b) The Trench Mortar Battery will wear black and white ribbon.
(c) Engineers will wear white tape on each shoulder strap.
(d) Mopping up and Carrying parties will wear distinguishing marks laid down in S.S.135.

LIAISON.

11. (a) O.C. "A" Company will detail the following liaison parties for the 8th N. Staffs. 57th Brigade at the following points :-
J.31.b.35.50.
J.31.b.7.3.
J.32.a.0.2. (after advance to BLUE LINE has begun)
(b) These parties will establish posts which will not be withdrawn before ZERO plus 8 hours.

COMMUNICATIONS.

12. (a) The Contact Aeroplane will be distinguished by a black and white fuselage, and small black board on lower left plane, and will fly over the area of attack from ZERO to ZERO plus 5½ hours.
(b) Brigade Forward Station will be established at the N.W. corner of BULGAR WOOD, and an advanced station at J.28.c.6.1.
(c) From Front line Companies to Support Company by Runner, from there to Battalion H.Q. by Fullerphone and Runner. In the event of the Support Company moving forward the Relay Post and Advanced Signal Station at their H.Q. will not move.

FLARES.

13. Flares will be lit (by leading Troops only) when called for by the Aeroplane. This call will be a succession of "A's" on the Klaxon and one White Very Light.
Troops will be particularly on the look-out for these signals on reaching each successive objective.
Flares are to be lit at the bottom of trenches and shell holes. Flares which can be seen by the enemy Ground Observers form excellent ranging marks for his Artillery.
Leading Troops who are without Flares when they are called on, will attract the attention of the Aeroplane by other means, i.e. Waving their Steel Helmets. If they make no response they are liable to be mistaken for enemy.

DRESS AND EQUIPMENT.

14. Fighting order, waterbottles filled. All waterbottles will be filled by ZERO. (Two will be carried on the man.)
Every man will carry the following :-
(1) 1 pair Socks.
   Towel and soap.
   Canteen.
   One complete day's rations.
   Iron rations.
   Waterproof sheet.
   Box Respirator.
   P.H. Helmet (the best method is to carry this over the shoulder and under the belt without crossing the chest).
   Haversack.
   Entrenching tool.
   2 Sandbags on the belt in front and not behind.
   2 Flares Front Line) Except Runners.
   Companies only   )
(2) Lewis Guns will be carried slung to prevent Lewis Gunners being picked out by enemy snipers.
No maps of any description showing our trenches will be taken over.
All Officers will wear men's jackets and waterproof sheets in the battle, and no raincoats are to be taken.
Platoon Commanders to carry rifles and bayonets.
No Officers to carry Sticks.
Packs will be stored at the present Quartermaster's Stores.

STORES.

15. GRENADE No. 20.   4 man loads (8 per load) per Rifle Bombing Section.
    MILLS No. 23.   4 man loads (8 per load) per Bombing Section.
    RIFLE GRENADE   1 per man of Rifle Bombing
    CUPS.   Section, Bombing Section, and 1 per Bucket.
    5 Blanks in a section of a Bandolier worn on the outside in front of the right bottom corner of coat.
    S.A.A.   One extra Bandolier per man exclusive of Runners.
    1" VERY LIGHTS.   12 per Company for Signalling.
    VERY LIGHT   6 per Company.
    PISTOLS 1".
    SHOVELS.   50% of every platoon will carry shovels with a proportion of picks.
    AUTHORISED STORES. All Authorised Stores as per Establishment will be carried.

DUMPS.

16. The following will be the situation of Dumps at ZERO :-
(a) RIFLE DUMP. Near RAVINE with one day's supply of S.A.A., Grenades, R.E. material, Rations and Water.
(b) SHERWOOD DUMP at ZWARTELEEN with another day's supply.
(c) 2 Companies 116th Brigade will carry forward RIFLE DUMP to the vicinity of the BRIGADE FORWARD STATION at ZERO plus 4 hours. This will be known as FORWARD DUMP.
Ammunition will be issued from it to any Platoon or Company.

5.

MEDICAL.	17.	R.A.P. at No. 1. Dugout, RAVINE. Further Orders will be issued later.
PRISONERS.	18.	All arms will be removed at once. Documents will be taken from Officers only. Escorts will be 5 men for 100 prisoners. All prisoners will be sent to Battalion H.Q.
SYNCHRONISATION.	19.	Watches will be synchronised at Battalion H.Q. at 7 p.m. daily.
ZERO.	20.	ZERO hour will be notified later.
REPORTS.	21.	To Battalion H.Q. at Nos. 2, 3 and 4 Dugouts, RAVINE.
NOTE.		Assembly will be carried out in silence, after assembly there will be no movement of any kind. Bayonets will be fixed at ZERO plus 2 minutes. Report of Assembly complete to Battalion H.Q. immediately on Assembly.

ACKNOWLEDGE.

(sd) F.D. Collen. Capt & A/Adjt.
18th September 1917.   17th Sherwood Foresters.

Copies to:-
- 117th Infantry Brigade   1
- 16th Sherwood Foresters   1
- 16th Rifle Brigade   1
- 9th N. Staffs.   1
- Commanding Officer   -
- O.C. A.B.C.D.HQ. Coys.   5
- Signalling Officer   1
- Medical Officer   1
- Adjutant   1
- War Diary   2
- Office Copy   1

"A" Form.
MESSAGES AND SIGNALS.

Army Form C.2121 (In pads of 100.)

Copy.

TO	16th Sherwood Foresters.	16th Rifle Bde.
	17th ditto.	117th M.G.Coy.
	17th K.R.R.C.	117th T.M.Battery.

Sender's Number.	Day of Month.	In reply to Number.	
* B.M/A166.	21.9.17.		AAA

Following telegram received from M.G.C. AAA
I congratulate you, your staff and the troops
under your Command on the great success you have
achieved today under difficult circumstances AAA
In forwarding this message the Brigadier wishes
to congratulate and thank all ranks for the
brilliant work they did yesterday.

From 117th Brigade.

E.Page. Capt.

"A" Form.
MESSAGES AND SIGNALS.

Army Form C.2121 (in pads of 100.)

TO { COPY.

Sender's Number.	Day of Month.	In reply to Number.	AAA
* B.M. 163.	30/9/17.		

ARTHUR wire begins AAA Following from Corps begins AAA Following received from Second Army to Lieut. General Sir T. Morland Commanding 10th Corps AAA Please accept and convey to your Divisions my hearty congratulations on the fresh success they have achieved today AAA From General Plumer AAA Ends AAA

From E.R. 56

R. Hall Capt.

"A" Form, MESSAGES AND SIGNALS.

Army Form C.2121 (in pads of 100.)

TO	16th Sherwood Foresters.	16th Rifle Brigade.
	17th ditto.	117th M.G. Coy.
	17th K.R.R.C.	117th T.M. Battery.

Sender's Number: *B.M./A169.
Day of Month: 21.9.17.

AAA

ARTHUR wire begins AAA The Major General Commanding has been directed by the Army Commander Second Army to convey to all ranks of the Division his appreciation of the manner in which the Division carried out the operations on the 20th September.

From 117th Brigade.

R. Hall. Capt.

REPORT on OPERATIONS on
September 20th/21st, 1917.

The Battalion moved up to the SHREWSBURY FOREST Sector on the night of the 18/19th and held the line with 3 Companies in their Battle positions, one Company remained in LARCH WOOD and moved up the following night.
Considerable Casualties occured on the way up from Shell Fire. The position of Deployment was successfully reconnoitred and taped out.

2.40 a.m.
Assembly of Battalion was complete on, was carried out on tapes about 70 yards East of the RAVINE on a bearing of 220° M. No Casualties occured during this manoeuvre.

5.40 a.m.
The Advance commenced on our Objective (THE RED LINE). The Enemy's reply to our Barrage was very prompt and he put a heavy Barrage down in NO MAN's LAND from which considerable casualties occured.
Opposition was at first met with between JULES FARM and BULGAR WOOD from enemy lying up in fortified shellholes. These were dealt with by our Lewis Gun fire. There was also considerable sniping from these positions and JORDAN TRENCH.
The Right Front Company were temporarily held up by strong opposition from Dugouts at WELBECK GRANGE but these were dealt with, with Rifle Grenades and Lewis Gun fire,and quickly overcome.
On the Left the Enemy put up a good deal of resistance from Dugouts on N.W. corner of BULGAR WOOD. On Rifle Grenades and Lewis Gun Fire being brought to bear on this point and with co-operation of the Centre Company these dugouts were captured, prisoners being taken and many killed.

5.55 a.m.
Support Company reached their Objective and consolidation started.

6.8 a.m.
Assaulting Companies reached their Objective and the consolidation commenced of the RED LINE.
During the Advance of the 16th Bn. Sherwood Foresters from the RED LINE to the BLUE it was noticed by our Support Company that small parties of the enemy were retiring and heavy Lewis Gun fire was able to be brought to bear on the Ridge in front, over the heads of the Advancing troops and it is believed several casualties were inflicted on the enemy by this fire also greatly assisting the advance.
Communication was established along the line and with both Battalions on our flanks, Support Company also reconnoitring positions forward.
At this period the enemy Machine Guns were very active from the Right Flank. Snipers were also very active from our Left Front, CHATSWORTH CASTLE and Dugouts in the BLUE LINE, most of this fire was very erratic.

7.45 a.m.
One platoon of Support Company was sent forward to reinforce Right Front Company who had suffered considerable casualties.
During this period shelling over the whole area was intermittent.

– 2 –

11.15 a.m. The Centre Company ("C" Company) which was after the capture and consolidation of the BLUE LINE under the immediate call of the O.C. 16th Bn. Sherwood Foresters, was ordered up by him into Close Support just in rear of the BLUE LINE where a position was taken up and consolidated.

5.10 p.m. O.C. "C" Company observed the enemy concentrating on the Ridge and in SUNKEN ROAD between points 16, 04 and 60 and in trench between 08 and 05, he at once sent this information back to O.C. 16th Bn. Sherwood Foresters and then personally advanced up with a Lewis Gun and opened fire on the enemy dispersing the enemy and inflicting heavy casualties. He estimated that at least 50 of them were hit. The Artillery then opened and the dispersion was completed.

7.20 p.m. Concentration of the enemy was again noticed at these points and S.O.S. was sent up by 16th Bn. Sherwood Foresters, "D" Company at once also being ordered to reinforce the front line. On the Artillery opening the concentration was again dispersed and no further movement was seen at these points.

The Artillery Barrage throughout was a great improvement on that of the 31st July 1917.

The following are the amount of Prisoners and Machine Guns captured during the operations :-

Machine Guns.   2.

A. Company.   34. Prisoners.
B. Company.   Nil.   "
C. Company.   42.   "   (Including 1 Officer).
D. Company.   40.   "

    Total,   116. Prisoners (including 1 Officer)

    Total,   2. Machine Guns.

23rd September 1917.   Cmdg. 17th Sherwood Foresters. Lt. Col.

R 3

17th Bn. SHERWOOD FORESTERS.

CASUALTIES 20.9.1917.

KILLED IN ACTION.
2nd.Lt. T. Bond.   20.9.17.
2nd.Lt. F.H. Williams.   do

DIED OF WOUNDS.   21.
2nd.Lt. T. Bracewell.   20.9.17.

WOUNDED.
Capt. W. . Burns.   20.9.17.
2nd.Lt. G.   .   21.9.17.

KILLED IN ACTION.

42125.	Sgt.	Coulo			7121.	L/Cpl.	Jeffreys	J.
7287.	L/Cpl.	Todd			28133.	L/Cpl.	Morton	
21221.	Pte.	Atterby			51811.	Pte.	Mason	
2478.	Pte.	Hobson			71246.	Pte.	Rothwell	
					235098.	Pte.	Wright	C.
77207.	Pte.	Casterton			7775.	L/Cpl.	Hobbs	
	Pte.	Potter			52281.	Pte.	Taylor	J.J.
	(19.9.17.)				(19.9.17.)			
72177.	Pte.	Ro			30129.	Pte.	Ripley	

DIED OF WOUNDS.

11046.	Sgt.	Redhouse			71507.	Pte.	Ladd	J.
7504.	Pte.	Oliver						
78811.	Pte.	Turn						
7 .	L/Cpl.	Spicer						
	(19.9.17.)							

WOUNDED.

8585.	CSM.	Siddons	H.	71507.	Pte.	Grundy	A.
90008.	Sgt.	Clarp	W.	27205.	Pte.	Gregory	C.
71077.	Sgt.	Gall	H.	71506.	Pte.	Griffiths	J.W.
57590.	Cpl. x	B.	18157.	Pte.	Jenkinson	S.
60134.	L/Cpl.	Turner	J.S.	71971.	Pte.	Martin	J.
27202.	L/Cpl.	Tootell	W.H.	9503.	Pte.	Middleton	L.G.
53210.	Pte.	Ancliffe	T.B.	24001.	Pte.	Powe	W.T.C.
91051.	Pte.	Sanders	H.	94429.	Pte.	Williams	W.O.
70034.	Pte.	Robinson	G.	15349.	Pte.	Smith	J.

23121.   Pte. Robinson E.H.

26957.   Pte. Bateman   A.
28256.   L/Cpl. Hatton   A.
20323.   Pte. Maltby   J.H.   235089. Pte. Pratt   F.L.
190688. Pte. Marsh   H.   268873. Pte. Sparrow   A.

47544.   Pte. Borough   J.
15361.   Pte. Green   J.   59658.   Pte. Pyne   W.
                               235093. Pte. Speight   A.

70576. Pte. Tongue   A.   71193. Pte. Yeomans   H.
(1914.)

LIST OF CASUALTIES.

17th (S) Bn. Notts & Derby.

| 42085. | Pte. | Holdon | A. | Killed in Action | 20.9.17. |
| 73071. | Pte. | Snyder | | Wounded. | do |

117th Machine Gun Company.

| 950?. | Pte. | ??? | | Missing. | 20.9.17. |

Attached 117th Brigade H.Q.

7?50?.	Pte.	Sharpe	G.A.	Missing.	20.9.17.
59417.	Pte.	Jackson	J.	Wounded.	do
59131.	Pte.	Dunn	C.	Wounded.	do
7?20?.	Pte.	Page		Wounded.	do

Attached 227th Field Coy. RE.

87711. Pte. Smith G.W. Wounded 24.9.17.

Lt. Colonel,
COMDG. 17th (S) Bn. SHERWOOD FORESTERS.

WAR DIARY
INTELLIGENCE SUMMARY

17th (SERV.) Bn. SHERWOOD FORESTERS. (NELBEEK RANGERS)

Army Form C. 2118.

Place	Date	Hour	Summary of Events and Information	Remarks and references to Appendices
Camp No 9a	1917 Sept 17th		Routine. Coys under Company officers. The following officers have been awarded the Military Cross for gallantry & devotion to duty. CAPT F R TURNER. CAPT F.D. COLLEN.	Wx. appdx 1
~ do ~	18th		The Batt relieved 2 Coys of the 13th Bn ROYAL SUSSEX REGT, taking up Battle positions B Coy in LARCHWOOD (SHEET 28). C & D Coys took out assembly positions.	Wx rainy
~ do ~	19th		Trenches. Situation Quiet. Men packed close together & no movement to & about concentration being detected by hostile aircraft. 2Lt WILLIAMS killed.	Wx fine
~ do ~	20th		Assembly Complete at 2.40 AM. Slight moon & very dark night. No casualties occurred during assembly. The 2nd Army to which the 39th Division belong is going to Attack on a wide front. The following Appendices are marked & attached which give an accurate account of the plan & attack on the enemy position. Operation Orders. Report on Operations. List of Casualties. Congratulations from C in C	Wx. Cold & fine. R 1 R 2 R 3 R 4

2449 Wt. W14957/M90 750,000 1/16 J.B.C. & A. Forms/C.2118/12.

Army Form C. 2118.

WAR DIARY
or
INTELLIGENCE SUMMARY

(Erase heading not required.)

17th (Serv.) Bn. SHERWOOD FORESTERS (WELBECK RANGERS)

Place	Date 1917	Hour	Summary of Events and Information	Remarks and references to Appendices
TRENCHES KLEIN ZILLEBEKE	SEPT 21ST		Yesterday the Battalion gained every objective yet in spite of strong resistance of groups of enemy in shell holes. We held it all day. The enemy formed up for three counter attacks but were beaten off each time & dispersed by our Artillery fire. Hostile shelling on forward area very heavy.	
~ do ~	22nd		Battalion still holds the ground captured. We are relieved tonight by the 1/1st HERTS REGT & proceed to BROOK CAMP (N10d) by Bus. Relief complete by 12.15 AM.	
BROOK CAMP	23rd		Reach Camp at 4 A.M. Routine. Coys under Company Commanders.	
~ do ~	24th		Routine. Coys under Company Commanders.	

.... Lt. Colonel
Comdg. 17th (S) Bn. SHERWOOD FORESTERS

Army Form C. 2118.

WAR DIARY
or
INTELLIGENCE SUMMARY

(Erase heading not required.)

11th (SERV) Bn. SHERWOOD FORESTERS (WELBECK RANGERS)

Place	Date 1917	Hour	Summary of Events and Information	Remarks and references to Appendices
BROIL CAMP	Sept 25th		The following Officers, WOs, NCO's & men have been recommended for Honours & Awards as stated for gallantry & devotion to duty during the action Sept 20th to Sept 22nd 1917.	
			DISTINGUISHED SERVICE ORDER.	
			Captain J.W.J Millar.	
			MILITARY CROSS.	
			2nd Lieut W.E Boswell. 2nd Lieut. H.Bracewell. Lieut N.S. Temple. Captain B.J Ross. Lt N.L Dexter.	
			DISTINGUISHED CONDUCT MEDAL.	
			3457 Pte. J Bowler, 27118 Cpl. T. Holmes, 22367 Pte. G Warrington, 13496 L/Cpl.F. Wright.	
			MILITARY MEDAL	
			9685 Sgt. R.Teer. 266659 Pte J Mayfield, 31253 L/Cpl. A South, 20903 A/CSM E.Moore, 18966 Pte W.H Bower.	

Lt.Col.
Comdg. 11th (S) Bn SHERWOOD FORESTERS

Army Form C. 2118.

WAR DIARY
INTELLIGENCE SUMMARY
(Erase heading not required.)

17th (SERV.) Bn. SHERWOOD FORESTERS (NELOCK RANGERS)

Place	Date 1917	Hour	Summary of Events and Information	Remarks and references to Appendices
BRODIR CAMP	Sept 25th (cont)		MILITARY MEDAL (CONT) 23501 Pte. W. BUSTIN, 22320 Pte. T. GREAVES, 11820 Cpl. J. DRURY, 13737 Pte. H. NEAIL. 70362 Pte. W. RAYMENT. 71091 Pte. A. GARLICK. The Battalion moved to RIDGE WOOD at 7pm tonight.	
RIDGE WOOD	26th		100 men told off as stretcher-bearers to be attached to the 116th Bde & 118th Bde for operations.	
		8P.M.	The Battalion was called upon to support the 116th Bde in the TOWER HAMLETS sector. (Sheet 28 NW)	
TRENCHES	27th		All the companies in the front line to help consolidation. Very heavy shell fire. Capt. B.J. ROSS, & 2nd Lieut MASSEY wounded. Relieved by the 13th ROYAL FUSILIERS. A & D Coy remained behind to complete consolidation until 2A.M. On relief the Battalion proceeded by Bus to LOCRE HOF FARM (28 N.9.c.)	

2449 Wt. W14957/M90 750,000 1/16 J.B.C. & A. Forms/C.2118/12.

Army Form C. 2118.

WAR DIARY
INTELLIGENCE SUMMARY

17th (SERV) Bn. SHERWOOD FORESTERS (WELBECK RANGERS)

(Erase heading not required.)

Place	Date 1917	Hour	Summary of Events and Information	Remarks and references to Appendices
LOCRE HOF FARM	Sept 28th		Routine Battalion cleaning up. Total casualties for past 24 hours in the trenches 2 officers 45 O.R.	
do	29th		Routine Battalion cleaning up.	
do	30th		Brigade inspected by Divisional Commander in morning. Baths in afternoon	

Army Form C. 2118.

WAR DIARY
INTELLIGENCE SUMMARY

(Erase heading not required.) 17th (SERV.) Bn. SHERWOOD FORESTERS. (Welbeck Rangers)

Place	Date	Hour	Summary of Events and Information	Remarks and references to Appendices
LOCREHOF FARM.	OCT 1ST		Routine. Companies under Company Commanders.	17th (S) Bn Sherwood Foresters
do	2nd		Routine. Companies under Company Commanders. Firing on range.	17th (S) Bn. Sherwood Foresters
do	3rd		Routine. Companies under Company Commanders. Sgt McCredie (Brigade Staff) took Companies in Physical & Bayonet Training	17th (S) Bn. Sherwood Foresters
do	4th		Routine. Companies under Company Commanders. Lewis Guns firing on Range.	17th (S) Bn Sherwood Foresters
do	5th		Routine. Companies under Company Commanders.	17th (S) Bn Sherwood Foresters
do	6th		Routine. Companies under Company Commanders. Firing on Range.	17th (S) Bn Sherwood Foresters
do	7th		Routine. Church Service in Cinema LOCRE.	

Mulford ....Lt. Colonel,
COMDG. 17th (S) Bn. SHERWOOD FORESTERS

Army Form C. 2118.

WAR DIARY
or
INTELLIGENCE SUMMARY

(Erase heading not required.) 17th (SERV.) Bn. SHERWOOD FORESTERS. (Welbeck Rangers)

Instructions regarding War Diaries and Intelligence Summaries are contained in F. S. Regs., Part II. and the Staff Manual respectively. Title Pages will be prepared in manuscript.

160

Place	Date	Hour	Summary of Events and Information	Remarks and references to Appendices
LOCREHOF FARM.	8th		Companies under Company Commanders. Platoon football in afternoon.	7th Capt/Adjt
~ do ~	9th		Routine. Companies under Company Commanders. Football in afternoon.	7th Capt. Adjt
~ do ~	10th		Routine. Companies under Company Commanders. Battalion Bathing	7th Capt/Adjt
~ do ~	11th		Routine. Battalion Route March. Divisional General Inspected	7th Capt/Adjt
~ do ~	12th		Battalion Training. Companies under Company Commanders.	7th Capt/Adjt
~ do ~	13th		Routine. Company Officers reconnoitred Support line in TOWER HAMLET Sector (28. NW M.p).	7th Capt/Adjt
~ do ~	14th		Sunday. Voluntary Church Services.	7th Capt/Adjt
~ do ~	15th		Battalion moved by Route March to VYVERBEEK CAMP (N.9.9.5 Sheet 28 S.W.)	7th Capt/Adjt

..............Lt. Colonel,
COMDG. 17th (S) Bn. SHERWOOD FORESTERS.

Army Form C. 2118.

WAR DIARY
INTELLIGENCE SUMMARY
(Erase heading not required.) 17th (SERV.) Bn. SHERWOOD FORESTERS. (Welbeck Rangers)

Place	Date 1917	Hour	Summary of Events and Information	Remarks and references to Appendices
VYVERBEEK CAMP	Oct 16th		Routine. Companies under Coy Officers. NCOs Musketry class in afternoon.	h.S.T. 1544/A/A
~ do ~	17th		Routine. Companies under Coy Officers. NCOs Musketry class in afternoon.	h.S.T. 1544/A/A
~ do ~	18th		Routine. Companies under Coy Officers. NCOs Musketry class in afternoon.	h.S.T. 1544/A/A
~ do ~	19th	9-11am	Routine. Companies under Coy Officers. Relieved 14th Hants Regt. In support Tower Hamlets Sector. B.H.Q. - BODMIN COPSE (J.19.d.55.60). Map 28. N.W. B C & D in the line. A to Brigade School (M.4.C)	h.S.T. dired A/A
TRENCHES (TOWER HAMLETS)	20th		Trench Routine. 100 men cable burying. "A" moved to VOORMEZEELE.	h.S.T. 1544/A/A
~ do ~	21st		Trench Routine. 100 men cable burying.	h.S.T. 1544/A/A

..................Lt. Colonel,
COMDG. 17th (S) Bn. SHERWOOD FORESTERS

WAR DIARY
or
INTELLIGENCE SUMMARY

(Erase heading not required.) 17th (SERV) Bn. SHERWOOD FORESTERS (Welbeck Rangers)

Army Form C. 2118.

Place	Date 1917	Hour	Summary of Events and Information	Remarks and references to Appendices
Trenches (Tower Hamlets)	Oct 22nd		Minor operation by two Platoons of "B" Coy. under 2/Lt Higgins. Against Dugouts at J.21.d.7.9. Owing to the bad going and strong resistance of the enemy the objective was not gained. A considerable amount of valuable information was obtained	Hist Rnd A/4
do	23rd		Trench Routine. 200 men working on cable burying. A Coy rigging Front line Dumps	Hist Rnd A/4
do	24th		Trench Routine. 200 men working on cable burying. A Coy rigging to Front line Dumps. Relieved as follows :- "B" by A Coy 13 & 2nd Border Regt "C" by A " 2nd Queens "D" by C " 2/1 Manchesters Embussed at SHRAPNEL CORNER (I.20.a.8.6.) at 2.30 pm Oct 25th. Arrived VIERBEEK CAMP (N9.a.4.9.) (Ref Map 5/W) Coys arrived to camp 4.30 pm Oct 24th	Hist Rnd A/4
VIERSTRAAT No 2 Camp	25th		Cleaning up. Inspection under Coy officers.	Hist I Rnd A/4
do	26th		Cleaning up. Inspection under Coy officers. Battalion bathing.	Hist Rnd A/4
do	27th		Routine. Inspection under Coy officers.	Hist Rnd A/4
do	28th		Battalion moved by Route March to hut 2 Camp VIERSTRAAT WOOD (N.11.b.1.9.)	Hist Rnd A/4

Lt. Colonel
COMDG. 17th (S) Bn. SHERWOOD FORESTERS.

WAR DIARY
or
INTELLIGENCE SUMMARY

(Erase heading not required.)

17th (SERV.) Bn. SHERWOOD FORESTERS. (W. & L. BE 9F. KM 7ER)

Army Form C. 2118.

Place	Date	Hour	Summary of Events and Information	Remarks and references to Appendices
No 2 Camp VIERSTRAAT	1917 Oct 29		Routine. Companies under Company Commanders. N.C.O's musketry classes in afternoon.	SC 21 July
	30		Routine. Companies under Company Commanders. Young S/ficers and N.C.O's musketry classes. The Battalion has been awarded the following decorations for the action at BULGAR WOOD on September 20th. Bar to D.S.O. a/lt.Col. A.P.H. LE PREVOST. D.S.O (atta 7th K.R.R.C.) D.S.O. Major. J.R. WEBSTER. M.C. (atta 16th S.F.) Captain. J.W. MILLAR Captain. B.J. ROSS. Lieut. N.S. TEMPLE. Lieut. N.L. DEXTER. Military Cross. D.C.M. 27118 L/corporal. HOLMES. T. 3857 Pte. BOWLER. J. 13496 A/cpl. WRIGHT. F.H.	SC 21 July
	31st		Routine. Coys under Coy Commanders. Box Respirator drill at night. Musketry	SC 21 July

COMDG. 17th (S) Bn. SHERWOOD FORESTERS .... Lt. Colonel.

Army Form C. 2118.

WAR DIARY
or
INTELLIGENCE SUMMARY

(Erase heading not required.) 17th (SERV.) Bn. SHERWOOD FORESTERS.

Place	Date	Hour	Summary of Events and Information	Remarks and references to Appendices
No 2 Camp VIERSTRAAT	1917 Nov 1st		Routine during morning. Bn paraded at 2.30 P.M. (300 strong) under Major Cassy proceeded to LAREN WOOD TUNNELS. Three parties of 100 each work till 9 P.M. on trenches, throwing up breastwork drawing and carrying timber, bad conditions owing to mud and gas shelling.	
	2nd		Baths allotted to two companies morning. Remainder of Bn on P.T. and Yukon Pack drills under company commanders.	
	3rd		Companies under respective commanders. Routine. Communication drills for N.C.Os. Musketry and P.T.	
	4th		Divine Service at 10.30 A.M. Working party of 100 employed on burying R.E. material to MOUNT SORREL during morning.	
	5th		Battalion moves by march route to E CAMP ERWA CAMP (Chippewa) relieving over then hour 7 HERTS REGT. Move complete by 12.30 P.M. Remainder of day spent in cleaning up.	
CHIPPEWA CAMP.	6th		Routine days under company commanders.	

Lt. Colonel
Comdg. 17th (S) Bn. SHERWOOD FORESTERS

Army Form C. 2118.

WAR DIARY
or
INTELLIGENCE SUMMARY
(Erase heading not required.) 17th (SERV.) Bn. SHERWOOD FORESTERS. (Welbeck Rangers)

Instructions regarding War Diaries and Intelligence Summaries are contained in F.S. Regs., Part II. and the Staff Manual respectively. Title Pages will be prepared in manuscript.

Place	Date	Hour	Summary of Events and Information	Remarks and references to Appendices
CHIPPEWA CAMP	Nov 7th 1917		Battalion moved by Bus to SHRAPNEL CORNER. Thence by march route to front line. Relieved the 14th Hamps Regt in the Left front of TOWER HAMLETS SECTOR. Battn H.Q. at I.20 b.8.1. Relief complete 10 P.M.	MCC41
Trenches	8th		Quiet day in line. Weather fine.	MCC41
"	9th		Quiet day in line. Lewis gun team of "D" Coy hit by shell, 3 killed & 3 wounded.	MCC41
"	10th		Gas projectiles fired on LEWIS HOUSES. Front line stand down the operation. Very wet all day. Trenches all waterlogged & sides falling in. Relieved by 16th Bn SHERWOOD FORESTERS. Relief complete 3 A.M. Battalion in support in CANADA ST TUNNELS.	MCC41
CANADA ST TUNNELS	11th		Battalion on working parties. The tunnels are very wet & the men are in danger of contracting Trench Foot.	MCC41

[signature] Lt Colonel
Comdg 17th (S) Bn. SHERWOOD FORESTERS

Army Form C. 2118.

WAR DIARY
or
INTELLIGENCE SUMMARY

(Erase heading not required.)

1/4th (Staff Bn. SHERWOOD FORESTERS) (Notts & Derby)

Place	Date	Hour	Summary of Events and Information	Remarks and references to Appendices
CANADA ST TUNNELS	Nov. 1917 12th		All battalion out on Working Parties. The sick are much in evidence, there being over 70 on sick parade mostly with foot trouble.	WORK
"	13th		Relieved by 1/4th Bn HANTS REGT. Relief complete by 5 P.M. Bn relief proceeded by March Route to RIDGE WOOD "D" Camp (Sh.28a.23).	WORK
RIDGE WOOD	14th		Routine. Day spent in cleaning up. The Camp is very muddy making it impossible for the men to keep clean.	WORK
"	15th		Bn Battalion Bathed at BRASSERIE BATHS.	WORK
"	16th		Battalion Relieved 1/1st CAMBS REGT in the Right Sub Sector of the POLDERHOEK SECTOR. Bn H.Q. J21.a.0.5. (Sheet 28)	WORK
"	17th		Quiet day in trenches. Weather fine & conditions much improved.	WORK

Major Comdg 1/4 Bn SHERWOOD FORESTERS

Army Form C. 2118.

WAR DIARY
or
INTELLIGENCE SUMMARY

(Erase heading not required.)

(16) (Welbeck Rangers) 17th (Serv.) Bn. SHERWOOD FORESTERS.

Place	Date 1917	Hour	Summary of Events and Information	Remarks and references to Appendices
Trenches	Nov 18		Battn relieved by 16th Bn SHERWOOD FORESTERS & on relief proceeded to support line in BODMIN COPSE. Bn HQ Jig 6 central.	AAA
"	19th		Battalion on carrying parties. Carrying RE material from CANADA ST to front line. Bn HQ very heavily shelled on any movement being shown.	AAA
"	20th		Battalion relieved by 4/5th BLACK WATCH & on relief proceeded to CHIPPEWA CAMP by light Railway. Relief complete by 10 PM.	AAA
CHIPPEWA CAMP	21st		All in camp by 9.30 PM. Routine companies cleaning up & inspections by Company Officers	AAA
"	22nd		Routine companies under Company Officers	AAA
"	23rd		Routine Battalion Bathing at CHIPPEWA BATHS. Companies under Company Officers.	AAA

[signature] Lt Col
17th (Serv) Bn SHERWOOD FORESTERS

Army Form C. 2118

WAR DIARY
or
INTELLIGENCE SUMMARY

(Erase heading not required.)

17th (SERV.) Bn. SHERWOOD FORESTERS (Welbeck Rangers)

Instructions regarding War Diaries and Intelligence Summaries are contained in F. S. Regs., Part II. and the Staff Manual respectively. Title Pages will be prepared in manuscript.

Place	Date	Hour	Summary of Events and Information	Remarks and references to Appendices
CHIPPEWA CAMP.	Nov 24th		Battalion moved by Train & Much Route to Watou Area. Billets very scattered & most of men in tents	
WATOU	25th		Battalion relieved 18th Bn Manchester Regt at St Jean for work under X Corps Heavy Artillery. Battalion proceeded by Mech. Transport. Route to Poperinghe thence by train to Ypres. Battalion Headquarters at English Farm C 27 d 5.3. (Sheet 28)	
ENGLISH FARM.	26th		300 Men on working Parties under the VIII Corps Heavy Artillery Groups. Hours of Work 7.30 am to 2 pm.	
"	27th		250 Men on working Parties. Serving shells, making tracks to gun positions.	
"	28th		250 Men on working Parties under the VIII Corps Heavy Artillery. Same work as yesterday	

2449 Wt. W14957/M90 750,000 1/16 J.B.C. & A. Forms/C.2118/12.

Army Form C. 2118.

WAR DIARY
INTELLIGENCE SUMMARY

(Erase heading not required.)

17th (SERV.) Bn. SHERWOOD FORESTERS. (Welbeck Rangers)

Place	Date 1917	Hour	Summary of Events and Information	Remarks and references to Appendices
ENGLISH FARM.	Nov. 29th		Battalion on working parties. Light duty men employed on improving camp.	300 per
"	30th		Battalion on working parties for VIII Corps Heavy Artillery.	300 per

Confidential

[Stamp: 117TH INFANTRY BRIGADE No. BM/308]

The appendix referred to under Sect. 2nd is not as interesting as I hoped it would be.

Please return early.

R Stable?
Bm 117 Bde

Jan 6th

H.Q.
117th Regt Bengal.

Refer Appendix +
~~attached~~
Herewith
This was forgotten by me

Reece Lt/Adjt
2nd Sherwood Foresters

6.1.08
3.11. P.M.

Army Form C. 2118.

WAR DIARY
— OR —
INTELLIGENCE SUMMARY

(Erase heading not required.)

17th (SERV.) Bn. SHERWOOD FORESTERS. (Welbeck Rangers)

Vol 22

Place	Date	Hour	Summary of Events and Information	Remarks and references to Appendices
ENGLISH FARM	Dec 1st 1917		300 Men on various Working Parties under VIII Corps Heavy Artillery.	22.0
do	Dec 2nd		Battalion at ½ hours notice to reinforce front line. All working parties cancelled. The Battalion were not called upon. Copy of Operation Orders attached.	S.1.
do	3rd		Working Parties under Artillery. Divisional guard in front the Camp. During to many Lorries & Limbers of RE material as are obtained a the Camp is much improved.	
do	4th		Working Parties under Artillery.	
do	5th		Working Parties under Artillery.	

2449 Wt. W14957/M90 750,000 1/16 J.B.C. & A. Forms/C.2118/12.

Army Form C. 2118.

WAR DIARY
or
INTELLIGENCE SUMMARY

(Erase heading not required.) 17th (SERV.) Bn. SHERWOOD FORESTERS Welbeck (Sherwood)

Place	Date 1917	Hour	Summary of Events and Information	Remarks and references to Appendices
ENGLISH FARM.	Dec 6th		Battalion on Working Parties under VIII Corps Artillery.	HVB2
~do~	7th		Battalion moved to WATOU Area (Sheet 27). By train from ST JEAN MVV4 to ABEELE thence by march route. Bn HQ. K.16 central Sheet 27.	MVV4 HVV8A2
~do~	8th		Battalion cleaning up.	
~do~	9th		Battalion moved to LUMBRES Area for training. By train from ABEELE to LOTTINGHEM. (Calais Sheet 13). Arrival on billets	HVV4A
		11.30 P.M.	Transport by road arrived 2.30 A.M. Billets very wet.	

[signature] Lt. Colonel,
17th (S) Bn. SHERWOOD FORESTERS.

Army Form C. 2118.

WAR DIARY
of
INTELLIGENCE SUMMARY

(Erase heading not required.) 17th (SERV.) Bn. SHERWOOD FORESTERS (Welbeck Rangers)

Instructions regarding War Diaries and Intelligence Summaries are contained in F. S. Regs., Part II. and the Staff Manual respectively. Title Pages will be prepared in manuscript.

(172)

Place	Date 1917	Hour	Summary of Events and Information	Remarks and references to Appendices
LOTTINGHEM	Dec 10th		Routine. Cleaning up & Inspections by Company Officers	400a Q
~ do ~	11th		Routine Cleaning up and Reorganisation of Sections and Platoons.	400a Q.
~ do ~	12th		Routine Training on Training Ground. Companies under Officers	400a
~ do ~	13th		Routine Training on Training Ground.	400a
~ do ~	14th		Routine Bayonet training in vicinity of Dubek owing to wet weather	400a
~ do ~	15th		Routine Companies on Training Ground under Officers	400a
~ do ~	16th		Routine Church Parade on Training Ground. Recreation in afternoon.	400a

Lt. Colonel
Comdg. 17th (S) Bn. SHERWOOD FORESTERS.

WAR DIARY or INTELLIGENCE SUMMARY

Army Form C. 2118.

17th (SERV.) Bn. SHERWOOD FORESTERS. (Welbeck Rangers)

Place	Date 1917	Hour	Summary of Events and Information	Remarks and references to Appendices
LOTTINGHEN	Dec 17th		Companies bathing at BELLES (about 1½ miles) Training in morning	
"	18th		of Bills. Afternoon Cross Country Run. O by first	
"	19th		Company Training during morning. Inter company football and Tug o' War in afternoon. Snow still thick and ground hard. Inter company finals Winter Parade and Company Training morning. Sturning morning. Football match played. A. wger. Snow still lying and freezing all day.	8 off or asp
"	20th		Lt Col J.A. MERNDEN 17th K.R.R.C. arrive to take command of Bn.	8 off (a asp) 8 off or asp
"	21st		Routine. Winter parade and company training during morning. Inspection by Brig General Army Page D.S.O. of whole Battalion. He complimented the C.O. on the smart turnout of the Bn. In afternoon transport at 11.30am ran took part in the Inf. Brig. Cross country run. This team were beaten by 16th Bn Sherwood Foresters by 80 points. First for Bn - Lieut ELSE. Baths in afternoon.	8 off or asp
"	22nd		Routine. Winter parade and company training during morning. Snow still lies and weather frosty.	8 off or asp
"	23rd		Routine. Winter parade and company training morning. B coy ran pulled over coy teams of 16th Sherwood Forester and 16th Rifle Brigade.	8 off or asp

J.B. Allwright
Lt. Col
17th (S) Bn. SHERWOOD FORESTERS.

WAR DIARY or INTELLIGENCE SUMMARY

Army Form C. 2118.

17th (SERV.) Bn. SHERWOOD FORESTERS (WELBECK RANGERS)

Place	Date	Hour	Summary of Events and Information	Remarks and references to Appendices
LOTTINGHEM	24		Routine. Muster parade and Company training in morning. 1 coy on Lewis gun firing practice. In afternoon B Coy Pug & Nor Team beat Coy Team of WELTS Regt but were beaten by Coy Team of HAMPSHIRE Reg. this being 2/0 in Divisional Competition. Major General FEETHAM. C.B. D.S.O. presented medals adm to the first two teams.	
"	25		XMAS DAY. Voluntary church parades in morning. Special dinner were given to all ranks (Port and Plumpudding). Brigadier General (late A.S.O.) went round the Battalion and wished the men a happy Christmas. In evening all officers had dinner together. Therewere 30 officers present.	
"	26		Company training in billets enough to achieve fall of snow. All games and sports postponed	
"	27		Company training in billets. All available men employed on clearing snow from roads.	
"	28		Bn marched to huts at SENNINGHEM and AFFRINGUES. Battalion arrived at 12 Noon. Transport and motor lorries delayed for several hours and had troops their last ration	
SENNINGHEM and AFFRINGUES	29		Battalion paraded at 4 A.M. and proceeded to march route to WIZERNES. Thence by train to ST JEAN. Bn. billeted in huts at BRISFAM and HILL TOP FARM at 1 P.M. Rations did not arrive till late at night and officers had no kit.	

Lt. Colonel
17th (S) Bn. SHERWOOD FORESTERS

SECRET. 17th. Bn. SHERWOOD FORESTERS. (Special) OPERATION ORDER No. 62.

Reference Sheet 28.

INFORMATION.	1. The Battalion comes under the Command of the 8th Division at 6 a.m. on December 2nd. 1917. and will be ready to move at half an hour's notice from 6 a.m. on the 2nd inst.
ORDER OF MOVE.	2. A. B. C. D. HQ. Platoons at 50 yards interval. Dress - Fighting Order, water bottles filled.
ROUTE.	3. OXFORD ROAD - No. 5. Track. Companies will not pass D.9.d.6.2. until Guides are met.
LEWIS GUNS.	4. Lewis Guns will be carried together with 20 Lewis Gun Magazines.
RATIONS.	5. Iron rations and one day's rations will be carried on the man.
REVEILLE.	6. Reveille will be at 5 a.m.
BREAKFASTS.	7. Breakfasts will be at 5.30 a.m.
STORES.	8. Drums will collect all stores, blankets, packs &c., and stack by the Quartermaster's Stores.
LIAISON.	9. 2nd. Lt. J.F. Powell will report to Brigade Headquarters at WIELTJE TUNNELS at 6 a.m.
SICK.	10. Sick Parade will be at 6.30 a.m.

NOTE. All water bottles will be filled overnight, and are not to be used until orders are issued.

1.12.17.

(sd) F.D. Collen. Capt & A/Adjt.
17th. Bn. Sherwood Foresters.

COPIES TO :-
8th Division.
O.C. A.B.C.D.HQ. Coys.
Transport Officer.
Quartermaster.
Office Copy.

WAR DIARY or INTELLIGENCE SUMMARY

Army Form C. 2118.

17th (SERV.) Bn. SHERWOOD FORESTERS. (WELBECK RANGERS)

July 23

Place	Date 1918	Hour	Summary of Events and Information	Remarks and references to Appendices
ALBERTA SECTOR	1.		Situation Quiet. Usual hostile shelling and M.G. fire. Enemy bombards to be burning and making merry at midnight and until early morning. S/Lt. company relief during night 1-2. (D to left but S.A.K rightforum). C Support. B Reserve. Situation Quiet. Shows still quiet. D Coy capture a pigeon at 11 P.M.	8RH Yeo
	2.			
	3rd		Situation Quiet. Bn relieved by 13th Bn SHERWOOD FORESTERS. Lt W.E. ELSE and by a sniper in post of left front Coy. Relief delayed till 11.30 P.M owing to an attempted raid on posts of left front Coy. Enemy dropped and caused no casualties. Bn in support positions in Corps line on LANGEMARCK RIDGE at 2.30 A.M. A, B & D Coys in Corps line. C Coy and B.H.Q on STEENBEEK. B.H.Q at 28.C.11.A.5.5.	8RH Yeo 8 U.Yeo
CORPSLINE and STEENBEEK	4th		Bn resting. Cleaning up and on working parties. 7 o'Nearly and 150 OR employed during a hours and evening on horses drawn and carrying at Col NETNOEM Sgts temporarily to command 117th Inf. Brigade. Captain F.O Bickering takes over command of Bn.	8 U.Yeo
	5.		Working parties. 6 officers and 150. OR employed as on working near front line. Also carrying parties and work on drainage and relief continued.	SKH Yeo 8RH Yeo
	6.		Working parties as on 5th. Bn rest self in divisional reserve.	8RH Yeo 82H Yeo

.... Lt. Col.
Comdg. 17th (S) Bn. SHERWOOD FORESTERS

WAR DIARY or INTELLIGENCE SUMMARY

Army Form C. 2118.

(Erase heading not required.) **17th (SERV.) Bn. SHERWOOD FORESTERS** (WELBECK RANGERS)

Place	Date 1918	Hour	Summary of Events and Information	Remarks and references to Appendices
ALBERT SECTOR	Jany 7th	7 PM	Working Parties. Bn relieved by 1st Notts Regt at 6 PM and proceeded by light railway to SIEGE CAMP (Sheet 28. B. 21. e.9) arriving camp at 9 PM.	SLV 7mp
Continuing and Strength				
SIEGE CAMP	8th		Bn. spent in cleaning up and inspection of kit. Snow fell during night.	
"	9th		Lt. Col. Matthews returned to Bn and took command.	8R 40 year
"	10th		Company Training and Working Parties. Lt. W. E. ELSE buried at VRAUCOURT MIL. Snow.	8R 40 year
"	11th		Company Training and Working Parties. 300 men working upwards were allocated working Parties. No training done since allocated men had been working the whole night before and did not return till 11 AM.	SN Hapgry SL 4 Yarp
"	12th		Company Training and working parties.	
"	13th		Brigade Church Parade and working party. Brigade into - company competition. 4 cog. taken by D.C.R.R.C. (C. 2. 3).	SLV 9min
"	14th		Football competition. Company Training and Working Parties attached to 257 Tunnelling Coy.	U. M. 1 Yarp.
	15th		Bn. relieved by 12th R. Sussex Regt at 2 PM & proceeded to IRISH FARM. All in Camp at 4.30 pm. Working parties	U. M. 1 Yarp.
IRISH FM	16th		Battalion not on working parties attached to 257 Tunnelling Company	W. K. Yarp.
"	17th		Working parties relieved & returned to IRISH FARM. All in by 7.30 pm.	W. K. Yarp.

Army Form C. 2118.

WAR DIARY
or
INTELLIGENCE SUMMARY

(Erase heading not required.) 17th (SERV.) Bn. SHERWOOD FORESTERS

Instructions regarding War Diaries and Intelligence Summaries are contained in F.S. Regs., Part II. and the Staff Manual respectively. Title Pages will be prepared in manuscript.

Place	Date 1916	Hour	Summary of Events and Information	Remarks and references to Appendices
IRISH FARM	18		Battalion cleaning up & working parties.	
"	19		All Companies out on working parties relieving 17th KRR	
"	20		Working parties & cleaning up. Few H.V. shells fell in the camp. no damage done	
"	21st		Battalion moved by train to Road Camp. All in Camp by 1 p.m.	
"	22nd		Cleaning up & inspection by Company Officers	
"	23rd		Company Training	
"	24th		Company Training	
"	25		Battalion moved by Rail at 7-30 a.m. to MERICOURT L'ABBE and arrived there at 11-30 p.m. Route March from Albert	
SUZANNE	26th		and to SUZANNE.	
"	27th		Cleaning up & settling down in new area.	
"	28th		Church Parade.	
"	29th		Company Training. Received letter from Gen Gough re Outstanding Battle of Messines	
"			Battalion moved by Rail & Road to WINCEAUX all in Camp	
	by 12 Noon.			
MURALAINS	30		Battalion moved by road to HEUDECOURT & relieve the 3/11 Bn. Queens. Rel. Relief Complete 7-45 p.m.	

A.W. [signature]

DOMDG. 17th (S) Bn. SHERWOOD FORESTERS

2449 Wt. W14957/M90 750,000 1/16 J.B.C. & A. Forms/C.2118/12.

WAR DIARY
or
INTELLIGENCE SUMMARY

Army Form C. 2118.

17th (SERV.) Bn. SHERWOOD FORESTERS. (WELBECK RANGERS)

Place	Date	Hour	Summary of Events and Information	Remarks and references to Appendices
ST JEAN	Jany 30		Battalion parades at 2.30 P.M. and proceeded to take over front line posn in ALBERTA SECTOR. B.M-Q at V.28.D.85.35. Bn relieved the 5/6. Bn. ROYAL SCOTS. Relief complete at 9.10. P.M.	8/Lt left Bn.
ALBERTA SECTOR	31st		Situation quiet. Some hostile shelling and enemy snipers and M.G. fire. From line shell hole posts. Coy HQs and B.HQ cut off by day. Situa settled on parties and fatigues 8/Lt left Bn. At 6. a.m. a considerable barrage was put up by the enemy. No counter action followed.	

17th (S.) Bn. SHERWOOD FORESTERS.

WAR DIARY
or
INTELLIGENCE SUMMARY

17th (SERV.) Bn. SHERWOOD FORESTERS

Army Form C. 2118.

Place	Date	Hour	Summary of Events and Information	Remarks and references to Appendices
Gouzeaucourt Sector	3/9		Very quiet period. Improvements of trenches carried out in our own and front line. Casualties nil.	

J.A. Mitchell Lt. Colonel
17th (S) Bn. SHERWOOD FORESTERS.

Army Form C. 2118.

WAR DIARY
or
INTELLIGENCE SUMMARY

(Erase heading not required.) **17th (SERV.) Bn. SHERWOOD FORESTERS**

Instructions regarding War Diaries and Intelligence Summaries are contained in F.S. Regs., Part II. and the Staff Manual respectively. Title Pages will be prepared in manuscript.

Vol 24

Place	Date	Hour	Summary of Events and Information	Remarks and references to Appendices
BEETOR	1.		Battalion quiet. Working on First Defence line. No sign of enemy. Aeroplane Recconaissance. Nil	
	2		Day very quiet. L.H. and Q of 2 Bn Sherwood Foresters v 10th Bde Bombers lined up for 3 hours. Enemy patrol 700 yards length. Enemy very quiet. Not engaged.	
	3		Battalion relieved by 15th Bn Sherwood Foresters all clear. 2.45 p.m. Battalion in Reserve at Tincourt. 9 p.m.	
?INCOURT	4		Battalion cleaning up & harried as Reserve Bn. Considerable Aeroplane activity. Very Quiet. Worked preparing moves.	
	5		Div General made a short inspection at Tincourt. Brig General Armyage ? Lt Col Methuen, Lee Han Division Congratulation on Col Methuen's speech. Battalion specially ready for moving up.	
	6		Very quiet. new Lewel Gunned. Officers & some Lewis Gunners joined preparing rolls for the Battn day of the Battle. 1st Dec ? Bn Sherwood Foresters.	
	7		Repeating of previous days and 2nd Draft left 12 noon from the 16th Bn Sherwood Foresters	

Jmmethuen .....Lt. Colonel,
COMDG. 17th (S) Bn. SHERWOOD FORESTERS.

WAR DIARY
or
INTELLIGENCE SUMMARY

(Erase heading not required.)

17th (SERV.) Bn. SHERWOOD FORESTERS

Army Form C. 2118.

Place	Date	Hour	Summary of Events and Information	Remarks and references to Appendices
HENDECOURT	1918 7		Fatal May of Hunt sectors & all refreshed men aligned to following Groups " to 2/3 " " to 3/5 " " to 4/4 " " to 10 " " to 9 "	
	8			
	9		Reported our Brigade formed PARTIES. Scouts, Potato perennial of hill near BIGNY SCHOOL	
	10		Rest of details proceeded to hrs respective units. Continued the training of B Battn.	
	11		Ditto	
	12		Ditto	
HAUT-ALLAINES	13		Moved by Road Route to HAUT-ALLAINES & attached to ALDWORTH REINFORCEMENT DEPOT. Remnants and small working party continued the affairs of Bunting up Battn. & Lt. Col. METHUEN preceded by 4 days course at R.F.C.	
	14		Ditto	
	15		Ditto	

J.C. Methuen Lt. Colonel,
Comdg. 17th (S) Bn. SHERWOOD FORESTERS

WAR DIARY or INTELLIGENCE SUMMARY

(Erase heading not required.) **17th (SERV.) Bn. SHERWOOD FORESTERS**

Army Form C. 2118.

Instructions regarding War Diaries and Intelligence Summaries are contained in F. S. Regs., Part II. and the Staff Manual respectively. Title Pages will be prepared in manuscript.

Place	Date	Hour	Summary of Events and Information	Remarks and references to Appendices
HAPP-ALLAINES	16th FEB		Moved by Route March to SOREL-LE-GRAND. Heavily bombed during the night. No casualties.	2/Capt. /Lieut
HAMEL	17th		Moved by lorry to HAMEL. Working party under the Canadian R.E.s	
	18th		At ROISEL. Lt Col METHUEN returned to the Battn. (Lt BROWN i/c command)	2/Lieut Briggs
	19th		Working party under R.E.s	2/Lieut Briggs
	20th		Working party whole armed - back at 3-45 from Camp. arrived	
			to HAUT-ALLAINES. Major COLLIN & Capt. BOOKER proceeded on 14 days leave	Lt Col Methuen
HAUT-ALLAINES	21st		Attached to 17th Entrenching Battn.	2/Lt Baffield
	22nd		Ditto	
	23rd		" (Capt C CLAYTON posted 1 months leave to U.K.)	Major Hedger

Lt Colonel
17th (3) Bn. SHERWOOD FORESTERS.

www.ingramcontent.com/pod-product-compliance
Lightning Source LLC
Chambersburg PA
CBHW080900230426
43663CB00013B/2588